AF531255

Hospitality Destination and Site Management

HOSPITALITY DESTINATION AND SITE MANAGEMENT

Dr. Ramesh Chand

CENTRUM PRESS
NEW DELHI-110002 (INDIA)

CENTRUM PRESS
H.O.: 4360/4, Ansari Road, Daryaganj,
New Delhi-110002 (India)
Tel: 23278000, 23261597, 23255577, 23286875

B.O.: No. 1015, Ist Main Road, BSK IIIrd Stage,
IIIrd Phase, IIIrd Block, Bengaluru-560085 (INDIA)
Tel: 080-41723429

Email: centrumpress@gmail.com
Visit us at: www.centrumpress.com

Hospitality Destination and Site Management

First Edition, 2013

ISBN 978-93-81460-20-7

PRINTED IN INDIA

Printed at Balaji Offset, Delhi.

Contents

Preface

The globalization processes in tourism, the fast and constant change of the tourist market, the more intensive competition between the tourist areas require faster and more flexible changes, reactions on behalf of the macro- and micro environment of tourism. That is the reason why the current management and operation process of tourism require some changes, they need to be renewed. The present structure of tourism management and operation get revaluated, it is replaced by the modern tourism management and operation system, the regional and organizational system of destination management. Destination management means the current practice of complex and integrated planning and operation of tourism with the difference that „the principle of regional concentration" – as one of the important means of the regional competitiveness –, and the regional co operations operating more consciously and reasonably are getting a more significant role in reconsidering the system of tourism in a more modern form. The principle of complexity is emphasised differently, which is meaning on the one hand the more effective use of the connection possibilities of tourism to other branches, on the other hand the more intensive development of the background infrastructure supporting tourism beside the tourist infra- and superstructure is taken for granted as well. The basic principles of the competitive developments are the sustainability and the innovative way of looking.

The principle of the regional concentration – as one of the important means of the regional competitiveness – and the co operations being organised more consciously have big parts in the development and operation of the tourist destination management. The principle of complexity is emphasised differently that means on the one hand the more effective use of the connection possibilities of tourism to other branches, on the other hand it takes for granted the development of the background infrastructure supporting tourism more intensively beside the development of the tourist infrastructure. The basic principle of the competitive developments are the sustainable developments and the innovative approach. Tourist destination can be identified with the tourist supply (product) from the elements of the tourist system: the tourist supply and the tourist destination are consisting just of the same elements. The difference is that the tourist product can be only one product and destination can be characterised as a complex pile of attractions and services being in connection with each other. The cooperation of the characters of destination are organised by the tourist value chain of which elements are the experiences in connection with the formation of the image, preparation of travel, travel, destination, return from the point of view of the tourist and the service providers of destination. Services of different level provided by the suppliers can influence the opinion and experience of the tourist in connection with destination negatively. The independent destination management system with suitable competence and specialists, running a coordinating activity can make a connection between the tourist and the receiving area. The destinations – as the organizational systems developing on the regional concentration and cooperation – have to be taken into connection with the economic processes in the world, one basic principle of which is that the durable industrial and business competitive advantages are appearing concentrated geographically more and more.

It is hoped that his book will not only meet the requirements of students but will also be useful as a guide to the academic professionals.

—Author

1

Introduction

Introduction

This paper draws the outlines of the notion and importance of the tourism history, by putting it in perspective of the more recent views of that discipline, which has gradually emerged as a separate entity within both historical, as well as tourism research. It has been the subject of interest with experts and scientists, especially those dealing with tourism which derives information from specific sources and by different methodology of research. Incorporated in social, economic and cultural environment, tourism followed a sequential path (subsequently accepted as a convention) assuming various shapes in its gradual development.

Historical research of tourism has also revealed distinctive indicators which are shared equally all over the world, Croatia including, where they have lately attracted a greater deal of attention. An already accepted scientific project entitled History of Croatian Tourism, as well as some other similar initiatives, particularly concerning the country's coastal area, substantiate that interest.

Research of any past, tourism past including, should at the end of the day be instrumental for both the present and the future, so the elaboration of this very complex issue should be perceived as an encouragement for a more intensive engagement in the research of an extremely rich Croatian tourism history.

A Retrospective of European Tourism

Historians are primarily concerned with the sequence of past events with the aim of getting to grips with social processes expressed in terms of changes seen in people, their ideas and institutions in a particular region. These transformations, regardless of different possible approaches to the historical science (positivism, humanism, structuralism and so on) remain its main preoccupation.

The key issue here, however, is: to what extent has historical research been incorporated in the serious tourism considerations and as such contributed to an understanding of both this important aspect of tourism as well as of the phenomenon as a whole? Few modern authors have undertaken research in this area and they will all agree that the share of this research in an enormous body of tourism literature is rather modest. On the other hand, there is an abundance of history-based tourism literature written by the authors who are not professional historians. In any case, history disciplines can certainly contribute towards clarification of a number of issues having bearing on the development of tourism. So far they have been grouped around the three following thematic units:

- history of travel and forerunners of tourism in the Old and Middle Ages
- research of the so-called Grand Tour
- development of spas and climatic resorts as the first modern tourism destinations.

Generally speaking, however; approaches to tourism history sources can be: geographic, socio- logical, thematic, institutional etc. With regard to the first group, there is a lavish literature on dating as far back as the period of

Ramses II, ancient Greece and Rome, otiums of slave-holders of Classical Antiquity and so on. After all, it is not difficult to agree with the statement that homo viator is one of the first forms of cultural enhancement of homo habilis.

Undoubtedly, both Old and Middle Ages abounded with tourism-like phenomena which have subsequently yielded themselves to research and provoked interest for the mere mysteriousness and mythical character of the ancient sources. It should suffice to remind ourselves of the most massive religious migrations of the time – pilgrimages–analysed from the point of view of history, not to mention classical Greek and Roman literature. The latter two very often describe dangerous travels of their famous protagonists (Ulysses and others). Biblical notion was held sacred, and the Greek words xenos and the Latin hospes denote both the guest and the host. However, although some speak of tourism prehistory, modern science mostly rejects various evolutionist theories according to which "tourism would be a sequence of some historical traces reaching far back into the Classical Antiquity". It is equally obvious that not even famous such as M. Polo or C. Columbus, or other explorers, seafarers, scientist and missionaries can fall into the category of tourists. Grand Tour of Europe, as the second major thematic unit in the historical research of travel, came into being in the 17th century (according to some as early as the end of 16th century) and lasted till the first decades of the 19th century. It became a popular subject of historical analyses, less commonly from the purely tourism point of view.

Those travels, described in general terms as touring some parts of Italy, France and Switzerland un-dertaken by young noblemen, mostly from England, for educational purposes, are nowadays considered a key development stage in the overall history of tourism. As such, it has been studied from the point of view of its participants' profile, temporal and spatial dynamics, and finally as bearing upon the formation of the future nuclei of tourist's offer. Grand Tour of Europe thus gradually assumed the characteristics of what is today known as tourism. Along the same lines, an exceptional interest in the study of those migrations has resulted in a substantial volume of literature, since the available historical data are quite abundant. Grand Tour was temporarily interrupted only by the 30-year War (1618-1648), and those migrations gave rise to the onset of tourism towards the thirties and forties of the 19th century in the countries involved.

A relatively short history of what is generally understood as tourism in the modern sense of the word does not start before the so-called aristocratic phase, some 180 years ago. Like all the previous phases it has been divided into rather similar periods by different authors who all agree that the next, democratic phase begins with the end of the First World War, and mass tourism appears in the fifties of this century. (In the meantime, the twenties are characterised by the conversion of seasons, and the thirties by the introduction of the legal right to paid holiday which gave a full swing to the so-called social tourism.) In all that historical research of long rural holidays of the privileged from the strata of the disappearing feudal class and the emerging bourgeoisie, which left a strong mark (certain Croatian regions being a typical example), plays an important role.

It is a period of radical social changes: fast economic growth and rapid urbanisation resulted not only in different conditions but also in different ways of life and emergence of a new leisure culture. Such a progress underlies the later prosperity of spas, and particularly of coastal and mountain climatic resorts, which are the origins of modern tourism history. Written documents from the period are mostly attribu to writers, poets, philosophers and even painters who travelled around leaving permanent artistic traces of their genius. It was particularly the romantic poets and landscape painters who indebted the humankind in such a way, and their works of art serve today not only to historians of tourism but to the historians of geography as well. The best known among those artists are Montaigne, Rousseau, Goethe, Châteaubriand, Stendhal, Byron, G. Sand, Heine, Ruskin, Taine and others.

Historiography of Tourism

In addition to the three above mentioned thematic units in the historical analyses of tourism, we should also mention a considerable interest in the retrospective research of leisure, which in part en- ters the corpus of tourism historiography. As a result of that we have ended up with a number of empirical studies in Europe, but also in Northern America, with understandable differences in terms of their number and more specific respective scopes of interest. Some authors plead for the whole segment of leisure to be included into the historical research in tourism, as well as for the tourism development of the less well established and more recently developed tourist destinations to become better known. Euro pocentrism of current research, which is often put forth as criticism, would be neutralised by the study of less well known, non-traditional destinations in other parts of the world. Often oversimplified tourist attitudes should be avoided and the horizons widened by adopting more profound notions, bearing in mind that tourism is not an independent attitude. The current trend implies looking at interactions within the social and cultural tissues of the environment and their mutations over the period of time. It has been the scope of certain projects and conferences on the history of travel and tourism.

Some significant initiatives in those terms come from Scandinavia, for example an outstanding conference held in Sweden in 199412, and a national project in Finland. Similar undertakings are still quite few, although the bibliography of titles dealing with tourism history published by C.H.E.T. of France comprised 12 volumes of mostly occasional documents. Sporadically one will come across a critical evaluation of historio graphic writings on leisure and tourism.

The available documents, for the most part, are not inter linked, and a comprehensive account of the history of tourism for particular countries, the Mediterranean or Europe is practically non-existent. Brief over views with the basic periodization can be found in almost every textbook on tourism, and only a few older authors have undertaken to encompass the global tourism history. More popular, however, are (fictionalised) biographies of famous characters from the tourism history like T. Cook, C. Ritz, C. Hilton, H. Negresco and others.

In any case, tourism history deserves to be more than a mere appendix or an illustration on the mar- gins of economic, geographic or sociological issues. Bringing to light historical facts can amongst other things inspire the local population's pride to their settlement or region, or even the entire country bound for tourist development. Therefore numerous sources, however fragmentary they may be, should be sought, usually on the spot, and used for such research.

Historical Research in Tourism in Croatia

Speaking about sources of historical research in tourism in general, what comes to mind first are written documents, although word of mouth should not be underestimated, especially when it comes to a more recent past. In that case it is perceived as being interwoven in the events of everyday life which stem from memories and personal experience. Historical documents, however, are neither so well known, nor so readily available in comparison with those intended for other types of research, which are both more frequent and more common. That is why theoretical papers on tourism mostly lack historical dimension and in depth approach. The same author proposes the following classification of the tourism history sources:

- statistical data

- personal documents
- mass communications
- Others: The first group comprises all the records on: demand, supply and consumption (visitors, over nights, facilities, receipts, etc.) which have been registered either by the administrative, police, health or other authorities, either by tourism, public or commercial organisations. The majority of such indicators have nowadays been standardised, but they used to be collected only scarcely or not at all. For example, in Croatia, then under Austro-Hungarian Empire, it was not until 1871 that the numbers of visitors started being recorded (for so-called Austrian coast and Dalmatia) whereas numbers of over nights were registered only rarely, starting as of a later date, at bathing and climatic resorts only.

Today so popular (opinion polls for example) visitor and host used to be an exception to the rule, which implies that historical research in tourism lacks a very valuable additional insight, impossible to gather by means of classical statistical methods.

Personal documents group refers to letters, diaries, travels (hand-written or printed) and the like. In addition to those, it comprises various mass publications: newspapers, magazines, guide books, posters, leaflets, etc. History of tourism would definitely be much poorer without a special genre of so called travel literature and geniuses such as those of Twain, Pushkin, Dickens, J. Austen, Gide, Chapek, Maugham and others. Croatian travel writers such as Matos, Mazuranic, Nazor, Cesarec, Krleza, Peic and others have left a permanent mark on the national literature, and represent an inexhaustible source for the study of tourism history. When the word tourist was still a novelty making it shyly into a small number of dictionaries, A. Nemcic Gostovinski, a prominent writer (Illyrian) uses it in his "Travel Trifles" – souvenirs of travel through Croatia and Northern Italy as early as 1845.

Finally, sources comprise archaeological findings of all shapes and forms, even the inscriptions and paintings on papyrus, stone or metal, buildings (summer houses, villas, inns), and especially various archives, including diplomatic correspondence. Various pictorials such as drawings, paintings, picture postcards, photographs and the like are also valuable sources of historical research.

At this point it is interesting to present The List of Documents for Croatian Tourism History proposed in these parts as early as 1967 with the principal aim of collecting and analysing such documents. The paper has not yet been made public, so it is here given in its shortened form.

List of Documents for Tourism History in Croatia

Written Documents

1. Minutes of constituent assemblies of tourism organisations
2. Minutes of annual assemblies of those organisations
3. Minutes of management boards of those organisations
4. Archives of those organisations: letters, reports, proposals etc.
5. Statistical reports and break-downs by month and year
6. Archives of communities relative to tourism, tourism organisation, catering, civil engineering
7. Hotel archives on their construction and operation
8. Archives of districts, and counties
9. Archives of steamship companies
10. Archives of bus companies
11. Archives of harbour-master's offices on the Adriatic
12. Tourism archives of Dubrovnik

Special Written Documents

1. Books of regulations of tourism organisations
2. Reports and other written papers by tourism associations on the Adriatic coast, PUTNIK, and their such organisations
3. Sailing and other time-tables
4. Price lists
5. Menus
6. Leaflets of all sorts
7. Posters

8. Guidebooks
9. Various tourist brochures
10. Tourist magazines, dailies and periodicals featuring tourism

Tourist Bibliography

1. Bibliography of books, brochures, magazines relative to tourism
2. Bibliography of articles on tourism in domestic and foreign print

Legacy of Tourist Officials

Recollection of Tourist Officials

Evidently historical research in this area is also quite limited not only by the unavailability but also by the reliability of the sources on hand, therefore a researcher is faced with the problem of making the right choice (selection), a problem common to all social sciences. Very often key (relevant) sources have not been preserved, so the mosaic is composed of various (auxiliary) parts. There are also differences in the basic approach adopted by historians as opposed to the approach of other social scientists. The former tends to interpret and reconstruct a past reality, whereas the latter do the same developing more general concepts of the society, in which historicity does not play a crucial role. The approach adopted by the latter scientists is considered to be more suited to the temporal dimension of tourism which, as an interdisciplinary phenomenon, penetrates all the pores of a society and consequently of social sciences. Tourism past, therefore, stems from the overall social and cultural framework of a specific environment.

Social and Cultural Context of Paleotourism in Croatia

Sociology of tourism, as a part of sociology of leisure, suggests that by their perceived value neither travel nor tourism can be regarded as neutral nor independent phenomena, without any impact on the environment. These impacts vary according to the area, and also to the period, therefore all those who undertake a research in tourism history should take them into account assessing their intensity and feedback. Modern theory furthermore recommends comparative studies which should help analyse the phenomenon from the point of view of the social groups which have become involved in tourism activities, and whose taste and behaviour have in turn been shaped by those activities. In that way we get to meet not only the guest, but the host as well, not only the visitor, but visited, a modern trend which has found its expression in various types of impact studies. Namely, limitations to a further tourism expansion often lie on the demand side, so in addition to the physical we quite often speak of the social saturation of a number of modern destinations, which was very uncommon in the past. Moreover, tourism was and still is under a very strong influence of technics and technology which have too often been boundary stones and turning points in its historical development. The same goes for fashion and other recognisable influences which have inspired tourism trends: the manner of travelling, the type of accommodation and the type of holiday.

Speaking about Croatian tourism history, particularly about the conditions prevailing in the first half of the 19th century when tourism emerged on the coast and in some parts of the hinterland, it was the era of late with all its socio-economic characteristics. A thin class of the bourgeoisie on the rise joined the country gentry in their extended leisure stays in a few resorts on the Adriatic or in spas during the winter months. Occasional visits from outstanding members of middle-European royal families were registered in Opatija, Losinj or Dubrovnik. Quite often they were the first promoters of those resorts in their home countries. They stayed at newly-built grand-hotels together with an entourage of their companions and servants. In general the new leisure-class was recruited mainly from foreigners and the local population in the beginning, didn't have much in common with the newcomers. Sociologically and culturally tourism was a totally new phenomenon in a rural environment.

Today however, at the end of the millennium, historical research in tourism should also incorporate mass tourism, which long ago stopped being a novelty. Although it will never disappear altogether, mass tourism is being pushed back for its mostly pejorative connotations. New ("post-industrial") or alternative forms with a number of variants of so-called sustainable tourism are being strongly encouraged. Like all the others before, the era of mass tourism has undoubtedly left numerous traces (sources) lending themselves to different types of research: However, the message those are bound to convey to the future generations is the one of a dehumanised of people who lived in the second half of the 20th century.

Adriatic – The Cradle of Croatian Tourism

Unfortunately so far the Croatian tourism has never been researched systematically and com-prehensively. The available research data mostly refer to the established tourist destinations (regions, cities, settlements) in different and sporadic periods of their development. Elements of such research can obviously be found in numerous historical, literary, sociological, geographic and other works, but also in original popular art and cultural heritage. There have been some individual attempts at presenting the tourism past in the works of J. Tadic, I. Peric who were writing about the Dubrovnik region, V. Jadresic, B. Juric and V. Mastrovic about the Zadar area,

Kojic about Losinj, S. Kabalin describing N. Vinodolski and L. Sudnik dealing with the environment of Zagreb, not to mention numerous papers dealing with Cavernoma and other coastal and island settlements, as well as those on the continent. There are also comprehensive scientific proceedings comprising valuable documents on the history of tourism in Rab, Kirk, Crikvenica, as well as some other places. Other useful sources are historical over views of segments of a broader phenomenon, for example the tourism organisation, the hotel industry, some types of transportation, travel agents, They allow for a detailed insight into the chronological sequence of development of a particular segment, corroborated by an abundance of facts.

Tourism was incorporated into the concrete Croatian Adriatic social reality quite early, becoming its inseparable part only a little later than it happened in the so-called classical tourist countries. First visits of foreigners had hardly any repercussions on the host environments, not noticeable at first, but subsequently gaining more and more prominence. First public houses, inns, hostels, and finally hotels contributed to the gradual development of other necessary infrastructure: transportation and communal systems, retail and entertainment facilities and so on.

In Croatia, like anywhere else for that matter, the history of tourism therefore cannot be separated from the regional planning and equipment of tourist resorts, those nuclei of development: from communications to horticulture, from beaches and ski slopes to pubs and restaurants. There from the richness of tourist life and distinctive atmosphere of such places in the past, very often and very readily depicted and ascribed to Opatija, Crikvenica, Kirk, Losinj, Rab, Zadar, Kastela, Haver,

Dubrovnik, and so many others. Such descriptions have mostly provided background for anniversaries of important events: opening of a hotel, founding of tourist boards or associations, opening of a road or the like. Brief information on commonplace events from the tourist past of a resort or a region tends to get a short mention in standard tourist guides, (illustrated) monographs, even in the so-called grey literature, sometimes containing inaccurate and non-verified data. Notwithstanding the notorious truth that it is not easy to determine the age of Croatian coastal tourism, some of its phases can easily be followed, or as contemporary foreign authors like to put it: follow the life cycle of tourist destinations

Fact-abounding historical accounts containing important dates, names of prominent tourist enthu- siasts, even anecdotes, can be invaluable for shedding light not only on the tourism past, but on the whole range of social, economic and cultural life of the period. The notion of hospitality and ancient autism, even in more primitive environments, places a special emphasis on getting together, associating and socialising, mostly in catering establishments which have always served as venues for discussions and important decision making. Health resorts, although mostly located in the hinterland were meeting-places of the then elite, who would spend a larger part of the year in spas and posh seaside resorts, and the first modern (Palace and Grand) hotels become the real monuments and witnesses to their time and to famous people who resided in them. Many of Croatian coastal villages and little towns had for years lived on maritime transport and trade, when the forties of the 19th century saw the introduction of steamers which provided them with opportunities to start accommodating excursionists and first partakers in the rudimentary forms of tourism, which would only later evolve into a mass phenomenon.

In Opatija, for example, the hundred fiftieth anniversary of tourism was celebrated in 1994. In Haver the first tourism organization named Society for Hygiene was founded in 1868 and in Kirk a similar body had existed even before that date. At other places tourism shot ahead thanks to a specific cult of thermal water or a healthy climate. Very often the history of providing health services is also the history of tourism of such climatic resorts, both on the coast as well as in the continental parts. Rab celebrated its century of tourism in 1989. The same year even two anniversaries were celebrated in Zadar: the eightieth of the Regional Association for the Promotion of Travel of Foreigners in Dalmatia and the ninetieth of the LIBURNIJA Mountain-climbing and Tourist. Association. Proceedings were published in Kastela near Split in 1966 on the occasion of the centenary of tourism, and similar publications could easily be found elsewhere as well. The first three modern hotels on the Adriatic coast, Opatija, Crikvenica and Imperial Dubrovnik were opened in 1884, 1894 and 1897 respectively. The last celebrated the centenary of its opening in 1997 with the publication of proceedings in which that event was accentuated as a turning point in the development of hotel industry in the town.

Some Significant Years from the Croatian Adriatic Tourism History

1837: steam-shipping line TRIEST-DUBROVNIK

1840: RIJEKA-VOLOSKO-OPATIJA-LOVRAN seaside promenade

1844: first villa and park in OPATIJA

1847: designs of OPATIJA as a health resort

1848: first small hotel in Haver

1849: Committee for renovation of cultural and historical monuments in Kirk

1857: VIENNA-TRIEST railway line

1866: Committee for embellishment of Kirk (unknown year of foundation)

1868: Society for Hygiene in Haver

1873: KARLOVAC-RIJEKA railway line

1878: First bathing place in NOVI VINODOLSKI

1880: First tourists visit MALINSKA

1882: Southern railways Inc. bought Villa Angiolina and started building modern OPATIJA

1883: Beginning of tourist statistics in OPATIJA

1884: First hotel Cavernoma in OPATIJA

1885: Committee for embellishment of M. LOSINJ

1886: Committee for embellishment of V. LOSINJ

1888: Bathing place in CRIKVENICA

1892: Committees for embellishment of OREBIC, SUPETAR and ZADAR

1894: Therapia hotel in CRIKVENICA

1897: Imperial hotel in DUBROVNIK

1899: LIBURNIJA Mountain-climbing and Tourist Association-first regional tourist association

1902: Committee for Embellishment of N. VINODOLSKI

1906: Health Care Act (passed by the Croatian Parliament)

1907: Regional association for promotion of foreign tourism in Austrian Coastal Region (in Istria)

1908: Island of Rab Bathing and health resort society (founded in Vienna)

Source: Antic, V. Razvitak turistickih organization U Jugoslavian, referat, Simpozij o tourism, Beograd, 1968. It is very difficult however and also most ungrateful to continue putting forth examples from the country's tourism past, for all of them are equally important and significant, and they have often served as the grounds for serious historical research. The results of this research, contained in the form of printed material, have not to the day been listed, let alone critically evaluated. Indeed, they are scattered in various libraries and archives or found in private possession. It would therefore be useful to catalogue them, if only in the form of a Bibliography for the future history of Croatian tourism, although some documents must have perished forever. One should not forget that invaluable historical documents on Croatian tourism are kept by the Tourist Documentation and Information Centre in Dubrovnik, which takes credit for collecting bib- liographic and other old publications (books, periodicals, etc.), which are today unique. In 1998 the sixtieth anniversary of the Centre's activity was celebrated and it was another incentive for a full appraisal of its still greatly unknown holdings in terms of historical evaluations.

Quite often one tends to forget that plenty of information for the history of tourism can be found incidentally in different works dealing with general history, history of transport, architecture, sports and others, but also in parish chronicles. It would therefore be recommendable to form local historical archives at the level of tourist associations and offices of particular places and counties, as referential collections of sources for the history of tourism. That would certainly encourage research, analysis and publication of papers dealing with the issue of tourism since the authorities on the subject would actually reside and work on the spot.

The task would be easier to perform in smaller and more homogenous areas, although the long-term comprehensive project History of Zagreb Tourism (within the Croatian Academy of Sciences and Arts- HAZU) has proved to be an exceedingly complex undertaking. A result of this project is an extremely well documented and lavishly illustrated publication whereas a number of monographic studies are still awaiting to be published. Already approved and launched project, also within HAZU, entitled History of Croatian Tourism, designed as a team work coordinated by the researchers all over Croatia, presents a great challenge to our tourism historiography. It is a pioneer work of utmost importance, which is not exploring the past just for the sake of searching for the roots, but rather to find an inspiration for the country's tourism future. Therefore the Croatian Tourist Association's appeal which was launched more than 30 years ago pleading for a comprehensive programme of collection, array and analysis of historical documents on tourist organisation and tourism on our territory is still very topical. On that occasion, amongst other things, it was recommended to do the following:

- search for and all the archives and other documentation covering the period from the very

  beginning of tourism to the First World War
- classify in detail all the material to be collected
- take into account libraries in private possession
- co-ordinate and their respective tasks, etc.

Unfortunately, there has been little concrete action undertaken in that respect, which makes the renewed project efforts so much more significant. The project should make up for failures and provide a comprehensive and systematic insight into the Croatian tourism past.

Conclusion

Study of tourism history is important for learning about key features of growth and specific characteristics of the host areas in the past with the aim of making vital decisions in the present, and even more so in the future. By ignoring or underestimating the tourism past of a destination which seeks a deeper-seated recognition on the market, one fails to take into account a favourable position it is very likely to have had in the past.

What is being neglected is the fact that some places and regions in Croatia used to be even better cared for, equipped and organised. Despite a quantitative growth in the number of tourist facilities and over nights, they have suffered an overall drop in quality and reputation.

Only sad fragments remain of once rich park architecture of Opatija and Lipik, and their past splendour, which placed them side by side with the most fashionable European bathing resorts and spas, is still mentioned as an unattainable goal. The refined environment dear to the heart of the affluent of the period has mostly been degraded. Degradation of natural wealth has been accompanied by a decline in the overall level of services and tourist offer, which reflects upon the type of clientele and overall business result.

For that reason it pays to value the past, not for nostalgic reasons but for the re-establishment of those traditions which can enhance the image and increase total economic and other (revival of forgotten attractions, local customs, old arts and crafts, sports, cuisine and so on). This will lead to the ascent from ordinariness and anonymity, so desirable in the new Croatian State which no longer has a reason to continue neglecting what used to be deliberately inhibited for over half a century. In that way the awareness of true historical values will help coastal regions as well as those on the continent in making the most of their affiliation with both Central European and Mediterranean culture circles, since by the profile of their tourist offer that is where they belong. It will undoubtedly be proven by the project History of Croatian Tourism.

International Tourism Receipts

In 2008, there were over 922 million international tourist arrivals, with a growth of 1.9% as compared to 2007. International tourism receipts grew to US$944 billion (euro 642 billion) in 2008, corresponding to an increase in real terms of 1.8% on 2007. When the export value of international passenger transport receipts is accounted for, total receipts in 2008 reached a record of US$1.1 trillion, or over US$3 billion a day.

The World Tourism Organization reports the following countries as the top ten tourism earners for the year 2008. It is noticeable that most of them are on the European continent, but the United States continues to be the top earner.

International Tourism Expenditures

The World Tourism Organization reports the following countries as the top ten biggest spenders on international tourism for the year 2008. For the fifth year in a row, German tourists continue as the top spenders.

History

Wealthy people have always travelled to distant parts of the world, to see great buildings, works of art, learn new languages, experience new cultures and to taste different cuisines. Long ago, at the time of the Roman Republic, places such as Baiae were popular coastal resorts for the rich. The word tourism was used by 1811 and tourist by 1840. In 1936, the League of Nations defined foreign tourist as "someone travelling abroad for at least twenty-four hours". Its successor, the United Nations, amended this definition in 1945, by including a maximum stay of six months.

Leisure Travel

Leisure travel was associated with the Industrial Revolution in the United Kingdom – the first European country to promote leisure time to the increasing industrial population. Initially, this applied to the owners of the machinery of production, the economic oligarchy, the factory owners and the traders. These comprised the new middle class. Cox & Kings was the first official travel company to be formed in 1758.

The British origin of this new industry is reflected in many place names. In Nice, France, one of the first and best-established holiday resorts on the French Riviera, the long esplanade along the seafront is known to this day as the Promenade des Angles; in many other historic resorts in continental Europe, old, well-established palace hotels have names like the Hotel Bristol, the Hotel Carlton or the Hotel Majestic – reflecting the dominance of English customers.

Many leisure-oriented tourists travel to the tropics, both in the summer and winter. Places often visited are: Cuba, the Dominican Republic, Thailand, North Queensland in Australia and Florida in the United States.

Winter Tourism

Major ski resorts are located in the various European countries (e.g. Austria, Bulgaria, Czech Republic, France, Germany, Iceland, Italy, Norway, Poland, Slovakia, Spain, Switzerland), Canada, the United States, Australia, New Zealand, Japan, Korea, Chile and Argentina.

Mass Tourism

Mass tourism could only have developed with the improvements in technology, allowing the transport of large numbers of people in a short space of time to places of leisure interest, so that greater numbers of people could begin to enjoy the benefits of leisure time. In the United States, the first seaside resorts in the European style were at Atlantic City, New Jersey and Long Island, New York. In Continental Europe, early resorts included: Ostend, popularized by the people of Brussels; Boulogne-sur-Mer (Pas-de-Calais) and Deauville (Calvados) for the Parisians; and Heiligendamm, founded in 1797, as the first seaside resort on the Baltic Sea.

Adjectival Tourism

For a more comprehensive list, see List of adjectival tourisms. Adjectival tourism refers to the numerous niche or specialty travel forms of tourism that have emerged over the years, each with its own adjective.

Many of these have come into common use by the tourism industry and academics. Others are emerging concepts that may or may not gain popular usage. Examples of the more common niche tourism markets include:

1. Agritourism
2. Culinary tourism
3. Cultural tourism
4. Eco-tourism
5. Heritage tourism
6. LGBT tourism
7. Medical tourism
8. Nautical tourism
9. Religious tourism
10. Space tourism
11. War tourism
12. Wildlife tourism.

Recent Developments

There has been an upmarket trend in the tourism over the last few decades, especially in Europe, where international travel for short breaks is common. Tourists have higher levels of disposable income and greater leisure time and they are also better-educated and have more sophisticated tastes.

There is now a demand for a better quality products, which has resulted in a fragmenting of the mass market for beach vacations; people want more specialised versions, such as Club 18-30, quieter resorts, family-oriented holidays or niche market-targeted destination hotels.

The developments in technology and transport infrastructure, such as jumbo jets, low-cost airlines and more accessible airports have made many types of tourism more affordable. WHO estimates that up to 500,000 people are on planes at any time. There have also been changes in lifestyle, such as retiree-age people who sustain year round tourism. This is facilitated by internet sales of tourism products. Some sites have now started to offer dynamic packaging, in which an inclusive price is quoted for a tailor-made package requested by the customer upon impulse.

There have been a few setbacks in tourism, such as the September 11 attacks and terrorist threats to tourist destinations, such as in Bali and several European cities. Also, on December 26,

2004, a tsunami, caused by the 2004 Indian Ocean earthquake, hit the Asian countries on the Indian Ocean, including the Maldives. Thousands of lives were lost and many tourists died.

This, together with the vast clean-up operation in place, has stopped or severely hampered tourism to the area.

The terms tourism and travel are sometimes used interchangeably. In this context, travel has a similar definition to tourism, but implies a more purposeful journey. The terms tourism and tourist are sometimes used pejoratively, to imply a shallow interest in the cultures or locations visited by tourists.

Sustainable Tourism

"Sustainable tourism is envisaged as leading to management of all resources in such a way that economic, social and aesthetic needs can be fulfilled while maintaining cultural integrity, essential ecological processes, biological diversity and life support systems." (World Tourism Organization)

Sustainable development implies "meeting the needs of the present without compromising the ability of future generations to meet their own needs" (World Commission on Environment and Development, 1987)

Eco-tourism

Medical Tourism

When there is a significant price difference between countries for a given medical procedure, particularly in Southeast Asia, India, Eastern Europe and where there are different regulatory regimes, in relation to particular medical procedures (e.g. dentistry), travelling to take advantage of the price or regulatory differences is often referred to as "medical tourism".

Educational Tourism

Educational tourism developed, because of the growing popularity of teaching and learning of knowledge and the enhancing of technical competency outside of the classroom environment. In educational tourism, the main focus of the tour or leisure activity includes visiting another country to learn about the culture, such as in Student Exchange Programs and Study Tours, or to work and apply skills learned inside the classroom in a different environment, such as in the International Practicum Training Program.

Creative Tourism

Creative tourism has existed as a form of cultural tourism, since the early beginnings of tourism itself. Its European roots date back to the time of the Grand Tour, which saw the sons of aristocratic families travelling for the purpose of mostly interactive, educational experiences.

More recently, creative tourism has been given its own name by Crispin Raymond and Greg Richards, who as members of the Association for Tourism and Leisure Education (ATLAS), have directed a number of projects for the European Commission, including cultural and crafts tourism, known as sustainable tourism. They have defined "creative tourism" as tourism related to the active participation of travellers in the culture of the host community, through interactive workshops and informal learning experiences.

Meanwhile, the concept of creative tourism has been picked up by high-profile organizations such as UNESCO, who through the Creative Cities Network, have endorsed creative tourism as an engaged, authentic experience that promotes an active understanding of the specific cultural features of a place.

More recently, creative tourism has gained popularity as a form of cultural tourism, drawing on active participation by travellers in the culture of the host communities they visit. Several countries offer examples of this type of tourism development, including the United Kingdom, the Bahamas, Jamaica, Spain, Italy and New Zealand.

Dark Tourism

One emerging area of special interest tourism has been identified by Lennon and Foley (2000) as "dark" tourism. This type of tourism involves visits to "dark" sites, such as battlegrounds, scenes of horrific crimes or acts of genocide, for example: concentration camps. Dark tourism poses severe ethical and moral dilemmas: should these sites be available for visitation and, if so, what should the nature of the publicity involved be. Dark tourism remains a small niche market, driven by varied motivations, such as mourning, remembrance, macabre curiosity or even entertainment. Its early origins are rooted in fairgrounds and medieval fairs.

Growth

The World Tourism Organization (UNWTO) forecasts that international tourism will continue growing at the average annual rate of 4 %. With the advent of e-commerce, tourism products have become one of the most traded items on the internet. Tourism products and services have been made available through intermediaries, although tourism providers (hotels, airlines, etc.) can sell their services directly. This has put pressure on intermediaries from both aniline and traditional shops.

It has been suggested there is a strong correlation between tourism expenditure per capita and the degree to which countries play in the global context. Not only as a result of the important economic contribution of the tourism industry, but also as an indicator of the degree of confidence with which global citizens leverage the resources of the globe for the benefit of their local economies. This is why any projections of growth in tourism may serve as an indication of the relative influence that each country will exercise in the future.

Space tourism is expected to "take off" in the first quarter of the 21st century, although compared with traditional destinations the number of tourists in orbit will remain low until technologies such as a space elevator make space travel cheap.

Technological improvement is likely to make possible air-ship hotels, based either on solar-powered airplanes or large dirigibles. Underwater hotels, such as Hydropolis, expected to open in Dubai in 2009, will be built. On the ocean, tourists will be welcomed by ever larger cruise ships and perhaps floating cities.

Latest Trends

As a result of the Late-2000s recession, international arrivals suffered a strong showdown beginning in June 2008. Growth from 2007 to 2008 was only 3.7% during the first eight months of 2008. The Asian and Pacific markets were affected and Europe stagnated during the boreal summer months, while the Americas performed better, reducing their expansion rate but keeping a 6% growth from January to August 2008. Only the Middle East continued its rapid growth during the same period, reaching a 17% growth as compared to the same period in 2007. This showdown on international tourism demand was also reflected in the air transport industry, with a negative growth in September 2008 and a 3.3% growth in passenger traffic through September.

The hotel industry also reports a showdown, as room occupancy continues to decline. As the global economic situation deteriorated dramatically during September and October as a result of the global financial crisis, growth of international tourism is expected to slow even further for the remaining of 2008, and this showdown in demand growth is forecasted to continue into 2009 as recession has already hit most of the top spender countries, with long-haul travel expected to be the most affected by the economic crisis.

This negative trend intensified as international tourist arrivals fell by 8% during the first four months of 2009, and the decline was exacerbated in some regions due to the outbreak of the influenza AH1N1 virus.

Economic Development of Tourism

Time is a valuable commodity for today's travellers. Dual-income families find it difficult to schedule vacation time; family members often have jobs or activities that conflict; or an individual's job makes long vacations impractical. As a result, more families and individuals are taking long weekend or holiday vacations, or extending business trips into short getaway vacations. Packaging is a popular technique used for attracting these customers, because packages make travel easier and more convenient. In the hospitality and tourism industry, "packaging" is the process of combining two or more related and complementary offerings into a single-price offering. A package may include a wide variety of services such as lodging, meals, entrance fees to attractions, entertainment, transportation costs (air, auto, train, cab or bus), guide services, or other similar activities.

Packaging can also create a variety of benefits for participating businesses. This publication will: Identify reasons for the increased popularity of packaging. Address issues a business should consider when developing a package. Describe the components of successful packages. Discuss the process of pricing a package.

Why Packages Are Popular

Travel packages have become increasingly popular over the years. They are attractive because they benefit both the customer and participating businesses; packaging provides convenience and value to the customer, and added revenue for participating businesses.

Items to Consider in Developing a Package

Before developing a tourism packaging program, the business should devise a marketing plan through practical marketing research. The business owner should ask him/herself the following questions: Are you willing to do market research to determine who your customers are and what they want? What are the potential attractions, businesses, or marketing service firms that could provide a part of the package? Meet with the managers of these businesses and public attractions to discuss their interests and ideas. What are potential marketing and promotional networks that will help spread the word about your product?

Convention and visitors bureaus, chambers of commerce, retail travel agents, clubs and organizations, state offices of tourism, and other attractions or travel businesses all have the potential to play an important role in merchandising your package. Will the physical appearance and service skills of your business match the target audience? Does your business have the ability to manage and service the customers you generate through your packaging program? Are you prepared for a risk? Because you will be including customer service activities that are not under your direct control, you will be required to develop formal, written agreements between the cooperating businesses.

Benefits to the Customer

Packaging can be an effective marketing tool to provide several customer benefits. These may include: Ability to budget for trips. Packages include most of the components a customer must pay for during a trip. The customer pays at one time and has a good idea of the trip's total cost. Increased convenience. Trips can be time consuming and difficult to arrange. Several telephone calls and letters may be required to arrange for tickets, accommodations, reservations, and other components of a trip. A package allows a customer to arrange many components of a trip with one call or letter and one payment, saving the customer time and aggravation.

Greater economy. Businesses that package can frequently purchase tickets, meals, and other package components at wholesale prices. The business can add in the cost of packaging and still provide a competitive price to the customer. Thus, the cost to the customer is usually more economical than purchasing the package components individually. Popular programs and activities. Visitors and travellers are often unfamiliar with many of the activities and attractions in an area: a package can help customers find them easily.

Specialized interests. Packaging provides a unique opportunity to design components of a package for specialized interests. These so-called "benefit bundles" can include a package component not readily available to individual customers. For example, a package weekend may feature a cooking demonstration by a well-known chef or a lecture by a well-known author. Benefits to Participating Businesses Packaging can be used by businesses to help improve profitability and build customer volume. Examples include:

Improved profitability. During peak or high-demand periods, use packaging to add value to an existing product. Purchasers may be required to stay a prescribed period or purchase a combination of goods and services. Packaging may also allow a business to price its product at a premium by adding special goods and services. Smooth business patterns. Use packaging during low demand periods to add attractive features to the business's service or product, thus generating additional business. Other businesses may also be willing, to discount their services during this time. Adding these services to the existing product mix may generate new business.

Joint marketing opportunities. Packaging can allow the business to reduce marketing costs or start a new program one could not normally afford by joining with one or more businesses to conduct a marketing or advertising program. This strategy can be especially effective if the businesses involved have similar customers. Improved target marketing. Packaging can be an effective tool to tailor tourism and travel products for specific target markets. Examples can be ski, sports, or theatre weekends.

Good market research is needed so an appropriate mix of tourism and travel services will meet the needs and desires of a target group of customers.

Greater holiday weekend business. Packaging can be used to highlight special holiday weekends by developing services appropriate to the theme of the weekend. New Year's, Valentine's Day, or Mother's Day are just a few of the holidays that can be used to develop special programs for parties, couples, or family gifts. Unique recurring events. Businesses can create their own events that can occur throughout the year. Events could be tournaments such as chess or bridge or crime re-enactments that let guests do the detective work. Events of this type will require imagination and inventiveness to take advantage of the wide variety of activities that take place in the community. This technique is often called "programming."

Redirected traffic to lesser-known attractions. Directing visitors to often overlooked attractions can help in two ways: heavily visited attractions may be offered some relief, while newly discovered attractions may thrive and prosper. Businesses can use many different strategies in designing a package product. Success will depend on good market research, an understanding of existing customers, research, an understanding of existing customers, and a good knowledge of the community and its activities.

Pricing a Package

Lodging or transportation—the most expensive parts of a package product-are usually the first contact points for customers who purchase a packaged vacation or travel product. Lodging operations or travel agents are usually the key to organizing a packaging program, even though an area's attractions may bring visitors to a community. Although accommodations and transportation are the basic ingredients of a package, tickets to attractions, dining, and other services are other key parts of the product mix that make the package marketable. It is necessary for a business to understand its target market and conduct basic practical market research in order to develop a successful package. Experimenting with a set of packages can also help you identify which sets of activities are most attractive to your customers. Issues to consider when pricing a package include: The package must be a good value and competitive in the market. Customers should not be able to purchase separate items in the package for less than the package price. A large user of package components should be able to receive discounts from businesses that provide them. Evaluate the role packaging can play in the business's marketing program. While packaging can be used to implement many different strategies, the basic intent is to generate additional business. Determine if the package is feasible by applying a break-even analysis to help determine how many packages a business must sell before earning a profit.

Break-Even Analysis

Break-even analysis is a tool used to determine total sales needed to recoup costs, hence the name "break-even." This analysis technique can also be used to evaluate alternative pricing levels.

Elements of a Successful Package

Putting together a successful package is not easy. However, by following the suggestions listed below, the chances of success will be greater. Include attractions or demand generators. Every package needs one or more core attractions. These could be tickets to a special event, specialized programming, or reduced prices. Provide value to the customer. Many travellers buy packages because they perceive they will receive greater value for the travel dollars they spend. For some, this translates into a package that costs less than the sum of the regular prices of individual elements. Almost everybody is interested in getting something for nothing or next to nothing. Be well planned and coordinated. A successful package must be well planned and coordinated. Each element should flow naturally from one to the next. Use a theme to hold the package together and create a positive experience for the tourist.

Offer consistent quality and compatibility among elements. Many customers buy packages because they expect consistency in quality. Combine only package components that are compatible and enhance the overall quality of the traveller's experience. Customer dissatisfaction with one part of the package will often spoil the entire experience. Provide a distinctive customer benefit. The best packages provide customers something they would not get if they purchased package elements separately. Sometimes this benefit is the offer of value, but in other cases, it is a component that is not readily available to individual customers. This might involve incorporating special lectures or appearances, unique dining experiences, or other activities. Cover all the details. The temptation might be to throw a package together, but the close attention to detail makes some packages more successful than others. Remember, it is often the little things a business does for guests that matter the most. Some things to consider include a policy on refunds and cancellations and complete information on all package elements included in the price, as well as items not included. Generate a profit. Clearly, packages offer a unique way to satisfy traveller needs and wants. Of course, the package should also be designed to generate a profit. The ideal time to offer packages is when demand is low and when the package will not displace customers who may generate higher revenues.

Tourism Contribution to Economic Conservation

The main positive economic impacts of tourism relate to foreign exchange earnings, contributions to government revenues, and generation of employment and business opportunities. These are discussed briefly here; further information on economic contributions from tourism can be found at the World Travel & Tourism Council's home page.

Foreign Exchange Earnings

Tourism expenditures and the export and import of related goods and services generate income to the host economy and can stimulate the investment necessary to finance growth in other economic sectors. Some countries seek to accelerate this growth by requiring visitors to bring in a certain amount of foreign currency for each day of their stay and do not allow them to take it out of the country again at the end of the trip. An important indicator of the role of international tourism is its generation of foreign exchange earnings. Tourism is one of the top five export categories for as many as 83% of countries and is a main source of foreign exchange earnings for at least 38% of countries.

Source: World Tourism Organization

Contribution to Government Revenues

Government revenues from the tourism sector can be

categorized as direct and indirect contributions. Direct contributions are generated by taxes on incomes from tourism employment and tourism businesses, and by direct levies on tourists such as departure taxes. Indirect contributions are those originated from taxes and duties levied on goods and services supplied to tourists. The United States National Park Service estimates that the 273 million visits to American national parks in 1993 generated direct and indirect expenditures of US$ 10 billion and 200,000 jobs. When visits to land managed by other agencies, and to state, local, and privately-managed parks, are added, parks were estimated to bring around US$ 22 billion annually to the US economy. These expenditures also generate significant tax revenues for the government. The World Travel and Tourism Council estimates that travel and tourism's direct, indirect, and personal tax contribution worldwide was over US$ 800 billion in 1998-a

Employment Generation

The rapid expansion of international tourism has led to significant employment creation. For example, the hotel accommodation sector alone provided around 11.3 million jobs worldwide in 1995. Tourism can generate jobs directly through hotels, restaurants, nightclubs, taxis, and souvenir sales, and indirectly through the supply of goods and services needed by tourism-related businesses. According to the WTO, tourism supports some 7% of the world's workers.

Stimulation of Infrastructure Investment

Tourism can induce the local government to make infrastructure improvements such as better water and sewage systems, roads, electricity, telephone and public transport networks, all of which can improve the quality of life for residents as well as facilitate tourism.

Contribution to Local Economies

Tourism can be a significant, even essential, part of the local economy. As the environment is a basic component of the tourism industry's assets, tourism revenues are often used to measure the economic value of protected areas. For example, Dorrigo National Park in New South Wales, Australia, has been estimated to contribute 7% of gross regional output and 8.4% of regional employment. The importance of tourism to local economies can also be illustrated by the impacts when it is disrupted: the catastrophic 1997 floods that closed Yosemite National Park in California cause locally severe economic losses to the areas around the park. In the most heavily impacted county, Mariposa County, 1997 personal income was reduced by an estimated US$1,159 per capita (US$18 million for the entire county)-a 6.6% decline. The county was also estimated to have lost US$1.67 million in county occupancy and sales tax revenues, and 956 jobs, a significant number in a county of fewer than 16,000 residents. There are other local revenues that are not easily quantified, as not all tourist expenditures are formally registered in the macro-economic statistics. Money is earned from tourism through informal employment such as street vendors, informal guides, rickshaw drivers, etc. The positive side of informal or unreported employment is that the money is returned to the local economy, and has a great multiplier effect as it is spent over and over again. The World Travel and Tourism Council estimates that tourism generates an indirect contribution equal to 100% of direct tourism expenditures.

The Economic Impacts of Eco-tourism

There are two related, but distinct, economic concepts in Eco-tourism: economic impact and economic value. This issues paper focusses on economic impact, which refers to the change in sales, income, jobs, or other parameter generated by Eco-tourism. A common Eco-tourism goal is the generation of economic benefits, whether they be profits for companies, jobs for communities, or revenues for parks. Eco-tourism plays a particularly important role because it can create jobs in remote regions that historically have benefited less from economic development programs than have more populous areas. Even a small number of jobs may be significant in communities where populations are low and alternatives are few. This economic impact can increase political and financial support for conservation.

Protected areas, and nature conservation generally, provide many benefits to society, including preservation of biodiversity, maintenance of watersheds, and so on. Unfortunately, many of these benefits are intangible. However, the benefits associated with recreation and tourism in protected areas tend to be tangible. For example, divers at a marine park spend money on lodging, food, and other goods and services, thereby providing employment for local and non-local residents. These positive economic impacts can lead to increased support for the protected areas with which they are associated. This is one reason why Eco-tourism has been embraced as a means for enhancing conservation of natural resources. Several studies in Australia and elsewhere have assessed the economic impacts of Eco-tourism.

Predictably, the level of benefits varies widely as a result of differences in the quality of the attraction, access, and so on. In some cases, the number of jobs created will be low, but in rural areas even a few jobs can make a big difference. Still, Eco-tourism benefits should not be oversold, or there may be a backlash as reality fails to live up to expectations. The impacts of Eco-tourism, or any economic activity, can be grouped into three categories: direct, indirect, and induced. Direct impacts are those arising from the initial tourism spending, such as money spent at a restaurant. The restaurant buys goods and services (inputs) from other businesses, thereby generating indirect impacts. In addition, the restaurant employees spend part of their wages to buy various goods and services, thereby generating induced impacts. Of course, if the restaurant purchases the goods and services from outside the region of interest, then the money provides no indirect impact to the region — it leaks away. By identifying the leakages, or conversely the linkages within the economy, the indirect and induced impacts of tourism can be estimated.

In addition, this information can be used to identify what goods are needed but are not being produced in the region, how much demand there is for such goods, and what the likely benefits of local production would be. This enables policy makers to determine priorities for developing inputs for use by the tourism or other industries. How, then, are these direct, indirect, and induced impacts to be estimated? For small areas with non-diverse economies, there are relatively few indirect and induced impacts, and there are relatively little data available for modelling these impacts. Therefore, surveys of visitors, residents, and/or businesses often are used to identify tourism's direct impacts. For larger areas, such as states or countries, economists have developed various techniques for estimating indirect and induced impacts, including computable general equilibrium (CGE) and input-output (IO) analysis.

Negative Economic Impacts of Tourism

There are many hidden costs to tourism, which can have unfavourable economic effects on the host community. Often rich countries are better able to profit from tourism than poor ones. Whereas the least developed countries have the most urgent need for income, employment and general rise of the standard of living by means of tourism, they are least able to realize these benefits. Among the reasons for this are large-scale transfer of tourism revenues out of the host country and exclusion of local businesses and products.

Leakage

The direct income for an area is the amount of tourist expenditure that remains locally after taxes, profits, and wages are paid outside the area and after imports are purchased; these subtracted amounts are called leakage. In most all-inclusive package tours, about 80% of travellers' expenditures go to the airlines, hotels and other international companies (who often have their headquarters in the travellers' home countries), and not to local businesses or workers. In addition, significant amounts of income actually retained at destination level can leave again through leakage. A study of tourism 'leakage' in Thailand estimated that 70% of all money spent by tourists ended up leaving Thailand (via foreign-owned tour operators, airlines, hotels, imported drinks and food, etc.). Estimates for other Third World countries range from 80% in the Caribbean to 40% in India.

Source: Sustainable Living

Of each US$ 100 spent on a vacation tour by a tourist from a developed country, only around US$ 5 actually stays in a developing-country destination's economy.

There are two main ways that leakage occurs: Import Leakage: This commonly occurs when tourists demand standards of equipment, food, and other products that the host country cannot supply. Especially in less-developed countries, food and drinks must often be imported, since local products are not up to the hotel's (i.e. tourist's) standards or the country simply doesn't have a supplying industry. Much of the income from tourism expenditures leaves the country again to pay for these imports.

The average import-related leakage for most developing countries today is between 40% and 50% of gross tourism earnings for small economies and between 10% and 20% for most advanced and diversified economies, according to UNCTAD. Even in developed regions, local producers are often unable to supply the tourism industry appropriately even if good will is present: the 64-room hotel "Kaiser im Tyrol" in Austria, an award-winning leader in sustainable practices, cannot find organic food suppliers in the local farming networks in the appropriate quantity, quality and reliability, as production cycles and processes are not compatible with its needs.

Source: Austrian Preparatory Conference for the International Year of Eco-tourism, September 2001 Export leakage Multinational corporations and large foreign businesses have a substantial share in the import leakage. Often, especially in poor developing destinations, they are the only ones that possess the necessary capital to invest in the construction of tourism infrastructure and facilities. As a consequence of this, an export leakage arises when overseas investors who finance the resorts and hotels take their profits back to their country of origin.

A 1996 UN report evaluating the contribution of tourism to national income, gross levels of incomes or gross foreign exchange, found that net earnings of tourism, after deductions were made for all necessary foreign exchange expenditures, were much more significant for the industry. This report found significant leakage associated with: (a) imports of materials and equipment for construction; (b) imports of consumer goods, particularly food and drinks; (c) repatriation of profits earned by foreign investors; (d) overseas promotional expenditures and (e) amortization of external debt incurred in the development of hotels and resorts. The impact of the leakage varied greatly across countries, depending on the structure of the economy and the tourism industry. From the data presented in this study on the Caribbean, St. Lucia had a foreign exchange leakage rate of 56% from its gross tourism receipts, Aruba had 41%, Antigua and Barbuda 25% and Jamaica 40%.

Source: Caribbean Voice

Enclave Tourism: Local businesses often see their chances to earn income from tourists severely reduced by the creation of "all-inclusive" vacation packages. When tourists remain for their entire stay at the same cruise ship or resort, which provides everything they need and where they will make all their expenditures, not much opportunity is left for local people to profit from tourism. The Organization of American States (OAS) carried out a survey of Jamaica's tourist industry that looked at the role of the all-inclusives compared to other types of accommodation. It found that 'All-inclusive hotels generate the largest amount of revenue but their impact on the economy is smaller per dollar of revenue than other accommodation subsectors.' It also concluded that all-inclusives imported more, and employed fewer people per dollar of revenue than other hotels. This information confirms the concern of those who have argued that all-inclusives have a smaller trickle-down effect on local economies. The cruise ship industry provides another example of economic enclave tourism. Non-river cruises carried some 8.7 million international passengers in 1999. On many ships, especially in the Caribbean (the world's most popular cruise destination with 44.5% of cruise passengers), guests are encouraged to spend most of their time and money on board, and opportunities to spend in some ports are closely managed and restricted.

Other Negative Impacts

Infrastructure Cost

Tourism development can cost the local government and local taxpayers a great deal of money. Developers may want the government to improve the airport, roads and other infrastructure, and possibly to provide tax breaks and other financial advantages, which are costly activities for the government. Public resources spent on subsidized infrastructure or tax breaks may reduce government investment in other critical areas such as education and health.

Increase in Prices

Increasing demand for basic services and goods from tourists will often cause price hikes that negatively affect local residents whose income does not increase proportionately. A San Francisco State University study of Belize found that, as a consequence of tourism development, the prices for locals increased by 8%. Tourism development and the related rise in real estate demand may dramatically increase building costs and land values. Not only does this make it more difficult for local people, especially in developing countries, to meet their basic daily needs, it can also result in a dominance by outsiders in land markets and in-migration that erodes economic opportunities for the locals, eventually dis empowering residents. In Costa Rica, close to 65% of the hotels belong to foreigners. Long-term tourists living in second homes, and the so-called amenity migrants (wealthy or retired people and liberal professionals moving to attractive destinations in order to enjoy the atmosphere and peaceful rhythms of life) cause price hikes in their new homes if their numbers attain a certain critical mass.

2

Destination Marketing System

International Tourism Demand for Turkey: A Dynamic Panel

Data Approach

Tourism has grown significantly since the creation of the commercial airline industry and the advent of the jet airplane in the 1950's. By 1992, it had become the largest industry and largest employer in the world. According to the World Travel & Tourism Council (WTTC), travel and tourism is the biggest industry in the world on virtually any economic measure, including gross output, value added, capital investment, employment, and tax contributions.

In 2003, the industry's gross output was estimated to be in excess of US$4.5 billion of economic activity, more than 10 percent of the total gross national product spending. The travel and tourism industry is one of the world's largest employers, with nearly 195 million jobs, or 7.6 percent of all employees. Furthermore, the World Tourism Travel Council (WTTC, 2005) expects that the scale of the world tourism industry, which made up approximately 10.4% of the world's GDP in 2004, will increase to 10.9% in 2014. When all components of the tourism industry are taken into account, i.e., investment, tourism consumption, government spending and exports, the industry grew 5.9% in 2004 alone, reaching US$5.5 trillion.

Furthermore, it is expected to contribute 3.6 % to Gross Domestic Product (GDP) in 2007 and 231.2 million jobs in 2007, 8.3% of total employment by WTTC. The 76.1 million T&T Industry jobs account for 2.7% of total employment in 2007 and are forecast to total 86.6 million or 2.8% of the total by 2017. This growth led to the development of a major new industry: tourism. In turn, international tourism became the concern of a number of world governments because it not only provided new employment opportunities, but it also produced a means of earning foreign exchange. For these reasons, thoroughly examining all aspects of tourism development and economic growth is tremendously significant for governments. Despite its importance for the world economy, applied economists have paid little attention to tourism as Papatheodorou (1999) and Balaguer et al., (2002) argue in their papers.

The current papers on this issue are Balaguer et al., (2002) for Spain, Dritsakis (2004) for Greece, Gunduz and Hatemi-J (2005) and Aslan (2008) for Turkey, Oh (2005) for Korea and Kim et al., (2006) for Taiwan. The possible causal relationship is analyzed between tourism and economic growth in a bivariate context by these papers; nevertheless, not all of them find evidence of the longrun causality from tourism to economic growth. Therefore, economic growth strongly contribute to tourism growth is a question not well answered at this moment in time. The purpose of this paper is to empirically examine the whether tourism growth causes the economic growth or not in Turkey by using dynamic panel data models based on the Generalized Method of Moment estimation (GMM). The main contributions of the present research can be found in the following: the estimated model, the applied methodology and the variables included in the model.

The rest of paper is organized as follows. The section 2 describes the importance of the tourism sector in economy. Section 3 describes the data, methodology and results from this empirical analysis. Section 4 presents the concluding discussion and further comments.

The Importance of the Tourism Sector in Turkey

In regards to the total tourist arrivals to Turkey, it seems that the number of foreign visitors has accelerated rapidly in the last two decades. In 1990, Turkey attracted 4.8 million foreign tourists, which generated an income of $3.4 billion but reached $18.2 billion in 2005 with 20.3 million visitors.

In addition, when taking into consideration top destinations for international tourism according to international tourism receipts and international tourist arrivals, Turkey has assured its position in recent years due to its cultural and natural attractions as the fourth most important destination in the Mediterranean region and the sixth in Europe after the tourism giants France, Spain, Italy, the UK and When comparing with 2004, the top ten destination rankings in 2005 remained unchanged. For international tourist arrivals and tourism receipt, the major change has been that Turkey entered the ranking in the ninth position in arrivals and eighth in receipt, as a result of its 21% and %14 increases in 2005.

Moreover according to the WTTC forecasts, real Turkish visitor exports growth will be 7.5% over the ten years (2001-2010), which is the highest rate in comparison to the EU countries. However, in contrast with the important role of the tourist industry in the Turkish economy, little attention has been paid to its quantitative analysis. Existing empirical research of the international tourism demand in Turkey is based on traditional econometric techniques without examining the stability situation of the estimated regression equations; see for example, Uysal and Crompton (1984), Var et al., (1998) and Akis (1998).

Uysal and Crompton (1984) have found the income variable to be statistically significant and the income elasticity to be generally above unity. In addition these finding for Turkey, Var et al. (1998) illustrated that the elasticity for all of the variables significantly vary from negative values to highly elastic measure. In another study, Akis (1998) concluded that there has been positive relationship between tourist arrivals and national income of tourist generating countries and a negative relationship between tourist arrivals and relative prices by using double-logarithmic functional form of the regression model.

Sample and Model Specification

In this paper, it is aimed to apply dynamic approach to the Turkey case by using panel data estimation. Since static regression models can suffer from a number of problems, including structural instability and spurious regression, in order to avoid these problems, dynamic analysis has started to be explored in the tourism field especially co-integration analysis such as the works by Sieddighi and Shearing (1997); Divisekera, (2003); Dritsakis (2004); Halicioglu (2004); Narayan (2004); Croes and Vanegas (2005); Han, et al., (2006); Munoz, (2006); Song and Witt (2003, 2006); and

Toh, et al., (2006); Munoz and Martin (2007). However, panel data estimations are relatively rare in the empirical literature, especially involving dynamics. The panel data approach is used to estimate the demand function of tourism in Turkey with respect to its nine major clients, Germany, Russia, United Kingdom, Holland, France, Austria, Iran, Bulgaria and Ukraine, for a period of 10 years (1995-2004). There are two main advantages in using this type of data. First, the use of annual data avoids the seasonality problems, which are dominant in this sector. Second, the utilization of a pooled timeseries or cross-sectional data set enables us to have more degrees of freedom than with time-series or cross-sectional data, and one can control for omitted variable bias and reduce the problem of multi colinearity, hence improving the accuracy of parameter estimates. Accordingly, the estimated demand function for tourism in Turkey involves the following variables;

Supply Dynamics

Supply conditions from the point of view of the hosting country are important factors in attracting more tourism inflows. It is introduced two main supply measures. The first is accommodation capacity (S) measured by the number of foundation available each year to host the tourists who visit Turkey. The data are collected from TURKSTAT, Tourism Statistics. The second is a more general supply measure related to infrastructures (airports, railways, roads, hospitals, and telecommunications). The ratio of public investment to GDP (PI) is used as a proxy to capture the welfare effects emanated from public infrastructure networks. The data for the public investment ratio in Turkey is collected from State Planning Organization, Public Investment Expenditures. Finally, two dummy variables (D99 and D01) are included to capture the influence of possible effects on tourism of the Marmara Earthquake in Turkey which takes a value of 1 in 1999 and 0 otherwise and September 11th events, which takes value of 1 in 2001 and 0 otherwise.

The empirical literature suggests that the most commonly specifications used for estimating the demand function of tourism are linear and log linear functions. Witt and Witt (1995) concluded that 75% of the analyzed models used a double log functional form. The preference given to the double log specification is due to more satisfactory estimation results obtained and easy interpretation of the estimated coefficients through the demand elasticity. In this paper, the dynamic structure of tourists' preferences is considered because knowledge about the destination spreads as people talk about their holiday, thus decreasing the uncertainty for potential visitors to that country. Because of this reason, if people are satisfied with a destination they may be more likely to come back and tell others about their favorable experiences related to the destination. That's why the parameter for the lagged dependent variable may be considered as a measure of habit formation and interdependent preferences.

Empirical Results and Policy Implication

In order to insert dynamics into the demand function of tourism in Turkey, it is introduced a lagged dependent variable as an explanatory factor to capture persistence effects of the tourists behaviour. However with this dynamic specification, it is faced that the correlation between the lagged variable and error term. Therefore the estimations with fixed effect (OLS) or random effects (GLS) would not be appropriate since the obtained estimates would be biased. One way suggested by Doornik et al., (2002) to solve this problem is to estimate dynamic panel data models based on the Generalized Method of Moment estimation (GMM).

In this methodology, it is assumed that there is no second-order autocorrelation in the errors; therefore a test for the previous hypotheses is needed. It is also conducted a test for autocorrelation and J statistic for the validity of instruments as derived by Hansen (1982). Failure to reject the null hypothesis in both tests gives support to model and the Wald test denotes the joint significance of the independent variables.

The value of the adjustment coefficient (72%) gives evidence of a rather low adjustment process between the actual variation of the demand for tourism and the desired long-run level. This means that the number of tourists visiting Turkey each year differs substantially from the previous years giving evidence of some kind of inertia or rigidity in the tourism inflows. As for the tourism demand studies, general conclusions indicate that income elasticity has commonly been found to be greater than one, confirming the luxury nature of tourism travel. However, contrary to expectations, income in nine major clients is positively related to the demand for tourism in Turkey with the elasticity less than one.

The estimated coefficient for the income variable suggests that the demand for tourism in Turkey is not dependent on the economic situation in nine major clients. This means that tourism in Turkey is considered by nine major clients as not a luxury. The own-price elasticity is normally negative, although magnitudes vary considerably among studies.

Generally elasticity estimates show negative values ranging from 0 to-1. Consistent with demand theory, relative prices are negatively related to tourism demand.

This means that %1 decrease in relative prices, demand for tourism rise around %0.2 However, contrary to expectations, the ratio of public investment to GDP (PI) which is used as a proxy to capture the welfare effects emanated from public infrastructure networks is negatively and Marmara Earthquake is positively related to the demand for tourism in Turkey. A possible explanation could be that public investment gains speed in summer. Therefore these actions make life difficult for tourists. On the other hand, a possible explanation of positive effect of Marmara Earthquake could be caused by important price dumping in Turkey.

Based on the above empirical studies that have carried out the calculation of elasticities in both the short- and long-run demonstrate that the values of both income and price elasticities in the long-run are greater than their short-run corresponding items, suggesting that tourists are more sensitive to income/price changes over the long-run.

The model was used to measure the performance of tourist arrivals from nine generating countries to Turkey between 1995 and 2004, and it was estimated by using the GMM-DIFF estimator proposed by Arellano and Bond (1991) for the case of dynamic panel data models. The dynamic model used in this study provides short and long-run elasticity for the variables of interest. This is an additional advantage over most studies of tourism demand, which are based on static models and only estimate long-run elasticity. This is a substantial improvement, since these models are only valid for short-term predictions. One of the main conclusions of the study is the significant value of the lagged dependent variable (0.28), which may be interpreted as a minor word-of-mouth effect on the consumer decision in favour of the destination.

The value of the adjustment coefficient (72%) gives evidence of a rather low adjustment process between the actual variation of the demand for tourism and the desired long-run level. This means that the number of tourists visiting Turkey each year differs substantially from the previous years giving evidence of some kind of inertia or rigidity in the tourism inflows.

The estimated values of the income elasticity suggest that the economic conditions of tourists who visit Turkey are not very important factor in determining tourism demand in Turkey. The estimated values of the income elasticity are not in line with the results of previous studies. Therefore tourism to Turkey is not a luxury good.

Moreover tourism to Turkey is not very sensitive to prices. According to the selected model, the estimated values for the own-price short- and long-run elasticities are –0.23 and -0.32, respectively. In order to capture the welfare effects emanated from public infrastructure, the ratio of public investment to GDP (PI) is used as a proxy. And finally, just as in other studies, it has been found that external and internal shocks (e.g., September 11th events and the Marmara Earthquake) may have an impact on tourism demand by using dummy variables. Contrary to expectations, public infrastructure networks are negatively Marmara Earthquake is positively related to the demand for tourism in Turkey and it is found that September 11th events affect negatively Turkey tourism.

International Tourism Demand: the Italian Tourist Flows to Ireland

Tourism is one of the world's major industries and in recent times its social and economic benefits have grown significantly and consistently. As tourism industry is highly competitive, destinations are more concerned about variables that influences tourism movements and moreover, in order to take advantage of tourism effects most destinations have implemented appropriate strategic and operational marketing activities and increased marketing expenditure.

Although, West European countries and North America have dominated previous research, with more than one hundred empirical studies among these only few attempts have been done to evaluate the marketing expenditure impact and moreover very scarce attention has been paid on identifying the determinants of international demand in the Irish market. The purpose of this study is to redress this situation in the Irish context analyzing both the importance of different determinants in explaining variations in tourism demand and the effect of Bord Failte's marketing expenditure. This empirical study is a country-tocountry regression model as it examines the outbound tourism demand from Italy to Ireland. Italy is the fifth most important market for Ireland and its growth is surprising if compared to other European origin countries. In this respect, the purposes of this study are to (a) identify major explanatory variables of Italian tourist arrivals to Ireland through a regression model; and (b) investigate the effect, on Italian market, of marketing variable by incorporating Bord Fáilte's marketing expenditure.

Model Specification and Estimation Procedure

Based on a review of literature in this study the authors selected income, relative prices, marketing expenditure and dummy variable (in order to evaluate terrorism effect) as the important determinants of Italian tourism demand to Ireland. Preliminary estimation indicated that the double-logarithm forms fitted the data better than did linear forms in terms of expected signs and statistical significance. Indeed, this functional form has had good empirical performance in most of the previous studies. Secondary data were used and the model was estimated using annual time series from 1989 to 2000.

This period and frequency were chosen because they provided the most consistent data set available to the authors at the time of writing. The *dependent variable* was measured as the number of total arrivals from Italy to Ireland divided by the Italian population in the same year. Data were supplied by Bord Failte and they are estimated based on (1) information from the Central Statistical Office's Country of Residence Survey-which is the best estimation and is based on count at frontiers-and (2) Bord Failte's Survey of Overseas travellers.

The choice of the *explanatory variables* was based on a meticulous analysis of previous studies findings but it was also influenced and limited by data and time constrains. *Income*. According to the economic theory, income is one of the most important variables in tourism demand and for this reason it was considered in this study. The Italian GDP was considered as the most representative variable for Italian income; it was included in the model in per capita form and at 1995-price. ISTAT supplied the Italian GDP and population data.

Relative prices. For the countries in consideration it was decided to include only the price of tourism in the form of cost of living in the destination country and in the substitute country. Moreover, as Italians tend to travel more in Italy than anywhere else, this study assumed that domestic tourism was the best and the only real substitute product in modeling Italian tourism demand.

An exchange-rate-adjusted-consumer-price-index was created dividing the Irish Consumer Price Index for the Italian Consumer Price Index and multiplying for the Exchange Rate between Italian lira and the Irish pound. Central Statistical Office of Ireland and ISTAT supplied data used herein. Both of CPIs were considered at 1995- price. The exchange rates used here were obtained from the Italian Office for Exchange (Ufficio Italiano Cambi).

Marketing expenditure. Marketing expenditure from the destination country to the origin country was the most important explanatory variable included in the model. Consistent with the previous literature that included marketing activity, it was considered the amount spent in market the destination by the National Tourism Organisations (NTOs) that is in this case Bord Failte who furnished the data used herein. In particular, data from 1989 to 1993 are our estimated based on European marketing expenditure while from 1994 the data are effective marketing expenditure in Italy.

A general-to-specific process was carried out and the equations were regressed using Ordinary Least Square and attention was paid to the: (a) estimated coefficients both at significance level (statistic) and sign coherency to the theory; (b) Adjusted R2; (c) F statistic to test the joint significance of all coefficients; (d) SSR, the sum of squared residuals. Initial results and a market analysis of the two countries under investigation showed that the static model could be an appropriate specification for modeling Italian tourists flows to Ireland. The results of this estimate showed that the Static model(3) was the most consistent with economic theory and it was parsimonious and encompassed all the other models considered in the analysis.

Results and Discussion

Two explanatory variables, relative prices and marketing expenditure, were statistically significant at the 5% level of significance and the signs were found as expected from the tourism demand theory. Using diagnostic tests for autocorrelation, heteroscedasticity, functional form and structural instability rigorous statistical analysis was performed.

The model fits the data reasonably well, was correctly specified and showed structural stability. There was no evidence of autocorrelation and heteroscedasticity although a suspicious of multicollinearity can arise, as in all previous studies, but it was unlikely that multicollinearity was serious. The suspect of the endogenicity of the marketing expenditure to the dependent variahle was not confirmed by the Wu-Hausman test.

Results indicate that income and the dummy variable for the cease-fire in 1994 may not be as important for Italians as expected. The estimated coefficient of the relative price is highly statistically significant and its sign is negative as expected. Italian tourism demand to Ireland is highly price elastic, as the absolute value of the price elasticity exceeds unity and this means that an increase of prices of 1% will result in a decrease of almost 5.2% in arrivals. The variable of marketing expenditure has the expected positive sign and it is highly statistically significant.

The results of the current study provide strong evidence of a link between the marketing variable and international tourism. However, NTOs are more interested in the amount of additional tourist expenditure than in the increase of arrivals. Consequently, the relationship between estimated marketing elasticity and its impact in terms of possible additional Italian expenditure during Italian holidays in Ireland was calculated showing an average increase in receipt of 1,222,000(4) (Irish Pound) when an increase of 1% of marketing expenditure was hypothesised.

Moreover, the ratio between increased tourism receipt and the increase in marketing expenditure necessary to generate the increase in receipts is 276:1(5). This result is in line with the results of Crouch, Schultz and Valerio (1992) and represents the highest benefit/cost ratio calculated to date. The aim of this chapter was to identify the determinants of Italian tourism demand to Ireland and to estimate the impact of Bord Failte's marketing expenditure on the number of tourist arrivals.

Results from the regression analysis indicate income and marketing expenditures as key determinants. The results of the model are consistent with findings of previous studies demonstrating the link between both economic and non-economic factors and tourism demand. Although, it is important to emphasise that caution should be used in interpreting these results overall, they provide some encouraging evidence on the cause-effect relationship between Irish marketing expenditure in Italy and Italian arrivals to Ireland.

Modelling and Forecasting Malaysia's Tourism Demand

Within the global tourism market, Malaysia can be considered as a relatively new tourist destination. Serious and integrated efforts to develop this industry were only started in the middle of the 1980s immediately after the world economic recession. The government has been playing a very important role to stimulate the growth and development of the tourism industry.

In 1987 the government had established the Ministry of Culture, Arts and Tourism and later upgraded it to the Ministry of Tourism in 2004 to manage, monitor, synchronize and ensure all tourism development activities and programs are in line with the National Tourism Master Plan. At the same time, various attractive incentives and assistance were given to private operators to encourage them to be directly involved in the tourism industry. The government was also allocated substantial amount of fund to this industry besides providing sufficient basic infrastructure. To further promote tourism, the government also involved in marketing by launching several Visit Malaysia Years. Malaysia is also fortunate for having abundant stock of natural tourism products.

Given the scenario above, the growth of Malaysian tourism was fantastic in the last two decades. In 1985, the total tourist arrivals were 3.11 million and increased to about 16.43 million in 2004. In terms of growth, within the last 20 years tourist arrivals to Malaysia had increased at an average of 14.9 per cent annually. According to WTO (2005), Malaysia was ranked as the thirteen world's top tourist destinations. Within ASEAN region Malaysia was the leading country in receiving inbound tourists by controlling about 32.37 percent of total arrivals in 2004 (WTO, 2006). In the same year the market share of Malaysia in the Asia and Pacific region was 15.7 per cent which was the third most visited destination after China and Hong Kong.

Increase in total tourist arrivals would also bring in more tourist receipts. From 1985 to 2005, tourist receipts had increased at an annual average of 16.4 per cent or from RM1.543 billion to RM31.954 billion. In 2006, tourism was the second largest contributor of foreign exchange earnings to the country after the manufacturing sector.

The major markets for Malaysian tourism are mostly from the ASEAN region, followed by the Far East, Australia and the UK markets. For example in 2006, out of 17.547 million arrivals, the four major ASEAN countries namely Singapore, Thailand, Indonesia and Brunei had contributed to more than 77 per cent, followed by China, Japan, Australia, United Kingdom, India and the United States of America which contributed slightly above 10 per cent. In order to diversify the economy, the government is trying hard to further stimulate the growth of the tourism industry. For this purpose, all stakeholders in tourism must be able to anticipate changes that might occur to tourist arrivals and respond to them accordingly. Prediction of the changing pattern in tourist arrivals can be done by knowing the factors that influence their arrival to this country.

The objectives of this paper are to model and investigate the most important factors that affect the inbound tourists to Malaysia and to forecast their arrivals in the next ten years using the most recent cointegration technique known as the Autoregressive Distributed Lagged (ARDL).

Tourism Demand Analysis: Variables and Data

Tourism Demand Analysis: Studies on tourism demand and forecasting have been carried out since the 1960s. However, most of the studies were based on the Ordinary Least Square (OLS) approach. Some of the studies used multiple regression using the Cochrane Orcutt (CO), Almost Ideal Demand Function (AIDS),

Generalized Least Square (GLS) etc. In the middle of the 1990s, emerged new approach. Most authors in the field of tourism demand have shifted to other methodologies, and most of them were using the dynamic approaches. One of the approach or method is a cointegration which is the most preferable. The details of other methodologies beside the importance of selected variables in tourism demand studies. The discussion is as follows:

Dependent Variables: Tourist arrivals have been used as a dependent variable in most studies on tourism demand. It has been supported by Witt and Witt (1995), Crouch et al. (1992), and Li (2004). Summary, that about 59 per cent of tourism demand model had used this variable. Other possible variables are tourist expenditure (32%), average length of stay (6%) and number of nights (3%).

Independent Variables: A survey of 100 empirical studies on tourism modeling by Lim (2004) found that income and price were the most commonly used explanatory variable. The importance of income (81%) and tourism price (65%) in tourism demand model. This is followed by travelling cost (53%), exchange rate (39%), dummy (29), time trend (18%), lagged dependent variables (16%) and population (13%), tourism price at substitute destinations (12%), marketing/advertisement (10%) and travelling cost to substitute destinations (3%).

Data: This study will also use some of the variables, and details are as follows:

Dependent variable: Tourist arrivals will be used as a proxy for the tourism demand. Annual data are used for the period from 1970-2004. Data on tourist arrivals were collected from the Malaysia Tourism Statistical Report.

Independent variables: The independent variables in this study are tourism price, travelling cost, income, tourism price at the alternative tourism destinations, exchange rates, lag dependent (repeat tourists) and the dummy variables. Details are as follows:

i) Tourism price refers to the price of all goods and services consumed by tourists at the destination. Since most countries do not have the price index for goods and services consumed by tourists, the next best alternative is the general Consumer Price Index (CPI) of that particular country. The calculation of tourism price is based on the consumer price index (CPI) of the visited country divided by the CPI of the origin country. In this study, the calculated ratio shows the cost of living in Malaysia relative to the origin country. It is expected that tourism price and arrivals will have a negative relationship.

ii) Transportation or travelling cost can be measured by air fares between the visited destination and the origin country; ferry fares and/or petrol costs for surface travel; and price of crude oil. In this study, the price of crude oil will be used. It is expected that the higher price of oil will reduce the arrivals.

iii) Tourism prices at the alternative tourism destinations are a substitute price. The calculation is similar to the estimating of tourism price, where the visiting destination now refers to the alternative tourism destination. In this study the alternative tourism destinations are Singapore, Thailand and Indonesia. Thus, tourism price at the alternative tourism destination will be the cost of living for tourists in Singapore, Thailand or Indonesia relative to the origin country. The important of substitute price has been proven in tourism study.

iv) The income variable refers to the real per capita income (RPI) or per capita gross domestic product. Income is the most popular variable included in the tourism demand function. Normally, the higher income will increase the total arrivals.

v) The exchange rate is the ratio of currency between the destination country and the origin country. The change in exchange rate will affect the currency value of the origin country. Any change in exchange rate will lead to an appreciation or depreciation of tourist currency. Any appreciation in tourist currency may encourage more people to travel.

vi) Lag dependent or repeat tourists variable is usually used on the international tourism demand as a proxy for informal promotion (word-of-mouth effect), since the knowledge about the destination will be spread as people talk about their holidays, and thereby reducing the uncertainty for potential visitors. Hence, it will encourage more tourists to come to that destination. In the dynamic model of tourism demand analysis, the lagged dependent variable (the previous year's number of tourist arrivals) must be included. If the impact of past tourism is neglected, the effect of the relevant variables considered will tend to be overestimated (as the estimated coefficients will involve direct and indirect effects). Several authors point out that tourism demand analysis will suffer from this neglect of the dynamic structure. Studies that include lagged dependent variables to explain tourism include those by Narayan (2004), Moòoz (2007) and Toh, Habibullah and Goh (2006).

vii) In this study the dummy variables have also been included. There are three dummies, which are the Asian economic crisis in 1997-98 (D97), the Gulf War in 1991 (D91), and the outbreak of SARS in 2003 (D03).

Most of the above data have been collected form World Development Indicator 2005.

The Long-run and Short-run Elasticities

Empirical estimation of the variables in the model indicate that most of them are statistically significant and consistent with the demand theory except for the exchange rates and Thailand as an alternative destination variable. In tourism, exchange rates may not play an important role especially with regard to the Malaysian Ringgit which is quite stable against other currencies.

Among the most important significant variables are tourism price, travelling cost, income and alternative destinations. For the tourism price almost all the countries show this variable is significant except for Japan and Australia. The sign of the variable is consistent with the economic theory except for Indonesia, Japan, the United Kingdom and Australia. For Japan, the United Kingdom and Australia the positive sign may indicate tourists from these countries are from rich countries and they are not really affected by the increasing of tourism cost in Malaysia. Furthermore, the tourism price in Malaysia is among the cheapest within the region.

Travelling costs from the origin countries to Malaysia are found to be significant for Singapore, Thailand, Brunei, China and Hong Kong while other countries are not significant. Most of these countries are a long-haul market.

The insignificance of this variable can be because to their arrival is not direct from their countries but that they visit Malaysia from nearby countries. Tourists from Thailand, Brunei, China, Hong Kong and the United States consider Singapore as a substitute destination for Malaysia.

Tourists from Indonesia, Japan, United Kingdom and Australia, on the other hand, consider Malaysia and Singapore as complementary destinations. Similarly, tourists from all countries put Indonesia as a substitute destination for Malaysia except for Hong Kong and the United Kingdom which consider Malaysia and Indonesia as complementary destinations. In this study, Singapore is the most significant an alternative tourism destination for Malaysia compare to Indonesia and Thailand.

As for income, it is significant in all countries except Indonesia and the most developed countries. Some countries consider Malaysia as an inferior destination due to its negative sign. In general, the majority of tourists from these countries visit Malaysia mainly to visit friends and relatives. For example, in 2003 about 47.2% tourist from Singapore visited their friends and relatives in Malaysia.

The magnitudes of the variables in the long run in general are acceptable and comparable to similar studies except for tourism price which can be considered as slightly high which implies tourist arrivals are quite sensitive to changes in prices of tourism services in this country.

The short-run relationships between tourist arrivals and its determinants have also been estimated. Following the general-to-specific approach Song and Witt (2003), only significant or close to significant variables will be included in the short run including the lagged dependent (repeat tourists) variable and the dummies.

In the short-run repeat tourists in all countries are statistically significant affected the tourism demand for Malaysia except for Singapore, China and the USA. Hong Kong and Australia however, show a negative sign, meaning that promotion (word-of-mouth effect) by repeat tourists is not effective. In order to make repeat tourists as an effective promotion agent, good tourism facilities and services must be provided at a very reasonable price. Their satisfaction while visiting Malaysia is very important because this experience will be shared with their friends and relatives, and indirectly will encourage or promote them to visit Malaysia in the future. This was supported by a survey conducted by MTPB which found that most tourists got information on Malaysia and visited the country through the encouragement of their friends and relatives.

The Gulf War (D91), Asian economic crisis 1997-98 (D97) and the outbreak of SARS in 2003 (D03) are expected to affect Malaysia tourism demand negatively. Dummy Asian economic crisis 1997-98 (D97) is significant in Singapore, Thailand, Hong Kong and Japan, which means that the Asian economic crisis did significantly decrease the volume of tourist arrivals to Malaysia. The outbreak of SARS (D03) which is significant in Singapore, Indonesia, Brunei, the United Kingdom, indicates that tourists from these countries were really concerned with the issue of safety. The Gulf War was only included in the USA market and it is significant.

A Panel Data Analysis of Demand for Tourism in Africa

Tourism is one of the most flourishing and emerging industry in the world with the international receipt growing by over 10 percent over the last ten years, while international tourism expenditure amounted to over US$525billion in 2003 (WTO, 2004). Despite its potential of creating many employment opportunities and foreign exchange in any economy, it is also a means of enhancing each country destination's infrastructural facilities as well as promoting cooperation and understanding among people all over the world.

Tourism has become a means by which many countries, especially the developing countries, improve their income base and at the same show case their traditional heritage. Tourism in

African continent has been seen as a means of enhancing economic growth and development as well as launching the image of the continent to the outside world.

According to Christie and Crompton (2001), the contribution of tourism industry in the gross domestic products (GDP) and exports in many African countries has been improving overtime. As identified by WTO (2004) report, there has been significant growth in the level of international tourist arrivals in Africa. The World Travel and Tourism Council (WTTC) also put the value of US$39.6billion as the amounted that was generated in 2003 from economic activities in the travel and tourism industry in sub-Saharan Africa The report also shows that about 2.5% of the GDP in the region is accounted for by tourism industry that has generated about 5.5% of all employment in the region.

However, in spite of Africa's potential in tourism, the continent's tourism endowments have been underdevelop and underutilized. WTO (2004) report indicates that Africa has attracted less than 5% of international tourist arrivals in 2004, and had received less than 3% of international tourism receipt. Africa in 2001 received about 27.7 million international tourist arrivals and got an international tourism receipts of US$11.7 billion, which implies that 3.7 arrivals per 100 of population that is compared poorly with the world average of 11 and the 44 per 100 in Europe. Furthermore, despite African potentials in tourism industry, there are limited empirical studies on issues concerning the hypothetical subject matter in the continent.

This is the reason why Christie and Crompton (2001) opined that the lack of appropriate empirical studies on tourism in Africa is what contributed to the inadequate policy guidance to the industry. It is against this background of shortage in empirical studies of tourism in Africa that we intend to contribute to the frontier of knowledge in tourism literature in Africa by including both endogenous and exogenous variables in explaining the factors that determine the demand for tourism in Africa through dynamic generalized method of moment (GMM) of panel data analysis between the period of 1995 to 2004 (an update of Naude and Saayman (2004) data paints).

Tourism in Africa

Tourism is one of the major global economic activities. Tourism is said to be an important ingredient for economic development through its impact on employment generation, enhancement of infrastructure provision, generation of income taxes, exports and by acceleration global peace. According to Sinclair (1998), the contribution of tourism to development is well documented and tourism is now among the fastest growing industries in the world. Competition among destinations has intensified to attract more and more tourists.

Tourism growth has been impressive in recent years and this shown in the number of tourism arrivals in all countries that increased from 25.3 million in 1950 to 69.3 million in 1960 and later to 165.8 million in 1970. Despite the drag in the growth rate of tourist arrivals since 1970, world tourist arrival multiplied by a sector of about 27 between 1950 and 2000. Thus, from 25.3 million in 1950, international tourist arrivals (now arrivals) reached 763.2 million in 2004, with an average annual growth rate of 6.4 percent.

In terms of global tourism receipts, the world witnessed an increase in tourism receipt from US$2.1 billion in 1950 to US$17.9 billion in 1970 and later rise to US$106.5 billion in 1980. Due to more and more arrivals in the world and with their accompany expenditure, international tourism receipts move from US$2.1 billion in 1980 to US$479.2 billion in twenty years after. This increasing trend continues till 2004, where the total global tourism receipts amounted to US$622.7 billion.

Thus, tourism is one of the most flourishing sectors in the world given that it global receipt have grown by 12 percent over the last ten years. This has led to the case where many countries are setting targets in attempts to gain the additional income, foreign currency, employment and tax revenue that the sector can provide.

It is as a result of this that many African countries have started tapping the potentialities that is embedded in tourism and hospitalities. According to Kester (2003), tourism has the potential to contribute significantly to economic growth and development in Africa. Naude and Saayman (2004) opined that Africa's cultural and natural resource endowment are such that it ought to be benefiting largely from tourism, while Christie and Crompton (2001) believe that African has an "exceptional" tourism potentials and that the it is increasingly contributing to the continent's gross domestic products (GDP) and exports.

International tourist arrivals to Africa destinations increase from just 500,000 in 1950 to over 15 million in 1990. This increase in arrivals continues, as it got to 28.2 million in 2000 and later rise to 33.2 million in 2004.

This really shows that Africa tourist arrivals have been growing overtime. According to WTO (2003) figures, Africa tourism has grown significantly since 1990. In terms of the continent receipts on global tourism, that African receipts on international tourism rise from US$100 million in 1950 to US$3.4 billion in 1980, which later increased to US$6.4 billion in 1990. By 2000, African tourism receipts have risen to US$10.6 billion and got to US$18.3 billion in 2004.

These incremental trends in African arrivals and receipts literarily depict that Africa is performance in term of tourism, but when we look at its share in the global tourism, we could sea that through it share in international tourist arrivals increased from 1.98 percent in 1950 to 4.25 in 2001, which is about 130 percent increment. This latter fall in 2002 to 4.21 percent and picked up by 2004 to 4.4 percent of the global tourist arrivals.. In terms of the growth rate, the continent witnessed a negative growth in 1960 of about 42 of its arrivals. This later change to a positive growth rate of about 81 percent in 1980 (the peak), afterwards, there the growth rate has been increasing at a decreasing rate up to 2004 when she witnessed a negative growth rate in arrivals of 6 percent.

The case of the growth rate of Africa's tourist arrivals is not that different with her receipts, as she experienced a negative growth rate of her receipt in 1960 (39 percent) and by 1990, it has reduced to –27percent and later to –0.7 percent in 2004.

Regionally, there are different in performance of these regions in the continent. According to WTO figure (2003), there has been considerable improvement in tourism in Africa, especially in 1990, especially that of southern Africa that has grown by about 300%

between 1990 and 2002. However, North Africa still remains the most attractive regional destination, capturing 1.5% of the total international tourism market share. Worth of noticing is that as the tourist arrivals in Africa increased in 2001 that of the world tourism decreased during the period. The report of WTO (2003c) indicates that there had been increasing trend in tourism in Africa despite the SARS virus that affected the Asia counties and the war in Iraq. Central Africa remains the least tourist arrivals destinations in the continent followed by the West African destinations. This might be due to the inadequate infrastructural facilities that are available for tourism in these destinations.

Literature Review

In general, the tourism literatures on the modelling of tourism demand focuses either on analyzing the impact of different determinants and/or on the accurate forecasting of the future tourism demand.

This study lies within the group focusing on the underlying determinants. The comprehensive reviews of the empirical literature on tourism demand by Crouch (1994a, 1994b, 1995), Witt and Witt (1995), Lim (1997, 1999) and Li et al (2005) Suggest a substantial agreement regarding both the tourism demand measures and the variables that are important in explaining international tourism flows. A lot of these existing empirical works have used tourist arrivals/departures and tourism receipts/ expenditures as dependent variables. The number of overnight the tourists stays in their destination countries and the average length of stay has also been studied, but much less frequently.

As for the explanatory variables, empirical models of tourism demand borrow heavily from the consumer theory, which predicts that the level of consumption depends on the consumer's income, the price of the good/service in question, the prices of related goods (substitutes and complements), and other demand shifters. As a result, income and prices are the most commonly used variables in terms of the major factors influencing tourism demand.

Given that the leisure tourism is generally regarded a luxury good, the income remaining after expenditures on necessities, or the so-called discretionary income would be the preterred income variable. However, discretionary income is a subjective variable and is not precisely measurable. Therefore, most researchers have relied on the nominal or real (per capital) personal, disposable, or national income, as well as GDP as measure for income in origin countries.

Apart from being sensitive to their own income, tourists are also sensitive to prices. The tourism includes two price elements: the cost of travel to the destination and the cost of living in the tourist destination.

Also, the literature shows that the most often employed variables aimed at measuring the cost of living at the tourist destination relative to the origin country (and possibly to alternative destinations) have been relative consumer price indices. However, their deficiency comes from the fact that the expenditure patterns of a tourist might be quite specific and therefore different from that of the average household in a certain country. As a result, some studies have used specific price indices such as hotel, drink and tobacco, shopping, meals, and entertainment and other variables. However, we should understand that the work of Martin and Witt (1987) has shown that such tourism-specific indices do not perform any better than the overall price indices.

Studies often use exchange rate in tourism demand model in addition to/or combined with the relative price variables. There is some group of authors that argued that tourists respond to exchange rate movements much more than to changes in relative inflation rates when they make decisions on the travel destination. However, Martin and Witt (1987) argued that the exchange rate alone is not an acceptable proxy for tourism costs. Most empirical works on tourism demand models have used the exchange rate adjusted for relative prices (i.e. real exchange rate) to capture the substitution between domestic vacations and international travel. In this way, the impacts of (relative) inflation and exchange rate movements are measured through a single variable.

There has been less attention on transportation costs in the literature due to the fact that there is lack of adequate measure of effective transportation costs. In countries where the most of the tourists arrive by car, the proxy are usually oil or gasoline prices while in the case of far-off destinations, airline fares represent the preferable alternative. In the latter case, according to Mervar and Payne (2007), data problems arise due to the pricing practices of airlines that often include "special" have that are difficult to collect and use for an empirical analysis. Furthermore, multicollinearity between the transportation cost and income variables presents an often cited reason for omitting the transportation cost variable from tourism studies.

Furthermore, the dynamics of tourism demand has been incorporated in a lot of studies to account for lagged effects of supply constraints in the form of shortages in hotel accommodation, passenger transportation capacity and trained staff, which cannot be adjusted rapidly. Sometimes, a time trend is included to capture qualitative factors in the tourist destination or changes in tourist faster for foreign travel. Also, during variables are employed in order to capture the impact of wars, political crises or natural disasters, as well as seasonal variations.

Given the above, tourism demand model is usually estimated as a function of income of tourists origin country, transportation costs between dimension and origin, exchange rates, relative prices, dummy variables and the deterministic trends. Despite the fact that in the literature, annual data is often used, there has been increasing use of quarterly data in recent literature, which is in line with the increasing interest in the seasonality of global tourism flows.

In terms of the estimation techniques, the log-linear regressions are the most frequently employed functional forms as the estimated coefficients can be interpreted as elasticities. However, while traditional econometric technique dominated studies up to the mid-1990s, the use of cointegration, vector autoregressive model, almost ideal demand systems, and time-varying parameter models have since become familiar approaches. Thus, given the fact that the trend parallels the overall trend in applied econometric studies since it has been shown that most time series data are not stationary and, therefore, the use of traditional econometric techniques may serious affect the credibility of the results. However, some studies have tried to forecast the demand for tourism for a particular period of time suing various for casting methods. Martin and Witt (1989) compared the accuracy of several quantitative methods in forecasting tourism demand in an international context; Johnson and Ashworth (1990) had survey articles on the determinants of tourism demand; Witt and Witt (1995) reviewed about sixty five empirical studies on the tourism demand; while Sinclair and Stables (1997) made a synthesis of several tourism analyses, discussing and particularly the use of different kinds of models, with explicit consideration of the single-equation and system of equations approaches, and their respective advantages and disadvantage.

Thus, studies on the determinants of tourism demand are subjected to specific problems. The reasons to the problems according to Mello et al. (1999) are twofold: the special nature of the demand for tourism, which can be attributed to the complexity of the motivational structure underlying the decision-making process, and the scarcity of relevant data that are fundamental in econometric modelling.

The quantitative studies of tourism demand require the framework of a formal mathematical model that can provide estimates of the sensitivity of demand to changes in the variables on which it depends. The econometric modelling also supplies a good basis for accurate forecasting that is of considerable value for policy purposes and an important element in public and private investment decisions.

However, tourism demand modelling is not easy due to the complexity of the decision-making process, the multiplicity and heterogeneity of the products and services specified, the fact that transportation plays a role in the consumption of tourism, the intertemporal dependence of current demand on its past and future values, and the nonseparability between leisure consumption and labour supply and/or between tourism demand and the demand for other goods and services.

These difficulties in the specification of a comprehensive and reliable model of demand for tourism arecompounded by the existence of unquantifiable factors influencing demand, as well as by the inaccuracy or unavailability of data for those that are, in principle, measurable.

Thus, the conceptual and practical problems underlying the empirical studies in this area accounted for the simplifying assumptions that investigators make in their attempts to specify econometric models for explaining the behaviour of tourism demand.

So long as the assumptions do not distort the estimated results, they perform an important role in facilitating the provision of information which can be useful for policy formation and decision making. When the assumptions are inadequate and questionable, they give rise to models that may embody misspecification bias, leading to accurate and unreliable estimation results that cannot be used for any sound inference and forecasting or policy purposes.

The major examples of this latter type of models can be found in the single equation approach within a static context. These adhoc models lack the theoretical basis within which the reasonable testable hypothesis of consumer theory can be included and often neglect the possible interdependencies among competing destinations Mello et al. (1999). Also, they usually ignore the dynamic nature of demand for tourism, disregarding the possibility that the sensitivity of tourism demand of its determinants may differ between different time periods.

Modelling procedures constrained by these theoretical faults lead to empirical inadequacies, such as the omission of relevant variables and incorrect functional form that result in misspecified models and biased estimates. Thus, given the above, we have discovered that in the literature of empirical studies of tourism, there are two main types. The first consists of those that prefer modern time series and cointegration techniques in the attempt of modelling and forecasting the dependant variable, between one or several pairs of countries, Kulenderan and Witt (2001), Seddighi and Theocharous (2002), Song et al. (2003 and Dritsakis (2004)). The second type includes those studies that estimate the determinants of international tourism demand using classical multivariate regressions, Witt and Witt (1995), and Lim (1997)).

Therefore, in this study we explore these two types of models, vis a vis, single equation and system of equation using annual panel data. The use of these two models will really afford us to make comparative analysis on the outcome of the two results so as to really know the model that suit the explanation of the demand for tourism.

This two stage least square only presents two different outcome, from fixed effect and none cross-sectional effect angle. We could see that we the system of equations, the result has drastically changed to that of OLS above. Here, all the outcomes show that the autonomous variable, constant, has negative effect on Africa's tourist arrivals. This means that if the regressors in the model are put into consideration and there is no encouragement,. Provision of infrastructure and political stability in the continent. Then the continent will not be attractive for tourists and there will be reduction in the number of arrivals.

Both outcomes of the two stage least square also show that the previous tourists number have statistically significant influence on the present tourist arrivals. Their degree of responsiveness is elastic, meaning that the prospective tourists are very significant to previous treatment and hospitality given to previous tourists. The two results show that tourists are very sensitive to prices in Africa, though the degree of responsiveness is inelastic. Exchange rate for both outcomes in the two stage least square is negatively related to tourist arrivals. This means that as the destination countries currencies get appreciated there will be loss of welfare to the tourists and this is in form of giving more of their domestic currencies to destinations currencies, and this will make their travels and adventures more expensive.

Their degree of responsiveness to exchange rate appreciation is elastic and statistically significant at the non cross-sectional effect level. The measure of infrastructure in both outcomes of two stage least square (Teline) has statistically significant direct effect on tourist arrivals. This means that as more and more infrastructural facilities are provided in the continent, tourists are eager to come and explore the opportunities and endowments that are embedded in Africa. The coefficient of the variable that stands for elasticities indicate that the variable is inelastic at both outcomes. Here, the political instabilities in different parts of the continent have adverse effects on tourist arrivals.

This shows that tourists are sensitive to what is happening in the polity before embarking on their trips. World income has an inverse relationship with arrivals under fixed effect, while direct effect in the none cross-sectional case. This reason for this is that since the fixed effect captures the individual destination effect and there are crises in same of these destinations in Africa, then even if the tourists have more income to spend on tourism, they will not prefer coming to the crises ridden destinations.

The result of the dynamic panel data techniques used in this study. The dynamic result gives four different outcomes of the technique vis a vis, fixed effect, random effect, difference and the orthogonal deviation. The dynamic results show that in all the four outcome of the model, consumer price index, a measure of relative price in the destinations is inversely related to the number of arrivals. The significant of this variable in all the outcomes except that of difference model, indicate that prices are important factors that tourists consider in their choice of destinations in Africa and the degree of responsiveness of tourist to changes in prices in inelastic in the models of the dynamic panel analysis. Exchange rate in all these models is also inversely related to tourist arrivals, indicating that appreciation of destinations currencies often discourage prospective tourists form coming to Africa. It is important to note that this variable is significant at 5 per cent level for all the models and it is highly inelastic. Crime rate in the continent also has an inverse effect with the tourist arrivals, that is, as the incidence of crime increases in the destinations, there will be reduction in the inflow of tourists to those destinations.

Source: Author's calculation The lagged value of tourist arrivals which is the number of previous tourist arrivals, the number of available telephone lines and world income all have direct effects on the number of tourist arrivals. The number of telephone lines for the four outcomes are statistically significant indication that it is an important factor that influences tourists' choice of destinations. The same can be said to the previous number of tourist arrivals in the continent, as all the outcomes show that this variable is relevant determinant of tourist demand and interesting thing here is that the autonomous variable indicates that if countries of destinations do not make efforts to develop tourism through improvement in infrastructure, crime rate and the political situation, there will be reduction in the number of tourist arrivals in Africa. These results contradict with those of the OLS results. Therefore, the results of this study have shown that the dynamic panel data analysis is a better technique in explaining the factors that influence tourism demand in Africa, since it is always used to correct for endogeneity problems, the issue of heteroscedasticity and dynamics of the variables.

Conclusion

We have tried in this study to econometrically determine factors that influence the demand for tourism in Africa. Analysis has been done on the structure, pattern and trend of African tourism overtime.

In selecting the variables for this study, we considered both the endogenous and exogenous variables. That is, we have selected the economic variables as well as the socio-political variables that influence the tourists' choice of destinations. In this study, we specified the single equation model and that of system of equations. The single equation model makes of OLS estimators with fixed and random effects, while the system of equation makes use of the two stage least square and the dynamic panel data technique. We find out from the analyses of this study that political instability, crime rate, exchange rate appreciation and consumer price index serve as signal to prospective tourists to the continent. However, the previous tourist arrivals, number of telephone lines, a measure of infrastructure, and world income, positively influence or determine tourist arrivals to Africa. Another interesting thing we found out in the study is that the results of system of equations are better than that of single equation model and this result was confirmed by Naude and Saayman (2004), Eilat and Einav (2003).

3

Impact Assessment of Environment

The quality of the environment, both natural and man-made, is essential to tourism. However, tourism's relationship with the environment is complex. It involves many activities that can have adverse environmental effects. Many of these impacts are linked with the construction of general infrastructure such as roads and airports, and of tourism facilities, including resorts, hotels, restaurants, shops, golf courses and marinas. The negative impacts of tourism development can gradually destroy the environmental resources on which it depends.

On the other hand, tourism has the potential to create beneficial effects on the environment by contributing to environmental protection and conservation. It is a way to raise awareness of environmental values and it can serve as a tool to finance protection of natural areas and increase their economic importance.

Three main impact areas: natural resources, pollution, and physical impacts

Three Main Impact Areas: Natural Resources, Pollution, and Physical Impacts

Tourism's Three Main Impact Areas

Negative impacts from tourism occur when the level of visitor use is greater than the environment's ability to cope with this use within the acceptable limits of change. Uncontrolled conventional tourism poses potential threats to many natural areas around the world. It can put enormous pressure on an area and lead to impacts such as soil erosion, increased pollution, discharges into the sea, natural habitat loss, increased pressure on endangered species and heightened vulnerability to forest fires. It often puts a strain on water resources, and it can force local populations to compete for the use of critical resources.

Depletion of Natural Resources

Tourism development can put pressure on natural resources when it increases consumption in areas where resources are already scarce.

Water Resources

Water, and especially fresh water, is one of the most critical natural resources. The tourism industry generally overuses water resources for hotels, swimming pools, golf courses and personal use of water by tourists. This can result in water shortages and degradation of water supplies, as well as generating a greater volume of waste water.. In dryer regions like the Mediterranean, the issue of water scarcity is of particular concern. Because of the hot climate and the tendency of tourists to consume more water when on holiday than they do at home, the amount used can run up to 440 liters a day. This is almost double what the inhabitants of an average Spanish city use.

Golf course maintenance can also deplete fresh water resources. In recent years golf tourism has increased in popularity and the number of golf courses has grown rapidly. Golf courses require an enormous amount of water every day and, as with other causes of excessive extraction of water, this can result in water scarcity. If the water comes from wells, overpumping can cause saline intrusion into groundwater. Golf resorts are more and more often situated in or near protected areas or areas where resources are limited, exacerbating their impacts.

Local Resources

Tourism can create great pressure on local resources like energy, food, and other raw materials that may already be in short supply. Greater extraction and transport of these resources exacerbates the physical impacts associated with their exploitation. Because of the seasonal character of the industry, many destinations have ten times more inhabitants in the high season as in the low season. A high demand is placed upon these resources to meet the high expectations tourists often have (proper heating, hot water, etc.).

Land Degradation

Important land resources include minerals, fossil fuels, fertile soil, forests, wetland and wildlife. Increased construction of tourism and recreational facilities has increased the pressure on these resources and on scenic landscapes. Direct impact on natural resources, both renewable and nonrenewable, in the provision of tourist facilities can be caused by the use of land for accommodation and other infrastructure provision, and the use of building materials.

Forests often suffer negative impacts of tourism in the form of deforestation caused by fuel wood collection and land clearing. For example, one trekking tourist in Nepal-and area already suffering the effects of deforestation-can use four to five kilograms of wood a day.

Pollution

Tourism can cause the same forms of pollution as any other industry: air emissions, noise, solid waste and littering, releases of sewage, oil and chemicals, even architectural/visual pollution.

Air Pollution and Noise

Transport by air, road, and rail is continuously increasing in response to the rising numbe reported that the number of international air passengers worldwide rose from 88 million in 1972 to 344 million in 1994. One consequence of this increase in air transport is that tourism now accounts for more than 60% of air travel and is therefore responsible for an important share of air emissions. One study estimated that a single transatlantic return flight emits almost half the CO2 emissions produced by all other sources (lighting, heating, car use, etc.) consumed by an average person yearly.

Transport emissions and emissions from energy production

and use are linked to acid rain, global warming and photochemical pollution. Air pollution from tourist transportation has impacts on the global level, especially from carbon dioxide (CO2) emissions related to transportation energy use. And it can contribute to severe local air pollution. Some of these impacts are quite specific to tourist activities. For example, especially in very hot or cold countries, tour buses often leave their motors running for hours while the tourists go out for an excursion because they want to return to a comfortably air-conditioned bus.

Noise pollution from airplanes, cars, and buses, as well as recreational vehicles such as snowmobiles and jet skis, is an ever-growing problem of modern life. In addition to causing annoyance, stress, and even hearing loss for it humans, it causes distress to wildlife, especially in sensitive areas. For instance, noise generated by snowmobiles can cause animals to alter their natural activity patterns.

Solid Waste and Littering

In areas with high concentrations of tourist activities and appealing natural attractions, waste disposal is a serious problem and improper disposal can be a major despoiler of the natural environment-rivers, scenic areas, and roadsides. For example, cruise ships in the Caribbean are estimated to produce more than 70,000 tons of waste each year. Today some cruise lines are actively working to reduce waste-related impacts. Solid waste and littering can degrade the physical appearance of the water and shoreline and cause the death of marine animals.

In mountain areas, trekking tourists generate a great deal of waste. Tourists on expedition leave behind their garbage, oxygen cylinders and even camping equipment. Such practices degrade the environment with all the detritus typical of the developed world, in remote areas that have few garbage collection or disposal facilities. Some trails in the Peruvian Andes and in Nepal frequently visited by tourists have been nicknamed "Coca-Cola trail" and "Toilet paper trail".

Sewage

Construction of hotels, recreation and other facilities often leads to increased sewage pollution. Wastewater has polluted seas and lakes surrounding tourist attractions, damaging the flora and fauna. Sewage runoff causes serious damage to coral reefs because it stimulates the growth of algae, which cover the filter-feeding corals, hindering their ability to survive. Changes in salinity and siltation can have wide-ranging impacts on coastal environments. And sewage pollution can threaten the health of humans and animals.

Aesthetic Pollution

Often tourism fails to integrate its structures with the natural features and indigenous architectural of the destination. Large, dominating resorts of disparate design can look out of place in any natural environment and may clash with the indigenous structural design.

A lack of land-use planning and building regulations in many destinations has facilitated sprawling developments along coastlines, valleys and scenic routes. The sprawl includes tourism facilities themselves and supporting infrastructure such as roads, employee housing, parking, service areas, and waste disposal.

Physical Impacts

Attractive landscape sites, such as sandy beaches, lakes, riversides, and mountain tops and slopes, are often transitional zones, characterized by species-rich ecosystems. Typical physical impacts include the degradation of such ecosystems.

An ecosystem is a geographic area including all the living organisms (people, plants, animals, and microorganisms), their physical surroundings (such as soil, water, and air), and the natural cycles that sustain them. The ecosystems most threatened with degradation are ecologically fragile areas such as alpine regions, rain forests, wetlands, mangroves, coral reefs and sea grass beds. The threats to and pressures on these ecosystems are often severe because such places are very attractive to both tourists and developers.

Physical impacts are caused not only by tourism-related land clearing and construction, but by continuing tourist activities and long-term changes in local economies and ecologies.

Physical Impacts of Tourism Development

Construction Activities and Infrastructure Development

The development of tourism facilities such as accommodation, water supplies, restaurants and recreation facilities can involve sand mining, beach and sand dune erosion, soil erosion and extensive paving. In addition, road and airport construction can lead to land degradation and loss of wildlife habitats and deterioration of scenery.

In Yosemite National Park (US), for instance, the number of roads and facilities have been increased to keep pace with the growing visitor numbers and to supply amenities, infrastructure and parking lots for all these tourists. These actions have caused habitat loss in the park and are accompanied by various forms of pollution including air pollution from automobile emissions; the Sierra Club has reported "smog so thick that Yosemite Valley could not be seen from airplanes". This occasional smog is harmful to all species and vegetation inside the Park.

Deforestation and Intensified or Unsustainable Use of Land

Construction of ski resort accommodation and facilities frequently requires clearing forested land. Coastal wetlands are often drained and filled due to lack of more suitable sites for construction of tourism facilities and infrastructure. These activities can cause severe disturbance and erosion of the local ecosystem, even destruction in the long term.

Marina Development

Development of marinas and breakwaters can cause changes in currents and coastlines. Furthermore, extraction of building materials such as sand affects coral reefs, mangroves, and hinterland forests, leading to erosion and destruction of habitats. In the Philippines and the Maldives, dynamiting and mining of coral for resort building materials has damaged fragile coral reefs and depleted the fisheries that sustain local people and attract tourists.

Overbuilding and extensive paving of shorelines can result in destruction of habitats and disruption of land-sea connections (such as sea-turtle nesting spots).

Coral reefs are especially fragile marine ecosystems and are suffering worldwide from reef-based tourism developments. Evidence suggests a variety of impacts to coral result from shoreline development, increased sediments in the water, trampling by tourists and divers, ship groundings, pollution from sewage, overfishing, and fishing with poisons and explosives that destroy coral habitat.

Physical Impacts from Tourist Activities

Anchoring and other Marine Activities

In marine areas (around coastal waters, reefs, beach and shoreline, offshore waters, uplands and lagoons) many tourist activities occur in or around fragile ecosystems. Anchoring, snorkeling, sport fishing and scuba diving, yachting, and cruising are some of the activities that can cause direct degradation of marine ecosystems such as coral reefs, and subsequent impacts on coastal protection and fisheries.

Trampling

Tourists using the same trail over and over again trample the vegetation and soil, eventually causing damage that can lead to loss of biodiversity and other impacts. Such damage can be even more extensive when visitors frequently stray off established trails.

Trampling Impacts on Vegetation	*Trampling Impacts on Soil*
Breakage and bruising of stems	Loss of organic matter
Reduced plant vigor	Reduction in soil macro porosity
Reduced regeneration	Decrease in air and water permeability
Loss of ground cover	Increase in run off
Change in species composition	Accelerated erosion

Source: University of Idaho

Alteration of Ecosystems by Tourist Activities

Habitat can be degraded by tourism leisure activities. For example, wildlife viewing can bring about stress for the animals and alter their natural behavior when tourists come too close. Safaris and wildlife watching activities have a degrading effect on habitat as they often are accompanied by the noise and commotion created by tourists as they chase wild animals in their trucks and aircraft.

This puts high pressure on animal habits and behaviors and tends to bring about behavioral changes. In some cases, as in Kenya, it has led to animals becoming so disturbed that at times they neglect their young or fail to mate.

Environmental Impacts at the Global Level

Loss of Biological Diversity

Biological diversity is the term given to the variety of life on Earth and the natural patterns it forms.

The effects of loss of biodiversity:

- It threatens our food supplies, opportunities for recreation and tourism, and sources of wood, medicines and energy.
- It interferes with essential ecological functions such as species balance, soil formation, and greenhouse gas absorption.
- It reduces the productivity of ecosystems, thereby shrinking nature's basket of goods and services, from which we constantly draw.
- It destabilizes ecosystems and weakens their ability to deal with natural disasters such as floods, droughts, and hurricanes, and with human-caused stresses, such as pollution and climate change.

Tourism, especially nature tourism, is closely linked to biodiversity and the attractions created by a rich and varied environment.

It can also cause loss of biodiversity when land and resources are strained by excessive use, and when impacts on vegetation, wildlife, mountain, marine and coastal environments and water resources exceed the carrying capacity. This loss of biodiversity in fact means loss of tourism potential.

Introduction of Exotic Species

Tourists and suppliers-often unwittingly-can bring in species (insects, wild and cultivated plants and diseases) that are not native to the local environment and that can cause enormous disruption and even destruction of ecosystems.

Depletion of the Ozone Layer

The ozone layer, which is situated in the upper atmosphere (or stratosphere) at an altitude of 12-50 kilometers, protects life on earth by absorbing the harmful wavelengths of the sun's ultraviolet (UV) radiation, which in high doses is dangerous to humans and animals. For instance, one of the reasons scientists have put forward for the global decrease of amphibian populations is increased exposure to UV radiation.

Ozone depleting substances (ODSs) such as CFCs (chlorofluorocarbon) and halons have contributed to the destruction of this layer. The tourism industry may be part of the problem; direct impacts start with the construction of new developments and continue during daily management and operations.

Refrigerators, air conditioners and propellants in aerosol spray cans, amongst others, contain ODSs and are widely used in the hotel and tourism industry. Emissions from jet aircraft are also a significant source of ODSs. According to Tourism Concern, scientists predict that by 2015 half of the annual destruction of the ozone layer will be caused by air travel.

UNEP's OzonAction Programme works with governments and industries, including the tourism industry, to phase out ODSs and find safer alternatives.

UNEP has developed extensive information and guidance on how many types of businesses can eliminate ODSs and contribute to preservation of the ozone layer. For further reading see the publication How the Hotel and Tourism Industry can Protect the Ozone Layer.

Climate Change

Climate scientists now generally agree that the Earth's surface temperatures have risen steadily in recent years because of an increase in the so-called greenhouse gases in the atmosphere, which trap heat from the sun. One of the most significant of these gases is carbon dioxide (CO2), which is generated when fossil fuels, such as coal, oil and natural gas are burned (e.g. in industry, electricity generation, and automobiles) and when there are changes in land use, such as deforestation.

In the long run, the accumulation of CO2 and other greenhouse gases in the atmosphere can cause global climate change-a process that may already be occurring.

Global tourism is closely linked to climate change. Tourism involves the movement of people from their homes to other destinations and accounts for about 50% of traffic movements; rapidly expanding air traffic contributes about 2.5% of the production of CO2. Tourism is thus a significant contributor to the increasing concentrations of greenhouse gases in the atmosphere.

Air travel itself is a major contributor to the greenhouse effect. Passenger jets are the fastest growing source of greenhouse gas emissions. The number of international travellers is expected to increase from 594 million in 1996 to 1.6 billion by 2020, adding greatly to the problem unless steps are taken to reduce emissions.

For more information on the relationship between energy and the environment, see UNEP's Energy Programme, which provides information and publications on energy efficiency and alternative energy sources to reduce the environmental impacts of energy use and of transportation.

How Global Environmental Impacts Affect Tourism

Natural Disasters

Catastrophes like floods, earthquakes, wildfires, volcanoes, avalanches, drought and diseases can have a serious effect on inbound and domestic tourism and thus on local tourism industries. The outbreak of the foot and mouth disease epidemic in England earlier this year (2001), for instance, has severely affected Great Britain's inbound tourism market. A BHA/Barclays Hospitality

Business Trends Survey found that 75% of hotels in England, 81% in Scotland and 85% in Wales continued to be affected by the foot and mouth outbreak, and over 60% forecast a decline in business in the June-September 2001 period.

Climate Change

Tourism not only contributes to climate change, but is affected by it as well. Climate change is likely to increase the severity and frequency of storms and severe weather events, which can have disastrous effects on tourism in the affected regions. Some of the other impacts that the world risks as a result of global warming are drought, diseases and heat waves.

These negative impacts can keep tourists away from the holiday destinations. Global warming may cause:

- Less snowfall at ski resorts, meaning a shorter skiing seasons in the Alpine region. In already hot areas like Asia and the Mediterranean, tourists will stay away because of immense heat, and out of fear of diseases and water shortages.
- Harm to vulnerable ecosystems such as rainforests and coral reefs because of rising temperatures and less rainfall. A major risk to coral reefs is bleaching, which occurs when coral is stressed by temperature increases, high or low levels of salinity, lower water quality, and an increase in suspended sediments. These conditions cause the zooxanthallae (the single-celled algae which forms the colours within the coral) to leave the coral. Without the algae, the coral appears white, or "bleached"-and rapidly dies. The Great Barrier Reef, which supports a US$ 640 million tourism industry, has been experiencing coral bleaching events for the last 20 years.
- Rising sea levels, the result of melting glaciers and polar ice. Higher sea levels will threaten coastal and marine areas with widespread floods in low-lying countries and island states, increasing the loss of coastal land. Beaches and islands that are major tourism attractions may be the first areas to be affected.

- Increased events of extreme weather, such as tornadoes, hurricanes and typhoons. These are already becoming more prevalent in tourist areas in the Caribbean and South East Asia. Hurricane Mitch in 1998, for instance, heavily affected tourism in the Caribbean. Wind damage, storm waves, heavy rains and flooding caused major losses in the local tourism sector.

Effects of Other Industries on Tourism

Impacts from other industries often have a more dramatic effect on the environment and can seriously affect tourism.

- Oil spills, like the oil tanker disaster that occurred off the Galapagos Islands (Ecuador) in January 2001, can cause severe short-term damage to tourist attractions. In that case, a freight ship loaded with 160,000 gallons of diesel fuel and 80,000 gallons of other petroleum products ran aground on the coast of San Cristobal and spilled nearly all of its load. Unique local marine and land species and the tourism potential of the area were badly affected.
- Agricultural runoff or industrial discharges can cause water pollution and may cause algae blooms like those that occurred in the Adriatic Sea in the early 1990s. In spite of improved control of sewage from tourism developments, the Mediterranean sea floor is increasingly carpeted with these quick-growing invaders, many rising 30 inches or more above anchoring runners. They appear equally adept at colonizing rock, mud, and sand in a virtually continuous swath that can extend from the beach out to a depth of about 150 feet, smothering coral reefs, fish and other sea flora and fauna in the process.
- Destructive practices such as blast fishing, fishing with poisonous chemicals like cyanide, and muroami netting (pounding reefs with weighted bags to scare fish out of crevices) directly destroy corals. They can also destroy a major draw for tourists.

How Tourism can Contribute to Environmental Conservation

- Direct financial contributions: Tourism can contribute directly to the conservation of sensitive areas and habitat. Revenue from park-entrance fees and similar sources can be allocated specifically to pay for the protection and management of environmentally sensitive areas. Special fees for park operations or conservation activities can be collected from tourists or tour operators.
- Contributions to government revenues: Some governments collect money in more far-reaching and indirect ways that are not linked to specific parks or conservation areas. User fees, income taxes, taxes on sales or rental of recreation equipment, and license fees for activities such as hunting and fishing can provide governments with the funds needed to manage natural resources. Such funds can be used for overall conservation programs and activities, such as park ranger salaries and park maintenance.

For Costa Rica, for example, tourism represents 72% of national monetary reserves, generates 140,000 jobs and produces 8.4% of the gross domestic product. The country has 25% of its territory classified under some category of conservation management. In 1999, protected areas welcomed 866,083 national and foreign tourists, who generated about US$ 2.5 million in admission fees and payment of services.

Improved Environmental Management and Planning

Sound environmental management of tourism facilities and especially hotels can increase the benefits to natural areas. But this requires careful planning for controlled development, based on analysis of the environmental resources of the area. Planning helps to make choices between conflicting uses, or to find ways to make them compatible.

By planning early for tourism development, damaging and expensive mistakes can be prevented, avoiding the gradual deterioration of environmental assets significant to tourism.

Cleaner production techniques can be important tools for planning and operating tourism facilities in a way that minimizes their environmental impacts.

For example, green building (using energy-efficient and non-polluting construction materials, sewage systems and energy sources) is an increasingly important way for the tourism industry to decrease its impact on the environment.

And because waste treatment and disposal are often major, long-term environmental problems in the tourism industry, pollution prevention and waste minimization techniques are especially important for the tourism industry. A guide to sources of information on cleaner production (free) is available here.

Environmental Awareness Raising

Tourism has the potential to increase public appreciation of the environment and to spread awareness of environmental problems when it brings people into closer contact with nature and the environment.

This confrontation may heighten awareness of the value of nature and lead to environmentally conscious behavior and activities to preserve the environment. For instance, Honduran schoolchildren from the capital city of Tegucigalpa are routinely taken to visit La Tigra cloud forest visitor centre, funded in part by eco-tourist dollars, to learn about the intricacies of the rainforest.

If it is to be sustainable in the long run, tourism must incorporate the principles and practices of sustainable consumption. Sustainable consumption includes building consumer demand for products that have been made using cleaner production techniques, and for services-including tourism services-that are provided in a way that minimizes environmental impacts.

The tourism industry can play a key role in providing environmental information and raising awareness among tourists of the environmental consequences of their actions.

Tourists and tourism-related businesses consume an enormous quantity of goods and services; moving them toward using those that are produced and provided in an environmentally sustainable way, from cradle to grave, could have an enormous positive impact on the planet's environment.

Protection and Preservation

Tourism can significantly contribute to environmental protection, conservation and restoration of biological diversity and sustainable use of natural resources. Because of their attractiveness, pristine sites and natural areas are identified as valuable and the need to keep the attraction alive can lead to creation of national parks and wildlife parks.

In Hawaii, new laws and regulations have been enacted to preserve the Hawaiian rainforest and to protect native species. The coral reefs around the islands and the marine life that depend on them for survival are also protected. Hawaii now has become an international centre for research on ecological systems-and the promotion and preservation of the islands' tourism industry was the main motivation for these actions.

Grupo Punta Cana, a resort in the Dominican Republic, offers an example of how luxury tourism development and conservation can be combined. The high-end resort was established with the goal of catering to luxury-class tourists while respecting the natural habitat of Punta Cana. The developers have set aside 10,000 hectares (24,700 acres) of land as a nature reserve and native fruit tree garden.

The Punta Cana Nature Reserve includes 11 fresh water springs surrounded by a subtropical forest where many species of unusual Caribbean flora and fauna live in their natural state. Guests can explore a "nature path" leading from the beach through mangroves, lagoons of fresh water springs and dozens of species of Caribbean bird and plant life.

The Punta Cana Ecological Foundation has begun reforesting some parts of the reserve that had been stripped of their native mahogany and other trees in the past. Other environmentally protective policies have been put into effect at the resort, such as programs to protect the offshore barrier reefs and the recycling of wastewater for use in irrigating the grounds. The fairways of the resort's new golf course were planted with a hybrid grass that can be irrigated with sea water The grass also requires less than half the usual amounts of fertilizer and pesticides. The resort has also established a biodiversity laboratory run by Cornell University.

Tourism has had a positive effect on wildlife preservation and protection efforts, notably in Africa but also in South America, Asia, Australia, and the South Pacific. Numerous animal and plant species have already become extinct or may become extinct soon. Many countries have therefore established wildlife reserves and enacted strict laws protecting the animals that draw nature-loving tourists. As a result of these measures, several endangered species have begun to thrive again.

4

Hills and Mountains Site

Introduction

Tourism has become one of the most important aspects of man's spatial behaviour in modern times. It is, as some say, the most important civil industry in the world growing at a phenomenal annual growth rate of 10-15%. According to some estimates it contributes around 10% of the global GDP and 7% of the work force. According to World Travel and Tourism Council, the total global capital investments, worldwide consumer spending (10.9%) and world's international trade in goods and services make tourism as one of the top three categories of trade.

In India also the 'white industry' is growing at a good pace thanks to the 'leisure revolution' and abundance of discretionary income. However, money making is not and has never been the best part of tourism. The social and cultural aspects, though less perceptible have more for reaching consequences. For a country like India endowed with vast natural wealth and human resources, tourism acquires a place of special importance. However, one should not turn a blind eye to ecological and environmental changes brought about by the increasing tourist traffic.

Tourism is normally seen as a money minting industry. With the kind of growth rate and the income generation abilities, it assumes a particular significance in India. In the absence of a trade surplus or a sound foreign exchange reserve, tourism is making a phenomenal though unplanned growth. But the returns of tourism should not obscure the long-term impacts of this smokeless industry on the local environment. In this Unit, we shall talk about the various aspects of hill tourism and try and analyse its impact on the environment. We will also try to explore the possible ingredients of a suitable management strategy. The present Unit is an attempt to analyse the varied impacts of tourism in the context of hills' and mountains' environment.

Mountains and Hills: Spiritual Abodes to Tourist Destinations

Hills and mountains have occupied an important place since ancient times, when they were considered abodes of gods. Sages and hermits would meditate and hence lot of reverence and divinity was attached to them in the Indian context. Some like Kailash, Meru, Kishkindha, Govardhan, Vaikuntha were particularly sacred. The modern concept of hill stations which transcends religious connotations and makes them commonly accessible owes much to British endeavours.

It arose with the expansion of European imperialism in the Orient in the nineteenth century. The French established Da Lat in Indo-China, the Spanish built Bagnio in Manila and the Dutch founded several similar centres in Indonesia. But no colonising power built more stations than the British in India. Their rapid growth was due to the real relief they provided from the heat and disease of the plains in summer, while later, after the struggle of 1857, they offered a place of refuge from the reality of life on the plains below.

Not all hill stations were established in a uniform manner. Most of the earliest stations were originally built as army cantonments and were meant to give European troops a breather from the pre-monsoon heat. Some of the more remote cantonments like Chakrata and Jalapahar lingered on in isolation while other more accessible ones attracted civilian attention and soon flourished as social and educational centres. The resorts nearer to large administrative centres also usually attracted local patronage. Thus, Ooty was summer capital for Madras, Murree for Rawalpindi, Nainital for Lucknow, etc. Others were popular with a particular clientele, e.g., Kotagiri acted as a magnet for planters and boxwallahs, Mussoorie attracted high-spirited young military cadets out for a good time, and Shimla was the preserve of the top military and civilian personnel.

Even the down-market stations enjoyed specialised patronage as Ranikhet catered principally to the signals and armoured corps and Almora drew survey, railway and telegraph staff. Madanapalle attracted mainly pensioned native officials, while Matheran served as a destination for wealthy Parshi merchants.

Kodaikanal was not established by the British but by ailing American missionaries. But two things were particularly there – firstly, hill stations attracted people from nearby or surrounding areas, maybe due to transport problems and secondly, that they had a loyal devoted clientele in the sense that visitors would visit the same place year after year.

The change, from hills catering to the affluent and the influential few to regular holidaymakers, was in part, a product of improved transport and communication networks. Other factors like increasing knowledge and awareness of hill stations, aggressive marketing by tourist agents, leisure time and availability of disposable income also played an important part.

Why Hills and Mountains?

Hills and mountains are unique ecosystems; their ecological and cultural attributes make them favourite tourist destinations. As 'zones of refugia' they offer ideal conditions for the three R's – rest, relaxation and recreation. They cater to the varied demands of a vast segment of society. Some of the main reasons behind hill tourism are:

a. Summer retreat – with their climatic and geomorphic conditions they offer ideal summer retreats from the scorching heat of the plains.
b. Natural surroundings – confluence of various ecosystems; hills, forests, snow, rocks and varied relief and ecological features attract naturalists, bio-scientists, academicians, poets, sightseers, photographers.
c. Pilgrimage centres – Some of the hill stations also happen

to be major pilgrim centres thus attracting huge tourist traffic. Vaishno Devi, Amarnath, Kedarnath, Badrinath, Gangotri, Yamunotri, are just a significant few.

d. Mountain sports – like mountaineering, trekking as in Leh, skiing, ice skating (as in Kufri, Patnitop), helicopter skiing, river rafting (as in Manali), gliding etc. attract sports enthusiasts.

e. Floral and faunal diversity – Wildlife and diversity of plant species make them ideal destinations for wildlife lovers. Bioprospectors have of late become a significant tourist component. Nanda Devi Sanctuary would be an example.

f. Adventurists and Explorers – The mountaneous terrain often lure many adventurers or explorers. Wanderlust accounts for but a small proportion of tourist traffic.

g. Miscellaneous – factors would include recreation, leave after work, desire to visit friends, relatives, honeymoons, etc.

Tourist Movements

G.R. Gruber primarily working in the context of Alps explains tourist movement through the following flow charts. As tourism is the movement of people – from say source 'A' to 'B' and then back, four kinds of movements are possible. Although 'A' and 'B' can be locations anywhere in the world for our purposes, let us assume 'B' as places in the highlands. Generally, tourist movement goes on throughout the year but there are two distinct phases of tourist movement.

a. When the summers are on their peak.

b. Early snowfall.

In additions, the Christmas and other long holidays also at times govern movement of tourist traffic.

Geographical Spread

The Indian subcontinent is dotted by mountain ranges all across; the Himalayas and the associated ranges in the north and northwest, Purvanchal groups in the northeast, the Aravalis in the northwest, the Satpuras, Vindhyas, Eastern and Western Ghats in the peninsular region.

There is thus an abundance of hill stations, some of which are not so well known. Graeme D. Westlake, "An Introduction to Hill Stations of India", divides them into four groups; the Himalayan, Central Western and Southern group for a convenient study.

Distribution of Indian Hill Stations and Cantonments

Himalayan Group

1. Ziarat
2. Sheikh Budin
3. Cherat
4. Murree
5. Khaira Gali
6. Nathia Gali
7. Dunga Gali
8. Gulmarg
9. Bakloh
10 Balun
11. Dalhousie
12. Dharmsala
13. Bharwain
14. Chail
15. Shimla
16. Jutogh
17. Sabathu
18. Solon
19. Dagshai
20. Kasauli
21. Chakrata

22. Mussoorie
23. Landour
24. Lansdowne
25. Nainital
26. Ranikhet
27. Almora
28. Chaubattia
29. Darjeeling
30. Lebong
31. Jabalpur
32. Kurseong
33. Shillong
34. Haflang

Central Group

35. Mount Abu
36. Chikalda
37. Panchmarhi
38. Ranchi
39. Hazaribagh
40. Parasnath

Western Group

41. Saputara
42. Khuldabad
43. Matheran
44. Lonavala
45. Khandala
46. Pune
47. Purandhar
48. Mahableshwar
49. Panchgani
50. Amboli

\Southern Group

51. Ramandurg
52. Horsley Hill
53. Nandidurg
54. Bangalore
55. Madanapalle
56. Yeracaud
58. Ootacamund (Ooty)
59. Wellington
60. Coonoor
61. Coimbatore
62. Palmaner
63. Kodaikanal
65. Courtallam
66. Ponmudi

Ceylon

67. Nuwara Eliya

Burma

68. Maymo

Westlake's map shows pre-1947 India and some additions might have been there nevertheless it serves as a useful tool for the distribution of hill stations.

The Himalayan resorts, at an average altitude of 6000 feet, offer magnificent views and range after range of jagged snowy peaks. The Western stations are not much over 2000 feet with the highest, Mahabaleshwar, reaching a modest 4700 feet above sea level. They do, however, provide scenic vies and pleasurable walking, not trekking though. These stations perch on the Western Ghats, a long ridge of volcanic rock running north to south and are full of snowfalls and rarely experience frost. At their southern extreme, the Ghats suddenly descend down into rolling downs and then rise again to plateaux of surprising height. Ootacamund

(Ooty) and Kodaikanal are higher than almost any other hill station save the Himalayan group and have a climate almost European in coolness and damp.

Impacts of Tourism on Mountain Environment

While dealing with the impacts certain things should be borne in mind:

a. Tourism does not necessarily have a negative impact, in many cases particularly in the economic field, it promises a huge growth potential. Having said that any analysis of the impacts has to be done with a long term agenda. In an strictly cost-benefit analysis the short term gains of tourism might be neutralised by long term losses.

b. Environment primarily does connote the physical ecological environment but a comprehensive analysis of the possible impacts would also involve treatment of the local society and economy of the region. The impacts thus generated are overlapping, e.g., ecological impact could well spill into the sociocultural or economic impact.

c. Generally speaking, however, it is the unrestrained mass tourism which leaves a trail of disasters. Ecotourism or sustainable tourism on the contrary, are being projected as having positive ramifications.

d. There are certain determinants (discussed subsequently) which influence the tourist-impact relationship. Purpose, profile, duration, etc. condition the possible impacts of tourism on the local environment.

Impact Determinants

The impact of tourism on hills and mountains is to a great extent conditioned by the following factors:

a. The number and duration of stay of the tourists; this is particularly true in the context of 'mass' or 'exploitative' tourism. Thus, the duration of stay in some cases becomes directly proportional to the impact on local environment.

b. The sphere of interests of the tourists: sports, relaxation, nature-watch, pilgrimage.

c. The fragility of the local environment, the accessibility of the region, the geo-morphological features and the nature of terrain.

d. The standard of living and the income of the tourists as well as the areas visited by the tourists (e.g., socioeconomic disparity).

e. The extent and type of infrastructural facilities, i.e., transport, accommodation, etc.

f. The tourists' awareness of the sociocultural and ecological environment and the resultant behaviour.

g. Existing government policies, regulations and guidelines.

While discussing the impacts of tourism on mountain environment another thing that has to be borne in mind is that the word mountain environment does not only connote the physical or the natural landscape, i.e., forests, rocks, ice, climate, but also the cultivated landscape (houses, villages, fields, infrastructural facilities) and the people as well (behaviour, customs, traditions). The net impact of tourism is different in different regions depending on the relative interplay of the factors discussed above. Let us now discuss some major impacts of tourism, both direct and induced on the hills and mountains. For the sake of convenience, let us divide these into three parts.

a. Ecological impacts.

b. Sociocultural impact.

c. Economic impact.

Ecological Impacts

Tourism's impact vis-a-vis physical environment has come in for a lot of debate. People are becoming ecologically more conscious day by day. Many humanists and sociologists like Elzeard Bouffier of France, Toyohiko Kagawa of Japan, Sunder Lal Bahuguna of India to name just very few have been raising environmental issues vigorously. Many reports, both national and international have also come up documenting tourism's impact on environment. The German Alpine Club's International Symposium in Munich (1983), and OECD Report on Impacts (1981) merely reflect some early attempts in this direction. While there may be a difference on the degree or intensity of the resultant problems, it is generally agreed that unregulated tourism tends to destroy forests, consume firewood, creates pollution and over-crowding, endangers ecological balance, threatens the floral and faunal diversity, produces garbage trails, overburdens environment with tourist structures and roads, causes at times natural hazards as also withdraws labour from agriculture, changes the land use pattern, etc. Let us analyse some of these impacts in greater details.

Forestation – By way of building of infrastructural and accommodation facilities or industrial requirements or grazing or firewood collection has led to reduction in forest cover in the hills and mountains. Rich forested slopes have been converted into barren rocks in the name of development activities like roads, hotels, tourist huts, and trekking trails.

Compare this situation with National Forest Policy recommendations which envisages 60% of the mountain areas to be covered with forests, whereas in the case of Himalayas, less than one fifth of the region is under snow cover, 3.7% under high meadow (Bugyals) and nearly 42.3% of the land is denuded of any vegetal cover. It is to be noted that only 4% of forest land comprises good quality trees.

The best coniferous forests are degenerating fast, there is a shrinkage in natural habitats and extermination of many plants and animal species. Musk deer, snow leopard, barasingha, etc. are becoming extinct. The dwindling Dal, Manasbal, Wular, Kounsernag Lakes and high incidence of floods in the rivers Jhelum, Sindh and Chenabl coupled with apparent change in marco and micro climatic conditions are some visible manifestations of misuse and mismanagement of various habitat types.

Degraded landscapes, ranging from glacial and peri-glacial areas with depleting snowfields to hill-slopes, foot hills and valleys are also reflective of the human interference. Recent studies of geo-ecosystems in Dhauladhar range and the adjoining areas south of the Punjab Himalayas as also in Uttar Pradesh and Eastern Himalayas have revealed 'erosion damage'. Owing to litho logical, structural, climatological and relief conditions, such areas are highly susceptible to erosional processes, being induced or accelerated by human activities such as over-grazing, tree logging, fuel wood-collection and improper constructions.

Loss of flora and fauna – Very much associated with deforestation (in fact it has been mentioned in passing earlier) increasing tourist menace is auguring danger for the floral and faunal wealth. In Nepal, several species like Rhododendron arboreum, Mynica esculenta, Cedrus deodaea, etc. are on the verge of extinction, whereas species like Akies spectabilis, Tsuga dumosa, Rhododendron nivale, etc. are under intense economic pressure. In Nepal mountaineering expeditions primarily account for decimation of biological wealth.

In the Uttarakhand part of Himalayas, the soils, biomass, flora and fauna and water have suffered a lot due to unplanned encroachment. Tourism and associated projects have been major destroyers. The Ramaganga dam has submerged a vast area falling under the natural habitat of tiger and other animal species. Tehri and Jamrani dams have also produced similar effects. Increasing construction at Gangotri is causing great loss to a number of plant species like Chir, Fur, Birch, etc. Heavy utilisation of open tracts adversely affects the biomass.

Trampling directly kills plants and causes soil compaction. Increased used of an area changes the microclimate and water balance and thus kills plants. These changes in the local biotic community can lead to eventual loss of the species. Plants are also lost by plucking of wild flowers and leaves by wanderers. Brahmakamal is one such greatly affected variety. Valley of flowers has been at the receiving end. In the case of animals, as has already been said, shrinkage in natural habitats, flourishing souvenir industry, contamination of ecosystems as well as in some places actual hunting have been primary decimating factors.

Garbage trails and pollution – Waste generation especially solid waste by the hotels like food, vegetable, paper, rags, clothes, bottles or the hospitals like glass, bottles, polythene, gloves, bandage, cotton, plastics, etc. is causing major damage to the local ecosystems. Most of the hill stations lack sewerage and waste disposal facilities. Of particular importance here is the fact that while some wastes are biodegradable others like soft drink bottles, polythene are non-biodegradable and cause immense harm to the environment. Surveys carried out in Kullu Manali Tourist Complex (KMTC) suggest huge amount of daily waste generation. Valley of Flowers also suffers from a similar problem.

In many cases water bodies are choked. Lakes, rivers and ponds become polluted. Dal Lake in Srinagar is heavily polluted, weeded and eutrophied thanks to release of an incredible amount of faecal matter and pathogenic materials from the houseboats. In addition, atmospheric pollution through motor vehicles, aircrafts, road and rail transportation, coal fuel, oil, natural gas, wood fuel and forest fires is also becoming increasingly prevalent. Of late, noise pollution is otherwise silent, serene ecosystems is also a problem to be taken into account.

Increasing instances of natural hazards due to disturbances in the fragile ecosystems of the hills and mountains are not unknown. A study conducted by James S. Gardner in Shimla is very illustrative. Increasing tourist traffic in Manali combined with the vulnerability of it's ecosystem has produced natural disasters.

In recent increase in the number of high density multi-storeyed hotels, constructions of buildings in the flood and erosion susceptible areas adjacent to Beas, the development of road network and winter recreation activities has elevated risks from natural hazards like snow avalanches, earthquakes, flash floods, rock slides, slope failures, etc. The Manali case shares many characteristics with similar situations elsewhere in India.

Mountain sports – like trekking, skiing, ice-skating, etc. are producing many undesirous results. Studies conducted in Nepal suggest that trekking and trekker related activities are leading to accelerating rate of deforestation in the Sagarmatha area, thereby destroying the habitat of numerous wild animals and high altitude plants.

In India, this has led to the need to close down the Nanda Devi Sanctuary for trekkers and shepherds. Markha valley in Laddakh has also borne the pressure of tourist menace. Likewise, water sports, involving diesel-powered speedboats and motor boats contribute to surface water pollution in many areas.

Deviations in land-use patterns are becoming common on many hill stations. The desire for 'quick gains' has led to regression of agricultural activities. In many cases tourism has overlapped agriculture thus creating a tourist monoculture. This is disastrous both, in the long run, both to the economy and ecology of the region. Likewise overcrowding, urban sprawl, shortage of civic amenities when incongruent with the carrying capacity of the region tend to produce harmful effects on the environment.

However, in many cases tourism has also served as a tool for conservation and environmental regeneration. If conducted properly tourism awakens ecological consciousness and the need for introducing measures of conservation in sensitive areas of nature monuments and wilderness. Retreat from hillside farming in the most marginal and dangerous areas is another gain.

Socio-Cultural Impacts

While dealing with sociocultural impacts let us first discuss the mechanisms of tourist-culture interface and then examine case studies if any. Local society and it's customs constitute an important tourism resource. Village lifestyle, traditional ceremonies and religious processions, arts and crafts are vigorously marketed by tourist organisations.

There is, however, much evidence to demonstrate that traditions and quality of life of the host society can be eroded by mass tourism. In one of the better known frameworks, Doxey has developed an irritation index which traces the local community's reaction, beginning with a level of euphoria associated with early tourist arrivals through to antagonism when a place becomes saturated with tourists.

Doxey suggests that the level of irritation was correlated with the degree of compatibility between host community and the visitors, the location of tourist accommodation and how much the locals directly benefit through employment and associated perks of the tourist industry. Also important in this regard is the configuration of the tourists. Mass package holiday-makers demanding facilities and levels of service matching metropolitan cities have little interest in understanding of local culture and history. Such tourists have little interaction with local residents. Studies have shown that tourism at many hill stations has been accompanied by higher prices for craft goods, greed and crime in societies.

In addition, the so-called demonstration effect involving the adoption by local residents, particularly younger people, of aspects of tourist life styles, is becoming increasingly common. High levels of expatriate ownership and management, together with resort development that has created private areas for tourists further alienates the local population receiving only limited benefits. Unregulated and insensitive tourism can also lead to dissolution of social cohesion, youth social conflicts, criminality, prostitution and immorality in the host society. Loss of cultural identity promoting commercialisation of tradition selling of antiques, vandalism and materialistic thinking also afflict the host society.

Tourism, however, also has a positive side when it comes to the host society. It entails behaviouristic change in the host society when the residents seek to improve their 'image'. It also, in many cases, delays out migration and provides motivation for learning. Preservation of cultural monuments, rediscovery of lost traditions, promotion of current culture, training of new craftsmen and contact with the outside world by way of infrastructure modernisation and urbanisation are other positive entailments of tourism development.

Let us now have a look at 'Leh' an important tourist destination in order to get a better picture of the state of affairs.

Leh in Laddakh was a forbidden land upto 1974. Subsequently it was marketed as 'The Little Tibet'. It is a classic example of how a unique cultural heritage could be ravaged by sudden tourist invasion. It goes on to show how tourism induced development in a backward economy can only result in marginal economic gains with major sociocultural losses. Proliferation of external entrepreneurs has led to economic dislocation of the local residents.

Some good work has been done by the way of restoration and renovation of monasteries and revival of some art traditions but otherwise Leh has paid a heavy price for the development of tourism. Only a small part of tourist earnings remain inside the region, the rest being siphoned either to the valley or the lowlands.

The sociological cultural front has borne the flood of tourist invasion in a major way. Lamas are increasingly coming under the influence of western culture. The younger generation has been uprooted from their age old tradition, and local pilgrims are discriminated against the better paying foreigners. Many religious olyeets have become 'wares' for sale and cultural assets and art olyeets have got commercialised and are either being sold or smuggled. In Tibetan culture, 'art' is not a saleable commodity. Leh's example clearly depicts the contradiction between tourism and tradition.

Economic Impacts

Recreational tourism induces growth at three levels – national, regional and local, although the quantum of this growth may be different at different levels. Let us have a look at some of the possible mechanisms through which tourism affects the economy of a region.

Tourism Related Industries and Employment Potential

Tourism is not a single industry but a loose confederation of number of these. It is usually classified in the tertiary sector, mainly a service sector. Geographers call it a 'landscape industry' since the products of tourism are made of natural beauty, dramatic landscape and cultural heritage. The development of various segments of tourist industry depends upon the importance and popularity of the tourist places.

Laying down of transport networks like roads, railway tracks, trek routes, rope ways all require a huge labour force for this construction and upkeep. Provision of better accommodation facilities by way of construction of classified hotels, indigenous hotels, tourist bunglows or other state establishments and other types specially tent houses, dharmasalas, etc. is another major responsibility of tourism industry. Souvenir making is another significant component of a good tourism policy. Thus, tourism, we see, is a labour intensive industry. A large number of seasonal works can seek employment such as the masons, carpenters, porters, rickshaw pullers, hotel guides, waiters, tourist guides, escorts, boatmen, pony owners, candi carriers, etc. These job opportunities sustain the hill economy to a great extent.

Income Aspects and Multiplier Effect

Tourism circulates existing wealth among social groups and geographic regions. The money spent by the tourists goes to the local business in a number of ways. This money in turn is spent on provision of goods and services to the tourists. Thus, through this multiplier effect one can explain the additional spending or job creation caused by a given level of tourist expenditure. However, the scope of multiplier effect is greatly reduced because of various leakages in the form of import of foreign goods, interest on foreign investments, etc.

Infrastructure and Regional Development

Tourism is an important mechanism to initiate and generate infrastructure development and improvement. The construction of roads, railway lines, airports, electricity and gas supplies, sanitation, water supply etc. which are mainly undertaken to attract the tourists benefit the local residents also by way of provision of civic amenities. Besides, the development of infrastructure prepares the basis for diversification of other economic activities. Thus, regional development is a natural corollary of development of tourism in a region. Foreign exchange, taxi revenues, impetus to local arts, economic diversification – are other accompaniments of development of tourist destinations.

However, there are certain negative aspects of tourism development which should not be ignored. It creates inflationary tendencies and seasonal dependency besides uneven economic development. Domination of external entrepreneurs, burden on commercial services and over-utilisation of scarce resources come along naturally.

What Needs to be Done?

While talking about possible remedial measures and suitable management strategies one could go on endlessly talking about the do's and the don'ts. Thanks to absence of preventing planning in India, we have reached a stage where things have become precarious. All the major hill stations are under tremendous ecological-cultural stress. The present state of affairs do not augur well for the long-term sustenance of this growing industry.

The basic dilemma with tourism and in particular mountain tourism is that the basic capital is landscape. Once it is degraded or damaged, it can hardly be repaired or redressed. The tragedy with mountain tourism is that as the mountainous regions are trying to emerge from their subsistence economy, they are seized up by modern exploitative forces causing rupture in the ecosystem. Tourism, which in a way was brought to mitigate socioeconomic disparities between highlands and the lowlands, has on the contrary widened the gap for the same region. In fact, market mechanism tends to destroy it's own resource. As it is rightly said "Tourism destroys tourism". The irony of the situation as Bilting says is that while the next of the landscape is being paid for, the long-term costs of presentation are not.

The need of the hour is to address the issue with urgent sincerity. There could be many possible suggestions in this direction like devising a tourism management plan for every region; a plan that encompasses all-important aspects and is interactive in nature. Such a plan should take into account:

(i) the ecological aspects, the nature of the terrain, the relative fragility of the ecosystem and the geo-morphic features.

(ii) the macro level tourism development plans should be integrated with the socioeconomic development at the micro-level. Integrated rural development schemes, non-conventional energy development, self-employment programmes conservation programmes and tourism development plane should work together as an integrated whole towards a common goal of development without sustainability disturbing the lives of the local people.

(iii) Building laws should be made more stringent in the mountainous areas. Multi-storeyed building unsuitable to the local landscape should not be allowed. All the buildings must be built on passive heating designs, so that the spare heating reliance on fuel-wood and imported fuels comes down. Solar waters could be encouraged.

(iv) Local people or their representatives should be involved while making tourism plans or administrative boards. Their wishes, aspirations, cultural values and economic necessities should necessarily be taken into consideration.

(v) The quantitative and qualitative aspects of tourism should be addressed sincerely. Controlling the number of tourists visiting a place could be a good starting point. Khajiar in Himachal Pradesh, the mini Switzerland of India is one good example in this regard. The formation of tourists boards on the lines of Vaishno Devi Management or Amarnath Shrine Boards could possibly regulate the tourist traffic. The quality aspect of tourism is equally important. Awareness generation and sensitisation of the tourists to local ecology, culture, economy, etc. could be useful. In fact, the tourist complexes could and should be used for diffusing information both to the tourists and the local populace. Another component of awareness generation could be orientation programmes. Mountaineering courses to promote expedition and the studies of glacial retreats, depleting snowfields, deforestation are being organised by Geological Survey of India and institutes like Wadia Institute of Himalayan Ecology. Such attempts need to be streamlined. Audiovisual media could also be used in enlightening the tourists.

(vi) A crucial link between the tourists and the local populace and ecosystems are the guides or escorts. Only trained tourist guides should be allowed to entertain tourists.

(vii) Diversion of tourist traffic to less frequented sites on a policy level could be of immense help. Development of alternative tourist spots on the likes of Laddakh Sarai near Leh or Span Resorts in Katrain between Kullu and Manali could be very fruitful.

(viii) At times regulations and legislations should supplement the efforts taken by other agencies.

Thus, any successful management strategy has to be very comprehensive in scope and address all possible ramifications of tourism development. The tourism industry has to take a serious view of this regard not merely through resolutions but through actual practice in their operations.

Nepal: A Case Study

Nepal is one of the dream tourist destinations. Ideal for trekking, wildlife, mountaineering, scientific expeditions geography, climatology, anthropology, sociology and linguistic archaeology, Nepal has a lot to offer. Tourism, thus, experienced a boom in this Himalayan kingdom. According to an ADB Report (1982) it took five years of tourist traffic to loose 15% of Nepal's forests. The impact of tourism has been analysed through a series of impactograms by T.K. Shrestha.

Let us Sum up

Mountain tourism has a good potential for growth in India. Efforts should be taken to mitigate the harmful effects of tourism on the hill environment. In fact, mountain tourism needs to be carefully organised. A proper planning focusing on the vital infrastructural areas will go a long way in harnessing its potential. We have noticed above the antiquity of hills as areas visited by pilgrims. We have also noticed the gradual shift from pilgrimage to modern day tourism in these hilly regions. But we also understand that an unbridled growth of tourism activity in these regions is replete with serious harmful consequences. Our hilly regions are eco-fragile and cannot sustain tourism activity beyond a certain point. Therefore, planning tourism activity in these regions in such manner as to take care of the harmful impact on the region is vitally necessary. Macro-planning for the region must account for ecological and sociocultural concerns of the people of the region. Possibly then we shall be in a position to adequately utilise this vast and valuable natural resource for tourism purposes.

Motivation for Holidaying

A review of tourism literature reveals an abundance of studies on motivation and satisfaction, however there is an apparent lack of research into the motivational factors which influence event tourists. Event tourism is globally important in terms of its popular appeal and ability to generate travel and tourism related benefits to destinations. Although research has been undertaken into the internal and external forces of the destinations attributes (i.e. climate, culture) and how they motivate travellers and the fact that there has been an increased interest in discovering what motivates tourists behaviour there has been an apparent lack of focus into defining what motivates event tourists. Hence the aim of this paper is to analyse the motivational factors which influence event tourists to attend an event.

What are Motivations?

To be motivated means *to be moved* to do something. A person who has no stimulus to act, is considered to be unmotivated. On the other hand a person who is moved to act is seen as motivated. Motivation can vary from the levels of motivation (how much motivation) and also the orientation of the motivation (what type of motivation). Underlying all behaviour are needs and motivations grounded in the basic physiological and socio-psychological wants of all humans. The standard theories of motivation applied to understanding leisure and tourism behaviour are (Murray's (1938) Needs Theory of Personality, Maslow's (1943) Hierarchical Theory of Needs and Berlyne's (1960) concept of optimal level of stimulation.

Murray (1938) explained that "A need is a stimulus – a force pushing an individual in a certain direction or to behave in a certain way' and identified 12 physiological needs which are viewed as primary needs, and include air, water, food and security, and also identified 28 psychological needs which are considered secondary needs and are connected to mental or emotional satisfaction. Murray postulated that needs are changeable and that they gain or lose importance as they are satisfied and in fact, suggested that there is a 'need cycle' and that needs can be dormant during the non-stimulated period, and are susceptible to stimuli during the ready period and so determine an individuals behaviour during the active period and also suggested that these needs work in combination with each other. A more structured approach was adopted in Maslows (1943) Hierarchical Theory of Needs which suggested that peoples behaviour is driven by both physiological and socio-psychological needs. However, Maslow had a more structured hierarchical order to the needs of activation and satisfaction. He believed that the lower-order needs (psychological needs followed by safety needs) had to be satisfied before an individual could work on the higher-order needs of love, belongingness and self-esteem. At the top of the hierarchy of needs is self-actualisation which is an opportunity for individuals to 'become everything that one is capable of becoming (Maslow, 1943).

Dispite this apparent difference Maslow (1970) agreed with the research by Murray (1938) that behaviour may be motivated by one or more needs and suggested that the hierarchy of needs may not be as rigid as it first implies. Research using both theories into tourism and leisure have found that the relationship between needs and activity choice is quite complex. This research has lea to the belief that behaviour is multidimensional and that the same activity may be motivated by a variety of needs at different times for the one individual or that one activity may have different meanings to another person at the same time. No matter how complex the relationships may be, the motivation theory still provides insights into why people choose to take part in certain events or activities i.e. being an event tourist.

Further research has indicated that motivation can be referred to as biological/psychological needs and wants, including forces that arouse, direct and integrate a person's behaviour and activity. Various disciplines have been used to explain the phenomena and characteristics related to motivation. However, they are very complex as they relate to human beings and human nature, which in itself is complex. Whilst in the disciplines of sociology and psychology, motivation is often directed towards cognitive and emotional motives or internal and external motives. Such internal motives are associated with feelings, instincts and drives whereas external motives involve mental representations such as beliefs or knowledge. MacCannell (1977) notes that from an anthropological viewpoint, tourists are motivated to escape the routine of daily life and seek authentic experiences. Whereas from a socio-psychological point of view, motivation is classified as seeking and avoidance behaviour.

Event tourists may relate to one or many of the areas mentioned above. They may be escaping their daily routine by seeking an authentic experience at a 'Sing Sing' (traditional song and dance) in the South Pacific. Or they may be attending a week long health clinic event to restore there inner strength.

What are Events?

Events range from small local events or festivals to what are known as mega events. As there several types of events and there may be different motivations for attending each type of event. Motivations may include 'keeping up with the Jones' to being the 'first on the block to attend an event' or just to escape the daily routine. One type of event is a special event and McDonnell, Allen & O'Toole (2002) considers a special event to usually be one-off or infrequent by nature. The special event could then be considered as a mega or hall mark event. Getz (1997) defines mega events as:

Their volume should exceed 1 million visits, their capital costs should be at least $500 million, and their reputation should be of a 'must see' event. Mega events, by way of their size or significance, are those that yield extraordinarily high levels of tourism, media coverage, prestige or economic impact for the host community or destination.

An example of a mega event would be the Olympic Games which fulfils all of the criteria to which Getz (1997) refers. The Olympics are significant as they yield extraordinary high levels of tourism and prestige and obtain a great deal of media coverage which in turn has further economic impacts on the host community and destination in general.

On the other hand, a hallmark event is considered to be smaller in scale than the mega event and generally has a special meaning or significance for a region or community. Allen, O'Toole, McDonnell & Harris (2002) defines hallmark events as:

> *A major one-time or recurring event of limited duration and often developed to enhance awareness, appeal or profitability of a tourism destination over a short time. However, Ritchie (1984) enlarges this definition viz: A major one-time or recurring event of limited duration, developed primarily to enhance awareness, appeal and*

> *profitability of a tourism destination in the short term and/or long term. Such events rely their success on uniqueness, status, and or timely significance to create interest and attract attention.*

The major point which both these definitions have in common is that they include a reason to celebrate, to bring various groups or individuals together to experience what the event has to offer. The event may last over several weeks or just a day. It may be a one time or recurring event and it may be a public or private sector event. Whichever type of event it is, there is the need to motivate people to take action to attend. Getz (1997) takes the general approach that people attend events to satisfy various personal needs.

Motivations to Attend an Event

There are several groups of motives proposed by McDonnell et al. (1999). The four main groups proposed by McDonnell et al. (1999) are *social motives, organisational motives, physiological motives and personal motives. Social motives* may include the opportunity to experience social interaction with others or of being part of the community spirit which takes place during an event. The event attendee may feel so moved by their social motives that they want to partake of good deeds and may become a volunteer at the event.

The second group are *organisational motives*. These generally include the need for status or recognition that they have been a participant at the event. For example, there is status and/or prestige connected with attending an event such as the Olympic Games. Organisational motives also include sponsorship or community support. For example, organisations want to appear to be supporting the community through their commitment to the event.

Physiological motives are the third group and these include the need for relaxation and or exercise depending on the type of event. An attendee at an event expects to eat, drink and to be entertained as part of the event process.

The final group are *personal motives*. These motives can be different for each attendee. Some of the personal motives could include the need to seek new experiences from the mundane. Or to fulfil an ambition i.e. to attend the Passion Play in Oberammergau, Germany. On the other hand it may related to personal development.

Actual attendance itself may be attributed to multiple motives or just a single motive.

Motivations of a Tourist

A review of the literature on tourism motivation shows that people travel because they are 'pushed' into making a travel decision by internal psychological forces, and 'pulled' by the external forces of the destination attributes. Tourists obviously have their own internal and external reasons for travelling. However, theses reasons could have positive or negative impacts on travel satisfaction which has as been used as a tool to assess the outcome of the travel experience. This concept of motivation can be divided into two groups which indicate that people travel because they are either pushed or pulled to do so by forces or factors. These factors illustrate how tourists are pushed by motivation variables into making travel decisions and then how they are pulled or attracted by a destination attributes. Whilst push motivations are related to the tourists' desire, the pull factors or motivations are aliened with the attributes of the destination choice. Put simply the push motivations are related to internal or emotional factors whilst pull motivations are connected to the external, cognitive or situational factors.

Crompton (1979) found that push motivations could be grouped into the following areas; escapism, rest and relaxation, prestige, health and fitness, adventure and social interaction, family togetherness and excitement. Tourists may travel to escape the monotony of their every day lives and for authentic experiences. The pull motivations are attributed to the overall attractiveness of the destination. Pull factors may include; beaches, cultural attractions, natural scenery, shopping and so forth. However, these push and pull factors may work in tandem and the destination attributes may stimulate and reinforce inherent push factors. Several research studies have been undertaken using these perspectives.

Further research by Iso-Ahola (1982) suggested that individuals perceive a leisure activity as having the potential to produce satisfaction for two reasons. The first reason is that the leisure activity may provide intrinsic rewards (such as mastery and competence) and secondly to escape from routine. In 1987 Kippendorf conducted similar research and found that tourists are motivated by 'going away from rather than going toward something' and that tourist motivation is generally self oriented.

Research into the needs, motivations and expectations of tourists has been conducted for several years. Whilst it does several researchers who have delved into this field. It is generally accepted that push and pull factors (as motivations) have generally been used in studying tourist behaviour. These studies have played a useful role in understanding the different needs and wants which motivate and influence the behaviour of tourists.

Although past explanations of tourist behaviour has been based on a unidementional approach, many tourism researchers are now moving to more than one motive or need which affects the tourists' behaviour.

Earlier studies acknowledged the following key motivation elements in relation to tourism. They are; the need to escape (for example a dreary home life) and to seek (new and exciting experiences). There is still acceptance of the undimentional approach to motivation on the understanding that a variety of behaviours can be explained as a response of a small number of motivational 'needs'. This appears to be the main view despite suggestions that motivation may be outdated since the decision process is a result of many experiences and knowledge of destinations. Gnoth (1997) suggests that motivation's two dimensions are lasting dispositions and object-specific elements. The interaction between motivation and the symbolic consumption of tourism experiences for its social or hedonic value, rather than functional utility was identified by Brown (1992).

Tourism Motivations Versus Event Motivations

Dann (1977; 1981) and Crompton (1979) have written extensively on 'push' and 'pull' tourist motivations noting that 'push' motivations are internal or emotional factors i.e. the tourists' desires. On the other hand they stressed that 'pull' motivations refer to the destination attributes i.e. external cognitive or situational factors. For example a tourist may want to visit great Grandmothers birth place in Ireland (push) and the airfares are two for the price of one (pull).

However, McDonnell et al. (1999) researched event motivations and divided them into four groups; social motivation (interaction), organisational motivation (status/recognition), physiological motives (relaxation/exercise), personal motives (new experiences/ personal achievement). This approach provides a broader explanatory capacity. When comparing the tourism motivations as postulated by Dann (1977; 1981) and Crompton (1979) and the event motivations put forward by McDonnell et al. (1999) it appears that no pull motivates have been applied to event motivations. In other words, the importance of beaches, cultural attractions, natural scenery and shopping (to name a few) have not been considered a motivational factor for event attendees. The question is then, will this be the case for event tourists or will pull factors play a part in their motivation to attend an event and if so how important will they be?

Developing A Motivational Typology

There are several proposed motivational typologies in the tourism literature for vacationers, tourists and travellers and many of these typologies are based on segmentation criteria which have been used to subdivide the travellers into homogeneous groups to assist in the development of targeting and positioning strategies. These criteria can be used separately or in combination. Often demographic criteria (such as age) is used, the benefits the traveller is seeking and the family life cycle.

Several researchers have studied behavioural variables such as holiday activities which tourists take part in when on holiday. Attention has also been given to researching the amount of expenditure distance travelled, chosen destination and frequency of the journeys. Whereas Swarbrooke & Horner (1999) suggested the more traditional criteria based on geography and economy should be used. Decrop & Snelders (2005) note that socio-psychological typologies offer a more integrated picture of the traveller because they connect descriptive aspects of the traveller with sociological or psychological variables. Decrop & Schnelders (2005) typology of socio-psychological variables with references to various researchers.

Whilst the issue of motivation of tourists has come under some scrutiny the typologies of Dann (1977;1981) and Crompton (1979) which provide the framework for developing an event tourism typology as it includes pull factors together with push factors. The categories include escape, self-exploration, social interaction, prestige, regression, relaxation and improvement in relationships together with external cognitive and situational factors. Recent research by Fairley (2003) noted that nostalgia is also a motivating factor for being an event tourist and should also be considered when developing a typology to define an event tourist.

Summary and Conclusion

In summary this paper has drawn attention to a number of significant gaps which have been identified in the literature in relation to event tourists. These are:

- A general reluctance by researchers to adopt a standardised definition of event tourists,
- A general lack of research examining the motivation of event tourists,
- The general lack of current research in providing relevant and reliable constructs known to predict motivations in relation to event tourism.

The limited published evidence available suggests that this could become a valuable source of insight into further development of the understanding of event tourism. As stated previously, limited research has been conducted into the motivational factors influencing event tourists and as it is a global phenomenon it is considered to be of great importance. More research therefore needs to be conducted into this area which will allow a typology to be developed of event tourists.

5

Destination Attractiveness in Second Homes

Recreational Properties

Many of us have fond childhood memories of dad loading up the station wagon or van and heading out of town for a long weekend. For some the destination was a lakeside campsite, but for many it was the summer cottage or cabin by the lake. For others it was a Winter activity that brought with it the long-anticipated excitement of driving up to the favourite mountain and throwing open the doors to a modest old ski lodge that one could call home for the next week or so. But unless one was lucky enough to inherit dad's cabin, the thought of purchasing one piece of recreational paradise can be daunting for most young families.

With prices still on the rise and demand for vacation homes brisk notwithstanding the general slowdown in real estate, there are a few bright lights for homeowners looking to pick up a second home or recreational property.

The Canadian Mortgage And Housing Corporation has instituted recently a new program that will provide Homeowner Mortgage Loan Insurance for borrowers with more than one residential property. This means that Purchasers can now obtain a mortgage insured by the Canadian Mortgage And Housing Corporation on a recreational property with as little as five percent down.

Traditionally getting institutional financing for a vacation property was a challenge, because lenders typically based their lending decisions on the risk of reselling this type of properties. As many second homes are located outside urban centres and, more often than not, in remote rural or coastal areas they might have limited resale potential, which from a mortgaging point of view increased the risk of financing. To mitigate this risk, lenders would require borrowers to put up more money down-as much as thirty-five percent or more, in fact. Even well-known and popular destinations such as Whistler, British Columbia required a minimum of twenty-five percent downpayment.

But lifestyles are changing and these changes affect decisions that real estate consumers make regarding how and where to live. So the Canadian Mortgage And Housing Corporation has made a move to put vacation properties within reach of more people. With a constant and steady increase in demand for this type of properties, the Canadian Mortgage And Housing Corporation has determined that the market is such that it is willing to insure lenders against potential losses. This is welcome news for those who have been longing to get a recreational property but did not want to wait until retirement to come up with the downpayment. All Canadian Mortgage And Housing Corporation's products are permitted to be used with the Homeowner Mortgage Loan Insurance and since most major institutional lenders already have their own recreational property mortgage products, consumers have the flexibility to choose the type of financing that is right for them.

However, as with most types of financing, there are some key limitations that is important to be clear on. The purpose of the Homeowner Mortgage Loan Insurance is to make it more feasible for consumers to purchase a second home. It is important to distinguish between a second home and a rental property. The Homeowner Mortgage Loan Insurance is not intended to allow an investor to purchase a rental property with five percent down. The guideline states that at initiation the real capital asset that secures a mortgage insured by Canadian Mortgage And Housing Corporation must be intended for occupancy at some point during the calendar year by the borrower or a relative of the borrower on a rent-free basis. If a rental income is anticipated from the property at a future date, it will not be calculated for the purpose of assisting the Purchaser to qualify for the loan. The location of the property is not restricted to major resorts or popular vacation spots, but there are some general requirements that apply as well. For instance, the recreational property must be suitable for and available for year-round occupancy. Properties that are constructed for seasonal use or have seasonal access are not eligible. As such, vacation cottages located on an island must have year-round bridge or ferry access. And finally, timeshare interests, life leases and properties in rental pools are not eligible.

Luigi Frascati

Luigi Frascati is a Real Estate Agent based in Vancouver, British Columbia. He holds a Bachelor Degree in Economics and maintains a weblog entitled the Real Estate Chronicle where you can find the full collection of his articles on Real Estate Economics and Finance. Luigi is associated with the Sutton Group, the largest real estate organization in Canada, and is based with Sutton-Centre Realty in Burnaby, BC.

Recreational Boaters of California [RBOC] is a nonprofit governmental advocacy organization that works to protect and enhance the interests of the state's recreational boaters before the legislative and executive branches of state and local government.

RBOC was formed as a statewide organization in 1968 and from that date forward has continued its commitment to promoting the enjoyment, protection, and responsible use of our waterways.

- Protecting your fuel tax dollars from diversion.
- Ensuring more dollars for boating law enforcement.
- Supporting education over regulation of boaters.
- Promoting legislation to fight growing infestations of invasive species clogging waterways.
- Saving interest deductions on boats as second homes.
- Reviewing all proposed legislation that affects boaters.
- Guiding and supporting local issues affecting your recreational boating and marina.

- Working in partnership with Boat U.S. on national boating legislation.

Recreation Properties Captivate Albertans

Mario Toneguzzi, Calgary Herald

Albertans are among the most willing in the country to make changes to their finances or lifestyle to own a cottage. And despite the economic downturn, many Canadians are still dreaming of owning a recreational property, both as a long-term investment and to enjoy with family and friends, adds a national real estate report released Thursday.

The 2009 Royal LePage Recreational Property Report said Canadians are willing to make sacrifices to own a cottage and more of them want to use their cottage, cabin or chalet year-round as a recreational property, although some want it as their primary residence.

"In Alberta, 69 per cent of residents agree that a cottage is a good long-term investment. At 62 per cent, Albertans are among the most willing in the country to make changes to their finances or lifestyle to own a cottage. One in five Albertans would purchase a fixer-upper, the highest score in the country, and 15 per cent would purchase a property with friends or family members," said the report. For Albertans, the three most important features of a cottage or recreational property are access to utilities (60 per cent), peace and quiet (51 per cent) and four-season use (33 percent). Access to boating and fishing (28 per cent) and proximity to amenities (22 per cent) also ranked high for Albertans.

Sixty per cent said a cottage on a lake would be their first choice, but 11 per cent would choose a resort condominium and another 11 per cent would choose a property in the woods, both significantly higher than the national average. In a report also released Thursday, Adrienne Warren, senior economist and real estate market specialist with Scotia Economics, said rising equity in principal residences and rising stock market wealth appear to have put second-home ownership within the reach of more Canadian families. "Demand for second homes/ vacation homes could slow over the coming decade as the large baby boom generation moves past its peak cottage buying years, and wealth gains fail to replicate the outsized increases of the past decade," she said. Warren said this suggests some easing in the steady upward pressure on recreational home prices seen over the past decade, but at the same time, the available supply of listings is likely to remain fairly tight. Royal LePage's nationwide survey showed the dream of owning a getaway property on the water to escape the pressures of city life is still alive and well across the country, said Phil Soper, president and chief executive of Royal LePage Real Estate Services. "Beyond the obvious lifestyle benefits, however, our research demonstrates Canadians see recreational property as a smart and safe long-term investment." Northwest Sonoma County and Southern Mendocino County Recreational, Second Homes, Retreats and Estate Sites All we do is country.

How we Operate

In effect, a Buyer or Seller or Both hire us. Our function is to bring information to a qualified prospect so they can make an intelligent decision. We try to create a package which gives you the information we would like if we were looking. Sometimes we also put together a brief package on another office's listing because of their not creating one or to correct inaccurate information. We offer good credibility without puffery.

We specialize in North Sonoma County and Southern Mendocino estate or recreational properties. We handle the majority of sales of large properties in this area. All of this area is under 3 hours from San Francisco. Appreciation has been strong. We have owned property here since 1975. We have the toys (four 4x4's, light stepping all-terrain vehicles with rubber tracks), the hindsight and a few skills like being able to fly airplanes or helicopters to help you buy or sell. Living in the centre of our market in the country, helps. We have over 300 acres adjacent to Lake Sonoma. Our neighbours are deer, pigs, quail, etc. Our water supply is a spring.

The properties in this area vary from remote weekend retreats to estate sites. The terrain varies from very rugged to rolling Sonoma Mountains. Most have spectacular views. The weather is very good. Very little fog. Rainfall from November through

February is heavy. Between storms is possibly the nicest time of the year. Many do not have PG&E. We can show you what the alternatives are.

The more you can paint me a word picture of what you see in your minds' eye of yourself needing or enjoying, the more I can help. I do see everything that is available in this area.

We will go out of our area as a Buyers Broker. Typically it is for a client who is strong on finances and short on time looking for a large property with a specific criteria such as hunting. I am capable of evaluating any property but it typically has been in the western United States. These are done with a separate contract covering the Buyers objectives and my income and expenses.

What does the Recreational Vehicle Supply List Look Like

If you are a person who loves vacationing and long distance travel, then you would be the right type of person who would love to have a recreational vehicle, since this would provide you with the basic comforts and amenities required for you to live on wheels. A well-maintained RV is actually as good as a second home; with the advantage that you can take it anywhere you like to go.

What Type of Recreational Vehicle Supply Do You Know About?

The RV is usually designed to become a second home for people who travel for indefinite periods, in hostile habitat's, and/ or rural places where accommodations are not easy to find. This will provide all the regular amenities of a home, such as gas stove, bed, bath, toilet, kitchen, fridge, DVD, music system and so on.

Depending on the budget and the RVs also come equipped with their own pedal power generation system, water harvesting system, radio communication, dish antenna and TV, computer with internet and other such amenities that can enable your independent function despite the local provisions.

When you decide to go for the purchase of a RV it would be good if you run a perfunctory glance at the recreational vehicle supply available in the market. Besides the different types of self-contained motor homes there are three different options. First, the travel trailer is a type of RV that is usually bigger and heavier than all the other RVs. It is usually pulled along with the help of a special hitch connection with the car/ truck you are driving.

Second, the truck camper is attached to the body of the car by means of a cradle; but it is smaller and becomes part of the body of the car/ truck

Finally, there is the fifth wheel travel trailer. As the name suggests, this type of RV is suspended over a fifth set of wheels while the front is attached to the main vehicle.

The type of recreational vehicle supply available in the market of a certain region is very dependent and limited to the demand of that region. The choice of recreational vehicle supply also depends upon the regions natural habitat. When the natural habitat is friendly and invites tourists, people tend to come and plan for longer stays, time during which some people decide to buy an RV. This too, in whatever small measure it may be, influences the recreational vehicle supply of the area

Recreation Property Market Expected to Regain Ground

A lack of interest in recreation or resort property is a "temporary condition," says a planning firm executive.

The issues clouding the property sector can be traced to a lack of consumer confidence based on current economic conditions, says Joe Miotto, vice-president of planning for NORR Architects and Planners. It will take a couple of years before the industry regains much of the ground it has lost, he says. Miotto was one of several industry insiders speaking at the recent Canadian Resort Investment Conference in Calgary.

Several projects have gone into receivership, or been shelved or cancelled, in the wake of the global recession and the reining in of spending by consumers.

"In many cases, the prospective real estate purchasers have the funds, but have become more conservative about real estate investment, perhaps due to worries associated with job loss, falling stock market prices and similar economic factors which reduce their confidence in real estate spending," says Miotto.

While the U.S. recreation property and resort segment has been pummelled, Canadian projects have not escaped unscathed, he says, adding that people are not losing interest in having a second home or recreation property, It's just the supply-demand curve at work. The market has been saturated with resort real estate product where supply has simply outran demand and real estate price continued to skyrocket.

"This has led to a need for a catch-up and price adjustment period which we are presently experiencing— which is more likely to occur, albeit slowly, over the next couple of years, especially with some of the price discounting that has been going on," says Miotto. There are three main reasons why he feels there will always be a strong demand for resort or recreation property.

- Because recreation property is usually in a limited supply due to the difficulties associated with land availability, lengthy land use approvals, and typically high infrastructure costs.
- Because of an "ever-present desire to improve lifestyle opportunities as a result of more frantic and challenging work environments."
- Because owning resort real estate typically represents a good investment. Values per square foot are usually very high compared to traditional real estate.

As the industry continues to improve along with the economy—and the level of consumer confidence —Miotto says there are two demographic markets that will show interest in second home or reproperty ownership.

The first is the baby-boomer crowd, those with money and time and living much more active lifestyles. The other emerging market is the children of the boomers—Generation X. Between 25 and 40 years old, these people are high-energy individuals, some with families, who are looking for a connection to the outdoors. They also stand to inherit significantly from their boomer parents, so they also have the income to invest in resort property.

As for the industry, itself, Miotto says it will be much more conservative in the future "as the recent years' phenomenon was not representative of normal market conditions."

Bottom of form

The basic need of the world is to save time for the own self and for their family members. There are also some of the people who see their children in week ends only!! Recreational Vehicles are specially made for those who never go for the vacations with their families for the burden of works. Recreational Vehicles facilitate them the facility and the room to make their jobs and to perform whatever they feel to and still the vehicle moves on. So, it's a road vehicle with the splendid services that any of the homes requires. So, RVs are the second option for the housing facilities and recently the Government of some states have made it legal to attend the RVs as the second homes. So, the RVS are becoming more and popular in the trend. People have started understanding the value of the time spending with the families and also the drawbacks of the lives of the people who were and are just living like a clock!!

But, there are so many different types of RVs and they are available in various models and also in various sizes. Motor homes are the most reputed types and people who are wishing to have a luxurious staying while driving can select the option of Motor homes. Motor homes for sale are the vehicles with the great superiority and spontaneously. They are also available in the online business and people are highly desperate in saving their time and money by owning the motor homes for sale.

Actually, all the RVs and the Motor homes are quite costlier option and they are available in the higher prices that are unbelievable. So, people have started demanding the used and second hand RVs that re cheaper in the rated and reasonable in the qualities. The Used RVs are better option for those who have lower cost of budget and still a good quality of the vehicle for the using.

So, to have the best of your life's experience, you should definitely go for the Recreational Vehicles that are better for the driving and journey purpose and best for the staying and accommodations purpose. They also are better for the money saving purpose of accommodations. Also they are better for the home liking purposes and give a good feel even on the wheels.

So, the RVs and Motor homes are the most appropriate and affordable options for the longer picnic with the families and also while going the country side. Have them, you'll have the comfort!!

Consider a Second Home as an Investment Property

Arizona has long been the preferred vacation destination for northerners looking for a break from the bitter cold of winter. Some of these tourists even purchased a second home in Arizona for their part-time residence. But second homes in Arizona are not just for the average "snow bird", and these second homes don't have to be a typical retirement property.

More and more people are considering a second home for an investment property. In fact, sales of second homes accounts for a third of all real estate sales in the last year. Unlike the typical retiree property, many second home properties are used as rental properties for investment gain. These home owners realize income from the rental, as well as tax benefits and appreciation in value.

As the population ages, there is a significant increase in the number of people considering a second home for investment potential. Many people consider these second homes as short-term investments, and long-term retirement potential.

These second-homes aren't necessarily small single-family properties or small apartment-like condominium. Instead these investment properties are often properties the investor can picture themselves living in long-term. This means the properties may offer amenities that are for more custom and appealing to a very active population. Investment properties are located close to golf courses and recreational properties, feature spectacular view, easy access to spas, right property in the right location can mean a steady stream of executive renters, and a great rental income. This second property can not only bring in income, but pay off the mortgage long before retirement.

Real estate investment is an excellent way to grow wealth. These second homes give owners a unique opportunity to accrue value. In Arizona, real estate prices have appreciated at a truly spectacular rate. While prices have cooled down from the lightening-hot rates of the past year, appreciation still remains extremely strong. When compared to other investment opportunities, it's clear that real estate is a stable and profitable investment.

There are a number of mortgage options that are quite unique to the second home market. For investors that are would like to pursue a second home, a quality mortgage agent can show you a number of options that make the second home not only possible, but extremely profitable.

European Cities: Towards a "Recreational Turn"?

Concepts and the Oretical Framework: Cities as Places in a "Regime of Dwelling"

Several concepts need to be defined and examined for their adequacy: "city," "recreation," "tourism," and "recreational turn." These concepts establish a theoretical horizon, in which the *spatial* dimensions of society are seen as crucial. As such, the concept of space as allowing cognitive operations of orientation, distance, arrangement, spatial organization, placement, recognition of various spatial qualities and so forth is a central point of analysis.

More precisely, it stems neither from an approach where space is seen as "naturally" built and explained by "natural laws" or closely related (such as in classical approaches of "distance decay"), nor from an approach in which space is seen as the material "surface" or Cartesian *res extensa* on which the social is projected. Rather, it is an approach where the central perspective is that of an actor-and practice-oriented "geography making" by various types of actors. More precisely, it is an approach whereby this geography making stems from practice in everyday life, in which the multifold relationships to space are at stake. This "doing with space," which I call "dwelling" (*Wohnen* in German and *habiter* in French), is addressed within a phenomenologically informed practice-based approach rooted in 20th century developments of social theory. The following concepts should be seen within this broader theoretical framework, in which actors fabricate space through their actions, while being embedded in situations where spatial dimensions—from the local to the global level, and from material to meta-geographical constructions—are Approaching the tourist dimensions of cities raises the question of the *kind* of places concerned, of their *quality*: How can the concept of "city" be defined in contemporary Europe? How can we speak of "cities" without speaking of places that are not cities?

This classical scientific problem is particularly difficult with regard to urban places because of confusion and difficulty in drawing adequate distinctions. One important question, often raised since Lefebvre (1974) or Castells (1973) in the late 1960s and early 1970s is: can we still speak of "the" city, or has the urban phenomenon become too manifold to assign one word to it? Many problems remain unsolved: 1) the urban/rural opposition: is the countryside an urban place for residence and recreation? 2) the "culturalist" definitions of the city in context: is there still a "European" city in the sense of a culturally different urban place, or do processes on the global level affect cities in Europe, Asia, Africa and South America in the same manner, thus no longer allowing us to give culture-based definitions of urban spaces? 3) the delimitation of city in comparison with agglomeration or "urban region", 4) the differentiated urban qualities of places, between global cities and small cities, industrial agglomerations, countryside, tourist resorts etc.

Within the framework of dwelling, a city is seen here as a place of specific qualities with which its inhabitants cope—i.e., mobilize as resources within their actions, recognize as problems within their practices, or give sense to by encoding a certain meaning through their practice. This meaning is constructed through the intentionality that guides the performed practice. Depending on the situation (the city is practiced in one way by the tourist and in another way by the resident), the individual experiences the city and the city makes sense as a place for specific practices. It is therefore the quality of the place, mediated through the specific situation, which is important for dwelling. The problem of defining the city, then, lies in the definition of a certain quality of place, as compared to other kinds of places (urban or non-urban), that is mobilized during an action.

Without probing deeper, we can use three important elements for the current purpose: (1) the distinction between different types of places where urbanness exists, at all levels of scale, making "city" one urban place among others; (2) on a local level of scale, seeing the "city" as designating the densest and most diverse organization of the urban; and (3) in comparison to tourist resorts, approaching cities as places with centrality that often have a poly-functional structure of urbanness (more diverse than resorts).

Tourism as a subsystem of dwelling and as a specific kind of recreation How do touristic dimensions contribute to the quality of the European city? How can tourism be defined? In order to fit into the actor-centred approach, the definition of tourism is one in which *tourists* are seen as essential. In fact, three interrelated issues are raised here: the definition of tourism, the question of recreation and the question of tourist places.

First, tourism is defined as a system of places, actors and practices, which has emerged in order to allow for inhabiting *other* places for the purpose of recreation. More narrowly, tourism could be defined as evolving in a sphere delineated by the various combinations of *displacement* and *recreation* of individual actors. It is therefore distinguished from other definitions of "visitors" for such multiple purposes as conferences, business and pilgrimage, visiting friends etc. The distinction is drawn between the everyday and the non-everyday, where the break with routine constitutes the essential experience.

This has been called "de-routinization" by Elias (1986). Tourist practices are therefore seen as a kind of de-routinization *based upon* a specific relationship with space: Through a displacement, a change of place, where alterity allows for a more efficient break with routine and recursive practices.

This allows for an understanding of different practices implying mobility, where familiar / other places and recursive and non-recursive practices are distinguished from each other. From a historical viewpoint, it seems important to see tourism as a relatively autonomous "sphere" or "domain" that has progressively emerged over time, between 1800 and 1850. It is this emergence of a new domain in human societies that contributes to understanding its relative importance in contemporary cities.

Second, recreation should be understood here as a break with the everyday in order to attain "controlled relaxing of self-control" through various practices. At this point of the argument, it should be acknowledged that this dichotomy of recreational practices does not fit numerous recreational practices: going frequently to a second home, or to visit a friend or a family, are practices where the strangeness of place is mediated through a familiar "technology." We might also question the relative importance of tourist practices in an age of mobility, where recreational displacement is no longer rare, such as in bourgeois and middle class tourism between 1850 and 1950. Thus, it might be more adequate to conceptualize a continuum of recreational practices, where the otherness plays a greater or lesser role.

Third, tourist places are nowadays highly differentiated places. Their touristic quality of space emerges not only through markers—through space designed *for* tourists—but also through the situated action of tourists. A tourist place can be defined as a place for tourist situations in the sense that the presence of tourists in a non-tourist place does not immediately transform the latter into a tourist place. Rather, the tourist place is a temporary result of the emergence and stabilization of tourist practices. As a first step towards a more differentiated approach, three elements might help to distinguish four fundamental types of tourist places.

The distinctions are threefold: the tourist site (*site touristique*) is distinguished from other tourist places by its lack of capacity to receive staying visitors (bed capacity). The tourist post (*comptoir touristique*) is distinguished from the resort and city by the absence of the local population in the former and its presence in the latter. Finally, the tourist resort (*station touristique*) is distinguished from the tourist city (*ville touristique*) in that the latter has diverse urban and tourist functions, while the former has monofunctional characteristics.

One element is therefore important in order to pinpoint a city where tourism is important: we need to look for diverse urban functions and centrality. The tourist city is therefore a specific kind of urban place and a specific kind of tourist place, defining a certain mode of urbanity.

The "recreational turn" is defined here as four interrelated processes: (1) the presence of tourists in urban places; (2) the desire, by local authorities or enterprises, to have tourists in their territory; (3) the rejection of tourism (i.e., a negative attitude towards tourism); and (4) a general interpretation scheme—a "gaze" in the Foucaldian sense—based on tourism, with which to interpret the world. It expresses itself in two main modalities, usually termed tourism and leisure.

This "recreational turn" could be related to the works of scholars like Dumazedier (1988) on the "civilisation of leisure" (*civilisation du loisir*) or Schulze (1997) on "society of experience" (*Erlebnisgesellschaft*). As the latter points out, the "aesthetic" is a certain way of giving meaning to numerous practices. As such, recreation is a way of giving meaning to practices through a particular stance and attitude. Indeed, we observe that although an "effort" is made, for example, climbing a mountain or going to an exhibition, that is not seen as work, but rather as "fun" and "relaxation." This attitude is by no means "natural"—in the nineteenth century, British alpinists were seen as "fools" by the indigenous inhabitants of Switzerland—but rather corresponds to the emergence of a new social value for practice. In this way, we can also understand that the activity of "shopping" is a playful one, whereas the veryday task of buying is not.

"Recreational turn" is therefore an expression that tries to back up the hypothesis of a greater importance of different forms of recreation in contemporary society, and more precisely in European cities. The fundamental idea is that of a change in the quality of the urban space affected by recreation. European cities develop a new quality by the relatively increased importance of recreation, and more specifically of tourism. The quality of urbanness depends to a great extent on the presence of tourists, of tourist-related business, of images informed by tourism. A "real" city –a place defined by a certain quality of urbanness – is essentially defined by its touristic quality.

The Context of the "Recreational turn" of European Cities

Several elements can be seen as essential in the ongoing process of recreationalization of urban space. Changing time budgets (working time down, leisure time up, especially the holiday: between four and six weeks a year, with the 1997 laws of reduction of labour time in France, even up to 11 weeks for senior executives), changing financial budgets (general rise in living standards between 1950 and 1970 in Europe), but also new ways of practising space, related to acquired tourist practices (more frequent but shorter holidays) are important elements.

That means the longterm holiday —the German *Sommerfrische* or the French *villégiature* of the 19th and first half of the 20th century— of one or two months is being replaced by more differentiated recreation practices: one or two weeks' holiday, short trips for the weekend, long weekends, shorter but more frequent, year-round holidays, etc. The tourist industry is aware of this change, and advertises products such as "city breaks" or "short breaks".

This new organization of the tourist practice is one important element of the rise of cities as places of recreation. This, by the way, invalidates the widespread thesis of tourist practices as "flight" from the cities to the countryside, mountains or seaside, developed by Enzensberger (1962) and widely acknowledged in the academic literature on tourism. What about the "flight" from the city to the city, or more precisely, from the (residential) suburb to the (touristic) centre of the city?

In press, *Hagar. Studies in Culture, Polity and Identities*. Preprint – please cite from local level, we find a huge discrepancy between different figures, and varying assumptions and counting principles from one source to another. For example, the cities, which are neither complete nor reliable.

The research group on tourism in European cities, based in Vienna, tries to address this problem. For Europe as a whole, the European Commission estimates 2.2 billion bed nights (ECT, 2001), the most important countries being Italy, Germany, Spain, France and the United Kingdom. These figures have the advantage of coming from the same source, but the disadvantage of being contradictory to other sources: for example, the statistical surveys of the United Kingdom count respectively 204 million foreigners' bed nights and 490 million nationals' bed nights, a figure well above that given by the European Commission; French surveys count 567 million foreigners' bed nights, which exceeds the overall figure and is five times higher than that for foreigners given by the European Commission.

Furthermore, these figures do not allow for a regional or local breakdown. Nevertheless, we can establish a cartographic construction known as a "cartogram" based on those figures. It constructs the cartographical surface of countries depending on the importance of tourism, rather than the area of the national territory. It allows for a visual appreciation of the importance of tourism in European countries. Irrespective of the problem of exact figures, the conclusion drawn is that the scale of European tourism has increased significantly. The elementary counting unit is nowadays the million bed nights in an increasing number of European cities.

Apart from those cities where tourism plays a key role, there are numerous cities where tourism is present, but on a much smaller scale. Yet, establishing the recreational turn by counting tourists or bed nights is not sufficient. As tourism can be defined as a system of places, practices, representations and actors with a relative autonomy, other elements besides beds, bed nights and flows would be required in order to establish the contemporary context of tourism in European cities.

Processes of Recreationalization

Several processes lead to the increased and differentiated recreational quality of European cities, following — and this is the main hypothesis— the initial quality of the place. Indeed, the initial quality can be that of a tourist resort or an industrial agglomeration or it can be tourist-oriented since the 19th century (Paris, Venice) or only recently (Bilbao). This historical element contributes to difference between European cities. Although there is no coherent theoretical framework for addressing these issues, the following processes can be observed. Festivalization Festivalization is one of the processes of the recreational turn in European cities. Festivals can be defined as musical, operatic or theatrical events, taking place every year, at the same place and at approximately the same time.

The concept has been extended to incorporate the question of "events". We find two kinds of urban places that are important in that scheme: capitals (Edinburgh, Budapest, Istanbul, Vienna, Berlin) or medium-sized cities (Aix-en-Provence, Salzburg) and smaller tourist cities (Granada, Orange) or quasi-rural places where the festival is the dominant urban attribute (Marciac Jazz Festival). Festivals are also used to boost "anciently constituted" tourist resorts: Garmisch-Partenkirchen, San Sebastian, Verbier, Gstaad, Montreux, Baden-Baden.

As a consequence, "festive cities" are created on the basis of *fêtes*: Paris (*Nuit Blanche* or *Paris-sur-Seine*), Reykjavik, Dublin, etc., directed not only towards the city's inhabitants, but, because of the increased geographical accessibility in terms of cost and time, to metropolitan inhabitants at the national and European levels too. Probably, the inspiring model for conceiving of an urban space as festive space is the case of Ibiza.

More generally, the attempt to create what are called "events" is more and more important, and is seen by promoters as one way to generate profit or to play with the image of the city. Sports events are exemplary for this process, because professional sport has grown in importance since the 1950s. Sportsmen and sportswomen have developed from amateurs to professionals, creating performances to be experienced as a spectacle by an ever greater audience.

The "sports system" is now a huge industry, with virtually no break throughout the year, and performing on a global scale. The pattern of distribution of sports events points to metropolises and anciently constituted tourist resorts.

In press, *Hagar. Studies in Culture, Polity and Identities*. Preprint – please cite from the original manufacturing has been replaced by tourism. This can be observed more and more in those cities or urban regions where a decline of the manufacturing sector has occurred since the 1950s. The most spectacular examples are British and Irish cities: Dublin, Glasgow, Liverpool, Manchester, Sheffield and Birmingham have made enormous efforts to change the city's image and/or its infrastructure and the practices of people. But also in France (Lille), Germany (Ruhr, Hamburg), Italy (Genova,

Torino) and Spain (Barcelona, Bilbao), the effects of a new recreational dynamic can be grasped. The processes taking place are differentiated, spanning from the constitution of industrial heritage to festivals, from sports to the display and imitation of lifestyle.

Liverpool is an interesting example because of the redefinition of what heritage might be: a malleable concept that can apply to virtually every situation. In the case of Liverpool, heritage defines the 19th century harbour facilities. It coincides with the urban regeneration towards the constitution of a tourist space. Two main operations were conducted: the preparation and recognition of parts of the city – the port and adjacent areas – as a "World heritage site" by UNESCO and the nomination as European Capital of Culture in 2008. The share of the hotel and catering sector in employment is about 5 %-which is relatively small compared to Benidorm, where it is 50%.

Barcelona is perhaps the model for all those transformation processes where tourists from all over Europe come to experience the leisure of the Barcelonese, and to stroll like them along the main street, the Ramblas. This was made possible through a politics of urban regeneration, "boosted" by the hosting of the Olympic Games in 1992.

Another process can be observed: the "heritageing" of inner cities. The result is what Ashworth and Tunbridge (1990) call "tourist-historic cities". This process is not entirely new and has its roots in the 19th century tourist development of Venice/Italy, Brugge/Belgium and Rothenburg ob der Tauber/Germany. It has expanded throughout the 20th century to more cities to the extent that few European cities are exempt from branding and image-construction through the slogan of "cultural heritage" This labelling raises the issue of a landmark that is worth visiting and fits in MacCannell's (1976) theory of a marker for a "thing" becoming a tourist attraction. The actors of this process are no longer local or the tourists themselves, which used to be the case in the 19th century. There are global or national actors, such as the UNESCO natural and cultural heritage project – roughly 1'000 "natural" or "cultural" sites are labelled, not to forget national laws for heritage protection. Nevertheless, the UNESCO labelling and accompanying discourse raises the problem of an adequate distinction between "cultural" and "natural".

Due to the aesthetic, tourist and heritaged gaze, the bio-physical elements, *e.g.* the Chinese karsts become cultural, because of the definition, by a special board of actors, of it *as* worth while seeing. Therefore, all those labelled things have become cultural. 15 This process of heritageing is most important for small and medium-sized cities and transforms profoundly the quality of space, such as in Trier/Germany, Toledo/Spain, Pisa/Italy, In press, *Hagar. Studies in Culture, Polity and Identities*. Preprint – please cite from the original Carcassonne/France. This process has extended to cities of the whole spectrum of the urban hierarchy, where more or less adequate historical layers are invented in order to display them to visitors. Nevertheless, this process of heritageing is not self-evident and creates conflicts on which elements of cities are "heritageable" and which are not.

Approaching the Modernity of Metropolises

The contemporary practice of short visits to cities – advertised as "short breaks" or "city breaks" – a trip lasting usually for a long weekend, is one element of the presence of tourists in cities. One observation or question can be made: those tourists being mostly "urbanites" themselves, how could we understand that they visit a *similar* place? Besides the experience of heritage, Duhamel (2006) identifies another fundamental process in the touristification of cities from the point of view of the tourist: to experience elements standing for *modernity*.

Since the London and Paris of the 19th century, the modernity of metropolises has been at the centre of the tourist agenda. Experiencing the urbanness of the city seems to constitute the key difference with resorts and heritage cities: the touristic practice of the city is based on its very urban, as a total experience, not of one element of it. This also allows for an understanding of the multiple ways of residing in a metropolis as a tourist: exchange of apartments or staying with inhabitants rather than in hotels are forms of contact with the otherness of the place. The objective is to experience the city not as an "outsider", but as an "insider", thus transforming the other place into a familiar place. It is different to seeing the tourist city as a collection of tourist sites. From resorts to cities: a specific kind of urbanization Finally, there is another kind of city which can be called a "tourist city": ancient tourist resorts – or "anciently constituted tourist resorts", as Knafou (1996) calls them more precisely–becoming cities through the development of centrality and diverse urban functions.

This is one kind of urban place completely overlooked in the literature, because it is either addressed as a "resort" or as a "normal" city without grasping the specificities of such a city with ancient tourist elements. They can be described as a development of a mono-functional resort into a more diverse city, where tourism continues to play a key role, often embedded in what Soane (1993) terms "resort regions". In Europe, there are two kinds of such "tourist cities". The bigger ones, such as Nice/France, Brighton & Hove/United Kingdom, Wiesbaden/Germany, and the smaller ones, such as Garmisch-Partenkirchen/Germany, Saint-Malo/France, Montreux/Switzerland etc. They have in common their emergence as tourist sites *before* the more recent rise of mass tourism.

This corresponds to the first and second periods of tourism's development: the first between 1780 and 1830, the second between 1830 and 192016. The process of urbanization is an interesting one: the diversification of recreational practices develops alongside population growth – both permanent and second homes – and the emergence of centrality in former non-central places. Vacation Home Sales to Surge, Study Says-Second Homes: Ecologists concerned about increased demand for resort properties in 1990s as baby boomers move into the age group that typically buys them.

In the next 10 years, droves of baby boomers may be heading for the hills. And for the mountains. And for the beaches. According to a new survey financed by the real estate and resort-development industry, demand for second homes may surge in the 1990s as baby boomers move into the age group that typically buys vacation properties. Demand for vacation properties may soar from its current level of about 135,000 purchases a year to as many as 450,000 a year, according to the study's authors. "Baby boomers generally are reaching that point in their lives where people historically have purchased vacation homes," said Steven S. Miner, research director of Eugene, Ore.-based Ragatz Associates Inc., which conducted the survey.

But the shift of development to the nation's hinterlands already is a matter of grave concern to environmentalists, who worry that more people and more traffic in once-pristine areas will damage wilderness areas. Now, in a new twist, some are advocating that the federal government take a new look at the ways in which it is helping to accelerate the process.

A U.S. Forest Service report, based on public hearings and backed by environmental groups, has suggested that the federal government should reconsider the tax breaks it gives to people who buy vacation homes in such ecologically important areas as New England's Northern Forest.

"The federal tax provision to deduct the interest on second-home mortgages may encourage the demand for recreational development and could be partially responsible for the increased rate of land conversion threatening the Northern Forest," the report said. "While the purpose of the deduction is to stimulate growth and construction, it may be having other effects in the Northern Forest." For many within the real estate industry, the mortgage-interest deduction is a key issue. Under current law, people who own second homes can deduct from their taxable incomes the mortgage interest they pay on the properties. In other words, depending on a household's tax bracket, the federal government will subsidize up to one-third of the cost of owning a vacation home.

Policy Document o Preserve it

The IRTRC policy was adopted on the 18th of December 2007 as a variation to the 2005-2011 Waterford County Development Plan.

Amendment to Existing Tourism Policy as per the County Development Plan 2005-2011

Proposals to develop low density residential developments for permanent accommodation or holiday home use removed from designated settlement centres were previously contrary to the policies of the Development Plan as set out in Chapter 3 (Settlement Strategy), Chapter 6 (Economic Development) and Chapter 9 (Development Standards). However it was considered that the development of golf courses, hotels, race courses and other tourist developments/leisure facilities located in rural unzoned areas, which provide an important local/national amenity, may form the basis for justifying limited on-site residential development. To allow this, however, some of the policies as set out in the County Development Plan 2005-2011 had to be amended as follows:

Rural Settlement Strategy

Should Read as Follows

The success of the County Settlement Strategy will be dependent on the ability of the Local Authority to channel development into the identified zoned settlements. Whilst the measures outlined in Section 3.6 will promote this, a key factor in the success of the County Development Strategy will be the degree to which development outside of the designated nodes can be controlled. To do this, it is necessary to establish a Rural Settlement Strategy, which will set out how it is envisaged that development will take place outside of the zoned areas. The Rural Settlement Strategy, as set out in the Plan is based on the National Spatial Strategy 2002-2020, the Regional Planning Guidelines and the Sustainable Rural Housing Guidelines for Planning Authorities issued by the DoEHLG. The strategy is also linked to other key elements such as the Housing Strategy, demonstrated development pressures, and associated projections such as future population levels, etc. This strategy will be implemented in parallel with the policy on the provision of housing in association with Integrated Rural Tourism and Recreational Complexes and medium sized tourism development and on tourism zoned lands.

Rural Tourism

It is recognised that the growth of the tourism industry is critical to the economy of the county. This is particularly true in the rural areas where employment opportunities are reducing and traditional employment levels in agriculture are in decline. While seeking to ensure that most tourism development with associated accommodation facilities, is located in or close to towns or villages or on tourism zoned lands, the council recognises that, by its nature, some tourism developments may require other locations. In this regard consideration will be given to the provision of Integrated Rural Tourism and Recreational Complexes *and* Medium sized developments at appropriate locations throughout the county.

Integrated Rural Tourism and Recreational Complexes

In recent years, there has been an increase in the demand for, and development of, Integrated Rural Tourism and Recreational Complexes and Golf Courses. Associated with this has been the demand for housing, either for temporary letting as holiday homes or for permanent residential use. It is acknowledged that the provision of accommodation of an individual unit nature, (self contained apartments, lodges, chalets or houses) is emerging as an integral element of the Integrated Rural Tourism and Recreational Complex (IRTRC). An Integrated Rural Tourism and Recreational Complex can be defined as a high quality tourism development located in a rural location which includes the following:-

- A quality hotel (min 50 beds); and
- A leisure centre/spa, conference centre or similar and
- Other facilities such as a 18 hole golf club or a similar major public facility such as an Adventure centre, marina, indoor recreation centre.

Such proposals may also include tourism related residential developments, which are ancillary to the main tourist attraction. The council also recognises that an element of permanent housing may be considered to balance seasonal fluctuations in population associated with such tourism developments, and to support the initial economic viability of such proposals, which will be important generators of employment in rural areas. Consideration will be given to the provision of IRTRCs where the developments comply with the following criteria:-

- Complies with the Scenic Landscape Evaluation and coastal development and landscape policies;
- Relates to the scale and level of activity in the locality;
- Will not have a significant adverse impact on the character or siting of settlements or the amenity of existing residents;
- Will not have a significant adverse affect on the character or appearance of the County's countryside and will generally retain the open nature of the land;
- Will not impact on road safety or the free flow of traffic;
- Will not have a significant adverse impact on sites of nature conservation value or archaeological importance or the built heritage;
- New dwellings are of a good standard of design and are sympathetic to the landscape in terms of their siting, design and materials;
- Include a phasing plan for the provision of the proposed facilities.

An IRTRC proposal should be a sustainable development, which demonstrated long term viability. Overall there should be an emphasis on innovation in design and layout providing for an integrated development linking units to open space and facilities. Existing site features, including trees and hedgerows should be retained as far as possible to form a comprehensive landscaping scheme. Applications for IRTRCs containing holiday homes should be accompanied by details of an agreement that the overall development will be retained in single Management or as a time share, short term letting of similar arrangement. In No instance shall the holiday homes/holiday units be sold for or used as permanent dwelling places. Permanent residences may be permitted in association with an IRTRC application and the criteria as set out in Section 9.4.2.

Medium Sized Tourism Developments and Associated Holiday Homes

Medium sized tourism developments of a local scale may have the capacity to accommodate holiday homes. A smaller tourism development may consist of the provision of any of the following:-

- a quality hotel (minimum of 50 bedrooms), or
- a golf course, or
- a major equestrian centre, holiday camp (similar to Trabolgan), marina, adventure centre, sporting activities with a maritime/estuarine location or
- similar type facility of regional attraction.

It is recommended that the paragraphs on 'Tourist accommodation and facilities', 'Holiday homes and second homes' and associated policies be amended as set out below:-

The paragraphs on 'Tourist accommodation and facilities', 'Holiday homes and second homes' and associated policies is amended as follows:

> *The development of tourism accommodation is crucial to the effective development of the tourism industry in the county. Apartment type developments are best located within the existing established tourism centres. Clustered holiday home developments will also be most appropriate in these centres, or in other settlements throughout the county where facilities and services are available or on tourism zoned lands or as part of IRTRC or medium sized tourism developments. In settlement areas outside of established tourism centres, it is important to ensure that holiday home developments will not impact negatively on the existing residential community (e.g seasonal fluctuations in population levels and the closure of services during winter months).*

In keeping with the Sustainable Rural Housing Guidelines for Planning Authorities, there will be a presumption against holiday home/ second home development in areas outside of settlements, in Visually Vulnerable and Sensitive Areas, and along Scenic Routes as designated in the Scenic Evaluation Map. However, consideration will be given to the development of appropriately scaled holiday homes on tourism zoned lands or as part of IRTRC or medium sized tourism developments. The council will encourage suitably scaled clusters of holiday homes in settlements and in IRTRCs, and will facilitate tourist houses in areas where such development will not contravene the council's Settlement Strategy as outlined in Chapter 3 and/or the Rural Tourism policy.

ED7: To support the development of appropriately scaled holiday home/second home development within existing settlements or on tourism zoned lands or in association with IRTRC or integrated into medium sized tourism developments in accordance with the Settlement Strategy set out in Chapter 3 or the Rural Tourism policy.

ED8: To support the development of appropriately scaled permanent home development in association with IRTRCs.

Tourism Development

The section of the Development Standards, which sets out the criteria for the assessment of residential tourism development, is amended as follows

The Council requires that planning applications for developments of this nature to demonstrate that the development provides for all year round usage. Any residential tourism development must demonstrate that it:-

- Does not place unsustainable demands upon the existing or planned infrastructure capacity of the area;
- Does not conflict with the maintenance of the natural and cultural heritage of the area;
- Is located within or adjacent to an established settlement node, on tourism zoned lands or in association with an IRTRC or a viable tourism facility; or medium sized tourism development.
- Reinforces the provision of non-residential tourism facilities in the county either through integration with established facilities or by the provision of new facilities; and
- Minimises the need for additional vehicular journeys to/ from visitor facilities in the immediate environs.

Development of an IRTRC and Housing on a Green Field Site

On a green field site, consideration shall only be given to the provision of dwellings/tourist accommodation units, where it is demonstrated that they are in accordance with the relevant criteria set out hereunder.

Development of Holiday Homes in Association with an IRTRC on a Green Field Site

The following standards shall be applied to holiday home development on green field sites:-

- The provision of holiday homes will only be considered where the total landholding is not less than 100 acres (40ha).
- The number of holiday homes permitted will be dependence on site specifics – area of site, location, degree of visibility, natural screening, scale of tourist facilities available/to be provided. Each case will be assessed on its merits.
- The building height/scale of the units shall be relative to the complex, the topography and screening of the site, etc.
- The holiday homes/units shall be clustered in an open plan layout with shared amenity space.
- The IRTRC and associated holiday homes/accommodation, excluding any related limited provision of permanent housing, should be developed and managed as a single unit.
- The holiday homes shall be used for short term occupation only and not used for permanent residential use. Where holiday homes are sold or transferred in ownership, the new owner shall be required to enter into a legal agreement with the Planning Authority that the unit shall not be used as a permanent home.
- The developer will be required to pay a special financial contribution towards the provision of social and affordability housing which will be calculated using a similar methodology to that applicable under Part V of the Planning and Development Act (2000-2006).

- All development shall have regard to the Scenic Landscape Evaluation and specific site suitability for development – drainage, access, etc.
- Provision of adequate water supply to serve the development and safe treatment and disposal of sewage, which would not prejudice the ground water quality in the area.

Development of Permanent Homes in Association with an IRTRC on a Green Field Site

The following standards shall be applied to permanent residential development on green field sites:-

- The provision of dwellings will only be considered where the total landholding is not less than 100 acres (40ha).
- The number of dwellings permitted will be dependence on site specifics – Location, topography, degree of visibility, natural screening, etc. Each case will be assessed on its merits. However in no case shall the number of dwellings provided exceed 1 unit per 8 acres (3 ha).
- Detached dwellings only will be considered (to avoid urban/suburban patterns of development which would be unsuitable in a rural setting).
- Minimum site size of 0.5 acres (0.2ha).
- All development shall be required to comply with the minimum development standards as set out in the County Development Plan 2005-2011, except where in conflict with the above specified standards.
- The developer will be required to pay a special financial contribution towards the provision of social and affordability housing which will be calculated using a similar methodology to that applicable under Part V of the Planning and Development Act (2000-2006).
- All development shall have regard to the Scenic Landscape Evaluation and specific site suitability for development – drainage, access, etc.

- Provision of adequate water supply to serve the development and safe treatment and disposal of sewage, which would not prejudice the ground water quality in the area.

Development of an IRTRC and Housing in Association with a Protected Structure

Consideration shall only be given to the provision of holiday homes and permanent dwellings where the Protected Structure or group of structures within the curtilage and/or attendant grounds are being refurbished and adapted for sustainable use. Such a decision shall be based on a full appraisal of the structure and setting. Appropriate subdivision of a structure may be also be an option. For both permanent and holiday home development of the Protected Structure or structures within the curtilage and /or attendant grounds of a Protected Structure, the standards set out above for green field sites will applied, in addition to the standards set out below:-

- The immediate grounds of the main structure/complex and the avenue/driveway/entrances of the main structure/ complexes shall be maintained free from housing development and associated works.
- New housing shall be screened from the Main Structure/ complex by either the topography of the site or existing mature landscaping. Where there is no existing screening arising from either topography or planting, a minimum separation distance of 500m will be required to be maintained (this is a minimum guideline only and a greater separation distance may be required in certain circumstances).
- The building height of the dwellings shall be relative to the complex, the topography and screening of the site, etc., but in no case will the building height of exceed that of the protected structure.
- Consideration could be given to the conversion of existing stone stable buildings/courtyard building to high quality tourist accommodation.

However, it should be borne in mind that these are indicative maximum thresholds and not the minimum expectation of the developer. Regardless of the above criteria, some sites may not be suitable for such development. The suitability of the site will be determined by the Planning Authority and will be based on reports, and the potential impact of the proposed developments on the character of the Protected Structure and its setting (if applicable).

Guidelines for Development of an IRTRC and Housing in Association with a Protected Structure

In all cases, prospective developers will be required to hold pre-planning discussions with the Planning Section, the Conservation Officer and the Heritage Officer. Preplanning with Bord Failte would be advisable. Information to be submitted with any such application should include:

- A Cultural Heritage Impact Assessment report of the Protected Structure, which may include a Building Conditions and Conservation Report; (This is dependent on the site and level of proposed development);
- Description of intervention works necessary to consolidate the PS;
- Description of proposed works necessary to ensure continued use of the building (change of use will be considered where appropriate);
- Description of proposed dwellings, including site specific designs of the proposed housing which demonstrates that regard was had to the topography, landscape features and the built heritage of the site.
- Assessment of impact of proposed housing on the Protected Structure, its curtilage, setting and its landscape features.
- Assessment of the impact of the proposed development on the natural heritage of the site. This may include a tree survey and flora and fauna survey. (In some cases, this may be included in the Cultural Heritage Impact Assessment).

- A Masterplan for the holistic approach to the development of the site is necessary as careful management of the house, gardens and demesnes, which should be considered assets, will benefit public and developers alike.

The complexity of the reports required would be dependence on the specific site and the level of development proposed. Prospective developers should comply with:-

- Appendix B; Architectural Heritage Impact Assessments, The Architectural Heritage Protection, Guidelines for Planning Authorities, DoEHLG, 2004.
- 'Guidance Notes for the Appraisal of Historic Gardens, Demesnes, Estates and their settings', Cork County Council, April 2007. This will be superseded by guidance notes, which are currently being prepared by our Conservation Officer.

Development of Medium Sized Tourism Developments and Associated Holiday Homes on Unzoned Lands

The following criteria would have to be complied with for the development of a medium sized tourism facility with associated holiday homes:-

- The provision of holiday homes will only be considered where the total landholding is not less than 30 acres (12ha).
- The number of holiday homes permitted will be dependence on site specifics – area of site, location, degree of visibility, natural screening, scale of tourist facilities available/to be provided. Each case will be assessed on its merits.
- A business plan shall be submitted with any application to demonstrate the long term viability and sustainability of the tourism development and associated holiday homes.
- The tourism development should not detract from any existing tourism facilities in the area.
- The tourism facility and any associated holiday homes shall be built and managed as a single unit by a management company.

- No permanent dwellings shall be permitted in association with the tourist facility/development.
- The developer will be required to pay a special financial contribution towards the provision of social and affordability housing which will be calculated using a similar methodology to that applicable under Part V of the Planning and Development Act (2000-2006).
- All development shall have regard to the Scenic Landscape Evaluation and specific site suitability for development – drainage, access, etc.
- The building height/scale of the holiday homes shall be relative to the topography and screening of the site, etc.
- The holiday homes/units shall be clustered in an open plan layout with shared amenity space.
- All development shall be required to comply with the minimum development standards as set out in the County Development Plan 2005-2011, except where in conflict with the above specified standards.
- The facility and units should be accessible to all, and fully compliant with Part M of the Building Regulations.

Regardless of the above criteria, some sites may not be suitable for such development. The suitability of the site will be determined by the Planning Authority during the planning application stage

Recreational & Second Properties Cabin Fever? Mortgaging for Recreation Properties

All across Canada we're seeing the recreational property market continue to go through the cedar-shingled roof. Industry experts predict another year in which buyers seeking a property may outnumber the recreational properties available. The boomers are in their peak income years and have benefited from an unprecedented climb in the valuations on their primary homes. And across the country, they're scouring every lake, ocean beach and ski slope-looking for the perfect getaway.

When cottages first became the vogue around the turn of the last century, those getaways were generally charmingly rustic structures designed to give their owners a taste of a simpler way of life for the summer season. But today, recreational property markets are reporting a stunning increase in teardowns and renovations-as rustic simplicity gives way to luxury accommodations. Today's recreational property mix covers the gamut from luxury waterfront homes, resort-style condominiums, ski chalets and timeshare properties. Many of the traditional-style cottages are still standing, of course... and they sell for top dollar on the rare occasions that they actually come on the market.

But more and more average Canadians have cabin fever: they're looking for a recreational property both as an investment and an enhancement to their own lifestyles. And for many, the goal is achievable: we've seen historically low mortgage rates over the last few years-and greater affordability for ordinary Canadians.

But financing a recreational property is more challenging than funding a principal residence. Traditional lending institutions typically find second homes a much less desirable investment. Purchasers are often advised to take out an equity loan or a second mortgage on their principal residence in order to buy the recreation property.

But the lending landscape has been changing in the past few years. We are beginning to see that some lenders have developed flexible new mortgage products and policies that are specifically designed for the recreational property market. The upshot is that Canad ians who are longing for that cottage or condo may now be able to bypass conventional lending criteria-opening the door to ownership much sooner than they imagined. Recreational property mortgages are available for owner-occupied second properties, including winterized and non-winterized, with as little as 15 per cent down for purchasers with good credit. And in some cases, 10 per cent down could get you into the recreational property market if you qualify.

And do your homework. In today's heated recreational property market, some purchasers have an edge in the marketplace because they are cash buyers. To level the playing field, buyers who are financing their purchase may want to consider talking to a professional to determine approximately how much they qualify for before launching their search. For some, recreational property is an attractive investment, with rentals providing an extra income stream. But the allure is usually more emotional: a cottage or condo often becomes a symbolic centre for family life, where families come together at all ages and stages in their lives to share common activities and traditions.

If you're dreaming of your own beach sunset or the perfect ski slope at your door, begin with a conversation with a mortgage professional. Your own getaway could be closer than yoWhat is a Recreational Vehicle and Its Classifications?

Are you the type of person who likes to travel to different places? Are you fond of camping and other recreational activities? Then, using a recreational vehicle would provide you with almost all the indispensable facilities that you will need on your travels.

In North America, people would rather define recreational vehicle as their second home. This is because they use the equipment as a means of transportation and at the same time a travel quarters.Generally, recreational vehicles are automobiles specially designed to serve as transitory home for people who are on travel, on a camping activity, or just about any activity that would require temporary dwelling at a certain time and place.

Most of the recreational vehicles consist of, but is not restricted to, a travel trailer, camping trailer, truck camper, and a fifth-wheel trailer. Actually, recreational vehicles can be set up like that of the truck campers, they can have their individual motor power like that of the motorhomes or they can be hauled by one more automobile just like the folding camping trailers and the travel trailers. Contrary to most popular belief, the basic description and definition of recreational vehicles do not include the mobile homes or the park trailers that are permanently manufactured to accommodate people for continuing dwelling, off-the-road motor vehicles, and conversion vehicles. To know more about recreational vehicles, here is a list of the different classifications of recreational vehicles:

1. Travel trailer. This refers to the recreational vehicle that has more weight than the other types of recreational

vehicle. It is especially made to be hauled by most automobiles through the use of a frame hitch or a bumper.

2. Truck camper. This is one type of recreational vehicle where the component is attached to the bodywork or the cradle of a pick-up truck. It is mainly used for recreational camping purposes.
3. Fifth Wheel Travel Trailer. This is the type of recreational vehicle that is extraordinarily made to be drawn by a pick-up truck furnished with an exceptional frame hitch in the truck cradle.

These are just a few of the many classifications of recreational vehicles. Whatever type you want to use, you can be sure that every recreational vehicle has its own storage areas, beds, food preparation areas, and tables. These facilities may vary depending on the size of the recreational vehicle.

Recreation, Tourism, and Rural Well-Being

While the economies of many rural areas in the United States have been sluggish in recent years, rural communities that have stressed recreation and tourism have experienced significant growth. This has not gone unnoticed by local officials and development organizations, which have increasingly turned to recreation and tourism as a vehicle for development.

However, not all observers are convinced that the benefits of this approach are worth the costs. There are concerns about the quality of the jobs created, rising housing costs, and potential adverse impacts on poverty, crime, and other social conditions. This report assesses the validity of these concerns by analyzing recent data on a wide range of socioeconomic conditions and trends in U.S. rural recreation areas. The purpose is to gain a better understanding of how recreation and tourism development affects rural wellbeing.

Recreation and tourism development has potential advantages and disadvantages for rural communities. Among the advantages, recreation and tourism can add to business growth and profitability. Landowners can benefit from rising land values. Growth can create jobs for those who are unemployed or underemployed, and this can help raise some of them out of poverty. Recreation and tourism can help diversify an economy, making the economy less cyclical and less dependent on the ups and downs of one or two industries.

It also gives underemployed manufacturing workers and farmers a way to supplement their incomes and remain in the community. Benefiting from growing tax revenues and growth-induced economies of scale, local governments may be able to improve public services. In addition, local residents may gain access to a broader array of private sector goods and services, such as medical care, shopping, and entertainment. While other types of growth can have similar benefits, rural recreation and tourism development may provide greater diversification, and, for many places, it may be easier to achieve than other kinds of development—such as high-tech development—because it does not require a highly educated workforce.

Many of the potential disadvantages of recreation-related development are associated with the rapid growth that these counties often experience; on average, "recreation counties" grew by 20 percent during the 1990s, nearly three times as fast as other rural counties. Rapid growth from any cause can erode local natural amenities, for example, by despoiling scenic views.

Cultural amenities, such as historic sites, can also be threatened. Growth can lead to pollution and related health problems, higher housing costs, road congestion, and more crowded schools, and it may strain the capacity of public services. Small businesses can be threatened by growth-induced "bigbox" commercial development, and farms can be burdened by increased property taxes. In addition, newcomers might have different values than existing residents, leading to conflicts over land use and public policies.

Growth can also erode residents' sense of place, which might reduce support for local institutions, schools, and public services. Aside from these general growth-related issues, some specific problems have been linked to tourism and recreation industries. These include the potential for higher poverty rates associated with low-wage, unskilled workers who are attracted to the area to work in hotels, restaurants, and recreation sites. Higher poverty rates could lead to various other social problems, including higher crime rates, lower levels of education, more health problems, and higher costs of providing public services.

With this mix of positive and negative impacts, it is understandable why experts on development policy may be uncertain about the value of rural tourism and recreation development strategies. Hence, it is important that policymakers have access to information about the nature and extent of the socioeconomic impacts of this type of development.

Past research has examined some of the impacts. Much of that research, however, is in the form of case studies, with only a few empirical studies examining nationwide rural impacts, such as the articles by English et al. (2000) and Deller et al. (2001). English et al. examined the impact of tourism on a variety of measures of local socioeconomic conditions (local income, employment, housing, economic structure, and demographic characteristics). Deller and his colleagues examined recreational amenities (including recreational infrastructure), local government finances, labour supply characteristics, and demographic demand characteristics, estimating their effects upon the growth of local population, employment, and income.

Our research used an approach similar to that of English and his colleagues, which identified a group of tourism-dependent counties and then used regression analysis to estimate the effect of tourism on various indicators of local rural conditions. Using the new ERS typology of rural recreation counties developed by Kenneth Johnson and Calvin Beale (2002), we identified differences between rural recreation counties and other nonmetro counties for various indicators of economic and social well-being.3 We also examined socioeconomic variations by type of recreation county.

We then used regression analysis to test statistically for the effect that dependence on recreation (including tourism and seasonal resident recreation) has on local socioeconomic conditions. Details about the regression analysis are provided in the appendix. We hoped to shed light on several important questions about this development strategy. Among these are:

- How does rural recreation development affect residents' ability to find jobs?
- How are local wages and incomes affected?
- How does recreation development affect housing costs and local cost of living?
- What effect does recreation development have on local social problems such as crime, congestion, and poverty?
- How are education and health affected?
- How do various types of recreation areas differ in socioeconomic characteristics?

What is a Recreation County?

In 1998, Beale and Johnson identified 285 nonmetropolitan recreation counties based on empirical measures of recreation activity, including levels of employment and income in tourism-related industries and the presence of seasonal housing. They modified and expanded their typology a few years later. Their 2002 typology identified 329 recreation counties that fell into 11 categories, varying by geographic location, natural amenities, and form of recreation. It is this typology that ERS has adopted as its recreation county typology. We used the 2002 typology, which covered only nonmetropolitan counties. To simplify our analysis, we excluded Alaska and Hawaii.4 This reduced the number of recreation counties in our study to 311.

One of the advantages of this typology is that it includes not only places with significant tourism-related activity but also those with a significant number of seasonal residents. Like tourists, most seasonal residents are attracted by opportunities for recreation, including some who come simply to relax in a scenic rural setting. In theory, seasonal residents should have a bigger economic impact on the local community than tourists because they stimulate the housing industry and their season-long presence significantly increases the demand for a wide range of local goods and services. In addition, seasonal residents often later become permanent residents. Because many seasonal residents first came to the area as tourists, it is difficult, if not impossible, to separate the long-term impact of tourists from seasonal residents. Our use of the ERS typology, which covers both tourism and seasonal recreational/residential development, thus seems ideal for estimating the long-term, overall impacts of tourism and recreation combined.

Another advantage of this typology is that it is derived from a continuous variable—a weighted average of tourism and seasonal housing dependence. In theory, this continuous variable may be used more effectively to estimate impacts than a simple recreation/ other nonmetro dichotomous variable because it allows us to examine variations in the extent of recreation. Similarly, the different types of recreation counties in the Johnson/Beale typology can be used to further elucidate and estimate the impacts of recreational activity on local socioeconomic conditions.

General Characteristics of Recreation Counties

The 311 recreation counties in our study are located in 43 States, but tend to be concentrated in the West, the Upper Great Lakes, and the Northeast. In the West, this reflects the ample opportunities for hiking, mountain climbing, fishing, and wintertime sports found in the many national parks and ski resorts there. By contrast, the high concentration of recreation counties in the Upper Great Lakes and Northeast—especially in New England and Upstate New York—is largely due to the popularity of long-established second homes in areas with lakes. Many of these areas also have significant wintertime recreation activities, including snowmobiling and skiing. Not surprisingly, recreation counties score higher (4.25) on ERS' natural amenities index than other nonmetro counties (3.34). Data from the 2000 Census reveal that recreation and other nonmetro counties average similar population sizes. However, during the last decade, the population of recreation counties has grown almost three times as fast (20 percent vs. 7 percent, on average). Recreation counties also have relatively low population densities, and more of their residents tend to live in rural parts of the county (those with less than 2,500 population).

Using the ERS 1993 county economic and policy typologies, we found that the economies in recreational counties were generally more diverse than in other nonmetro counties. For example, only 30 percent of recreation counties were highly dependent on a single major industry (agriculture, mining, or manufacturing), while 58 percent of other nonmetro counties were highly dependent on just one of these industries. Recreation counties also were slightly less dependent on neighbouring counties for employment; only 13 percent of recreation counties were identified as commuting counties (with a high percentage of their resident workforce commuting outside the county for employment), compared with 17 percent of other nonmetro counties. We also found that about a third (32 percent) of recreation counties were retirement-destination places vs. only 4 percent of other nonmetro counties.

How Were Recreation Counties Identified?

The 2002 Johnson/Beale typology covered only nonmetropolitan counties, using the 1993 Office of Management and Budget (OMB) definitions of metropolitan areas. Johnson and Beale began by examining a sample of wellknown recreation areas to determine which economic indicators were most appropriate for identifying other such counties.

They then computed the percentage share of wage and salary employment from the Census Bureau's 1999 County Business Patterns data and personal income from Bureau of Economic Analysis data as these data apply to recreation-related industries, i.e., entertainment and recreation, accommodations, eating and drinking places, and real estate. They also computed a third measure: the percentage share of housing units of seasonal or occasional use, from 2000 Census data.

They then constructed a weighted average of the standardized Z-scores of these three main indicators (0.3 employment + 0.3 income + 0.4 seasonal homes). Counties scoring greater than 0.67 on this recreation dependency measure were considered recreation counties. Next, they added several large nonmetro counties that did not make the cut but had relatively high hotel and motel receipts from 1997 Census of Business data. Additional counties were accepted if the weighted average of the three combined indicators exceeded the mean and at least 25 percent of the county's housing was seasonal. Then Johnson and Beale deleted 14 counties that lacked any known recreational function but appeared to qualify "either because they were very small in population with inadequate and misleading County Business Patterns coverage or because they reflected high travel activity without recreational purpose, i.e., overnight motel and eating place clusters on major highways."

These calculations produced their final set of 329 recreation counties. In 2004, ERS established these recreation counties as one of its county typologies. By 2004, some of these counties had changed their metropolitan status based on the new 2003 OMB definitions of metropolitan areas.

Many recreation counties (38 percent) were Federal land counties, meaning that at least 30 percent of the county's land was federally owned; only 7 percent of other nonmetro counties had that much Federal land. In addition, relatively few recreation counties (10 percent) had experienced persistently high levels of poverty, whereas about a fourth (26 percent) of other nonmetro counties fell into this category. Because recreation counties are not homogeneous with respect to these and other characteristics, the averages we present for all recreation counties mask considerable variation.

Economic Impacts

The conventional wisdom among researchers in recent years has been that recreation and tourism have both positive and negative economic impacts for recreation areas. On the positive side, recreation development helps to diversify the local economy, and it generates economic growth. It achieves this partly by acting as a kind of export industry, attracting money from the outside to spend on goods and services produced locally. It also stimulates the local economy through other means. Infrastructure, such as airports and highways and water systems, often must be upgraded to meet the needs of tourists, and such improvements can help foster the growth of nonrecreation industries in the area by attracting entrepreneurs and labour and by providing direct inputs to these industries.

Recreation development can involve significant economic leakages, however, in that many of the goods and services it requires come from outside the community—for example, temporary foreign workers often are drawn to the area to fill jobs in hotels, ski resorts, etc.—and many of the recreation-related establishments (restaurants, hotels, tour and travel companies) are owned by national or regional companies that export the profits. Thus, part of the money from tourists and seasonal residents ends up leaving the locality. Another economic drawback involves the seasonality of recreation activities, which can create problems for workers and businesses during off-seasons, though this may actually be a plus for places where seasonal recreation jobs are timely, coming when farmers and other workers normally have an off-season.

The greatest economic concern is that recreation development may be less desirable than traditional forms of rural development because it increases the incidence of service employment with relatively low wages. According to Deller et al. (2001), "There is a perception that substituting traditional jobs in resource-extractive industries and manufacturing with more serviceoriented jobs yields inferior earning power, benefits, and advancement potential" and that this may lead to "higher levels of local underemployment, lower income levels, and generally lower overall economic wellbeing."

In addition, many researchers are concerned that recreation may result in a less equitable distribution of income. These problems may be compounded by the higher housing costs in some recreation areas. These concerns reflect findings from individual case studies. Only a few studies have attempted to estimate how rural recreation areas nationwide differ on economic measures. Deller et al. (2001) found that rural tourism and amenity-based development contributed to growth in per capita income and employment, and concluded that as a result of the positive impact on income "the concern expressed about the quality of jobs created ... appears to be misplaced." English et al. (2000) also found that rural tourism was associated with higher per capita incomes, and with a higher percent increase in per capita income, although they found no significant relationship for household income. English and his colleagues also found housing costs and the change in housing costs over time to be significantly related to rural tourism. On the other hand, they found no evidence that the distribution of income was less equal due to rural tourism. To address these economic issues, we examined a variety of indicators reflecting employment, earnings, income, and housing costs.

Employment

Two employment measures, the local employment growth rate and the local employment-population ratio (percentage of working-age resident population employed in 2000) are particularly illuminating.

Recreation counties, on average, had more than double the rate of employment growth of other rural areas during the 1990s: 24 percent vs. 10 percent. The regression analysis, moreover, indicated that the extent to which a recreation county was dependent on recreation was positively and significantly related to the rate of local employment growth. Employment growth generally offers residents more job opportunities, enabling some unemployed residents to find jobs and employed residents to find better jobs. However, job growth does not necessarily improve job conditions for current residents. If too many people come into the area seeking employment, and if those newcomers aggressively compete with locally unemployed (or underemployed) residents, the resident job seekers may end up having greater difficulty gaining employment. Thus, we need to look closely at employment data to determine how recreation affects the local ability to find jobs.

Data Sources

The source for most of our data is the Decennial Census (Census Bureau, U.S. Department of Commerce). Other sources include:

- The Bureau of Economic Analysis, U.S. Department of Commerce, for data on earnings per job, and the Bureau of Labour Statistics, U.S. Department of Labour, Local Area Unemployment Statistics, for employment growth.
- The Uniform Crime Reporting Program (an unpublished data source available on an annual basis from the Federal

Bureau of Investigation (FBI)), for data on serious crimes. Note: These data have not been adjusted by the FBI to reflect underreporting, which could affect comparability over time or among geographic areas.

- The Area Resource File (a county-specific health resources information system maintained by Quality Resource Systems, under contract to the Health Resources and Services Administration, U.S. Department of Health and Human Services), for the age-adjusted death rate, the number of physicians, and the area (in square miles) used to compute population densities for regression analysis.
- Kenneth Johnson and Calvin Beale for the recreation county types and the measure of recreation dependency used in their 2002 article.

To measure the ability of residents to find jobs, we examined the percentage of the working-age population that was employed. For our study, we broke this into three separate rates covering three groups of the working-age population: ages 18-24, 25-64, and 65 and over. We hypothesized that recreation counties might be particularly advantageous for younger and older populations that may have a harder time competing in places with less job growth.

In addition, younger and older groups may find it more convenient to work in recreation counties, which are thought to provide more part-time and seasonal jobs than most other places. As expected, we found higher employment-population rates in recreation counties for both the younger and older age groups. However, the difference was less than 1 percentage point. The main working-age employment rate (ages 25-64) was roughly the same for both recreation and other nonmetro counties in 2000. However, for each of these age groups, the upward trend in the employment-population rate during the 1990s favoured recreation counties. Our regression analysis indicates that recreation had a positive and statistically significant impact on the employment rates for all three age categories in 2000. Recreation also had a positive and statistically significant impact on the increase in the employment rate during the 1990s, except for the older age group.

Earnings

Conventional wisdom suggests that a main drawback of tourism is that many of the jobs it creates are in restaurants, motels, and other businesses that tend to offer relatively low wages and few fringe benefits. But does this mean that rural recreation development generally leads to low-paying jobs?

To address this question, we examined average annual earnings per job (which include wages and salaries and other labour and proprietor income, but exclude unearned income and fringe benefits). We found that average earnings per job were $22,334 in 2000 for recreation counties—about $450 less than in other rural counties. The difference, though only about 2 percent, is consistent with the low-wage hypothesis. On the other hand, our finding that earnings per job increased faster in recreation counties than in other rural counties in the 1990s was not consistent with the conventional wisdom, but again, the difference was relatively small ($200).

Our regression analysis, however, found no statistically significant relationship between earnings per job and recreation dependency, at least no simple linear relationship. With regard to change in earnings per job during the 1990s, the regression analysis found that recreation had a positive and statistically significant impact on earnings per job. So these findings do not support the conventional wisdom that recreation results in generally lowpaying jobs.

The data on earnings per job covered all jobs in the county, including those filled by nonresidents. A different picture emerges when we look only at earnings per resident worker. Aside from excluding nonresidents employed in the county (who, in theory, might be lowering the average earnings per job in recreation counties), this measure totals the income workers receive from all the jobs they have. This is important because recreation counties often provide numerous part-time and seasonal jobs, potentially allowing more of their residents to have multiple jobs than the residents of other counties. The average worker's earnings from multiple jobs exceeded the average earnings per job. In recreation counties, earnings amounted to $29,593 per resident worker (16 years or older) in 1999—about $2,000 more than in other rural counties—an 8-percent difference. Our regression analysis found recreation had a positive and statistically significant effect on earnings per resident worker. Thus, some residents may work more hours in recreation counties, but on average they end up earning more than residents of other nonmetro counties.

Income

Earnings are only one source of income. Other sources include interest receipts, capital gains, and retirement benefits like social security. Because many recreation areas have attracted wealthy individuals—including retirees, whose earnings are only a small part of their incomes—we expected recreation county income levels to be higher than in other rural areas. Consistent with this expectation, we found average per capita income was 10 percent higher in recreation counties than in other nonmetro counties. Moreover, per capita income levels were growing more rapidly during the 1990s in recreation counties than in other nonmetro counties. These findings were reflected in our regression analysis, which found recreation had a positive and statistically significant effect on both the level of per capita income and the change in per capita income over time. This should also benefit the community as a whole, because higher incomes mean an increase in demand for local goods and services, as well as increased local government tax collections and contributions to local charities and other social organizations. One problem in interpreting per capita incomes is that they average together the incomes of the wealthiest and the poorest individuals. Thus, a small number of extremely wealthy people could make the community seem much better off than with other measures, for instance, the income of the typical (or median) person in the county. If recreation counties had more wealthy individuals than other rural counties, the per capita measure might be a misleading indicator of how the average family or household in each of these counties differed in income. For this reason, we include a second income measure: median household income in the county in 1999.

Using this measure, we found that median household income was 10 percent higher in recreation counties than in other rural counties. The recreation county advantage amounted to $3,185 per year for the median household. The regression analysis reflected this finding, showing a positive and statistically significant relationship between recreation and both the level and change in median family income.

Housing Costs

One of the main complaints about recreation areas is that the cost of living in them is often higher, offsetting much of the advantage that residents might obtain from their higher incomes. Of particular concern is that high living costs could become a significant hardship for people struggling to raise families on minimum-wage jobs. A high cost of living could force some lower paid workers (including some longtime residents) to look for housing outside the area.

The cost of housing is one of the most important contributors to the cost of living. According to Census data in 2000, median monthly rents for housing averaged $474 in recreation counties, 23 percent higher than the $384 median rent in other nonmetro counties. Our regression analysis also found a positive and statistically significant effect of recreation on median rent. Rents also increased faster during the 1990s in recreation counties, with the extent of recreation positively and significantly related to the extent of rent increase.

Though recreation counties had higher rents than other nonmetro counties, over the course of a year this amounted to a difference of only $1,080 per household—about a third of the $3,185 advantage we found in median household income in recreation counties. So after deducting for their higher rents, we found that households in recreation counties still had a significant income advantage over those in other rural counties.

It is difficult to draw conclusions from this kind of information, for several reasons. First, rents show only part of the housing cost picture. Most housing units in the nonmetro counties we studied (in both recreation and other nonmetro counties) are owner-occupied rather than rented. Assuming that higher rents reflect higher home prices and greater equity in homes, higher home prices should increase the wealth of homeowners in recreation counties. In addition, higher rents and home prices may reflect better housing quality in recreation counties, rather than simply higher costs. This might be expected because more of the housing in these rapidly growing places is likely to be relatively new (and hence more valuable), and recreation county residents, having generally higher incomes, may demand better housing than residents of other nonmetro counties. Higher home values also increase the local tax base, which may lead to higher tax collections, enabling local governments to increase public services. Thus, on balance, it is unclear whether these higher housing costs are a plus or minus for the community.

Social Impacts

Various researchers have examined the relationship between nonmetro recreation and social conditions in a community. Page et al. (2001) note that rapid population growth in nonmetro recreation counties has resulted in overcrowded conditions and traffic congestion.

Recreation may also affect local poverty rates. Some authors have argued that recreation activity creates new sources of employment, helping to raise the poor from poverty. Others have pointed to the low-wage, seasonal, and part-time nature of many tourism jobs, arguing that tourism may actually add to the number of poor in the community. Recreation affects social conditions in other ways.

For example, Page et al. argue that tourism and recreation activity may help to maintain or improve local services, such as health facilities, entertainment, banking, and public transportation, because of the increased demand that tourists generate for these activities. The relationship between recreation and crime has also been explored by a number of researchers, with a popular question being whether casinos increase criminal activity.

To address social impact concerns, we identified eight social indicators. Two involve conditions associated with rapid population growth; one identifies a population subgroup (persons in poverty) that may present special challenges; two relate to education; two deal with health-related concerns; and one measures crime.

Population Growth

The first social variable we examined was the county population growth rate during the 1990s. Population growth can be beneficial for stagnant or declining rural areas looking for new sources of employment and income, but in some places it can bring problems.

This is particularly true if growth occurs rapidly and haphazardly, contributing to sprawl, traffic congestion, environmental degradation, increased housing costs, school overcrowding, a decrease in open land, and loss of a "sense of place" for local residents. Perhaps because of their natural amenities and tourist attractions, recreation counties experienced a 20.2-percent rate of population growth between 1990-2000, nearly triple the 6.9-percent rate for other nonmetro counties during the same period.

These results are consistent with our linear regression analysis, which found a positive and statistically significant relationship between recreation and the county population growth rate. Further analysis revealed an apparent curvilinear relationship, in which recreation counties with moderate recreation dependencies experienced higher growth rates than those with smaller and larger recreation dependencies.

Travel Time to Work

This variable was included to test the hypothesis that growth in recreation counties may lead to increasing traffic congestion. We found that mean commute times for recreation and other rural counties were not significantly different in 2000. Moreover, during the 1990s, commute times increased at roughly the same rate (4.4 percent for recreation counties vs. 4.3 percent for other rural counties). The regression analysis, however, revealed a significant negative relationship between recreation dependence and change in travel time to work during the 1990s. One explanation may be that expanded economic opportunities in recreation counties during the 1990s meant that residents had to travel shorter distances for jobs.

Poverty Rate

Poverty poses a problem for communities by increasing the

costs of providing public services and contributing to crime rates, health problems, and neighbourhood blight. Previous research has found that an expanding tourist industry is linked with a decreasing rate of poverty. Given that many recreation counties have attracted well-off retirees and that average income levels have risen in recreation counties, the counties might, on average, be expected to have fewer individuals living in poverty than other nonmetro counties.

However, as noted earlier, some have argued that tourism, by expanding the number of lowpaying, part-time jobs, could increase the number of individuals living in poverty in these counties. We found that the poverty rate was substantially lower in recreation counties than in other rural counties. In 1999, 13.2 percent of all residents in recreation counties were living in poverty, compared with 15.7 percent in other nonmetro counties. Mirroring the national trend of declining poverty rates during the 1990s, the proportion of residents living in poverty during the decade declined (at approximately the same rate) in both recreation and other rural counties. Our regression analysis also found a significantly negative relationship between recreation and the poverty rate. In addition, the regression analysis found a statistically significant negative relationship between recreation and the change in the poverty rate.

Educational Attainment

Previous research has identified the central role that education plays in rural poverty. Education is important, not only because it contributes to the economy, but also because it can affect the quality of life in rural communities and can help raise people out of poverty.

Nonmetro areas with lower levels of education tend to be poorer and offer fewer economic opportunities for their residents. Migration (movement to another area) tends to increase with higher levels of education. Hence, recreation counties, which have had many in-migrants in recent years, may be expected to have higher levels of educational attainment than other nonmetro counties. English et al. (2000) found rural tourism to be associated with higher levels of educational attainment. We examined educational attainment at two levels: high school and college. Our results show that residents in recreation counties have higher levels of education than other nonmetro residents.

Recreation counties have both a smaller share of residents 25 years or older without a high school education, and a higher share of those with at least a bachelor's degree, than residents of other nonmetro counties. In 2000, 18.4 percent of residents age 25 or older in recreation counties did not have a high school diploma, compared with 25 percent in other nonmetro counties. For the same year, 19.2 percent of recreation county residents age 25 or older had a 4-year college degree or higher, compared with 13.6 percent in other nonmetro counties. During the 1990s, educational attainment on both measures improved in recreation as well as other nonmetro counties. These findings are supported by our regression analysis, which found that recreation had a significant negative correlation with the share of residents without a high school diploma and a significant positive correlation with the share of residents with a bachelor's degree or higher. In addition, a statistically significant relationship was found between recreation and an increase in the share of college-educated residents during the 1990s. However, the change in the share of high school graduates during the 1990s, although positive, was not significantly related to recreation.

Health Measures

Health is important for quality of life. In some recreation counties, many individuals moving in are retirees who demand more from health services than younger people; this could result in improved health services in these places. Many recreation counties are in pristine locations with clean air and water, which might also lead to better overall health. In addition, residents in recreation areas are probably more likely to be involved in outdoor activities than individuals in other nonmetro areas, which may also promote better overall health.

Our indicators of local health conditions—the number of physicians available and the age-adjusted mortality rate—support the view that recreation county residents have better health and health services than other nonmetro residents. In 2003, recreation counties had 123 physicians per 100,000 residents, compared with 83.4 per 100,000 residents in other nonmetro counties.

The analysis also shows that the age-adjusted death rate (computed as a 3-year average) was almost 10 percent lower in recreation than in other nonmetro counties. Our regression results show that recreation had a significantly negative correlation with the age-adjusted death rate. However, the relationship between recreation and the number of physicians, although positive, was statistically insignificant.

Crime Rate

Many researchers have looked at the link between recreation activity and crime. Some types of recreation counties attract criminals who prey on tourists inseason and rob unoccupied houses during the off-season. Also, some low income residents of these counties may commit crimes of opportunity, taking advantage of the influx of well-off outsiders. Some researchers have argued that crime may be particularly associated with casinos.

The results of our analysis indicate that recreation counties had nearly a 17-percent higher rate of serious crime (murder and non-negligent manslaughter, forcible rape, robbery, and aggravated assault) than other nonmetro counties. In 1999, the overall rate of serious crime in recreation counties was 2.8 incidents per 100 residents, compared with 2.4 incidents per 100 residents in other nonmetro counties, a statistically significant difference. These results are consistent with our regression analysis, which found that a significantly positive relationship exists between recreation and the crime rate.

However, the meaning of this finding is not clear because the crime rate is a biased measure in recreation areas, due to the fact that crimes committed against tourists and seasonal residents are included in the total number of crimes (the numerator of the crime rate), while tourists and seasonal residents are not included in the base number of residents (the denominator of the crime rate). So the crime rate is expected to be higher in recreation areas, even if residents of these areas are not more likely to be crime victims than residents of other rural areas.

Variations by Type of Recreation County

As noted, Johnson and Beale (2002) categorized each recreation county as belonging to 1 of 11 mutually exclusive recreational groupings, a classification that provides greater insight into the recreational component of each county. The single most common category is the Midwest Lake and Second Home, accounting for 70 counties and overwhelmingly concentrated in central and northern Michigan, Minnesota, and Wisconsin. The Northeast Mountain, Lake, and Second Home group, a closely related category, is mainly concentrated in northern New England (Maine, New Hampshire, and Vermont) and in portions of New York and Pennsylvania. Together, these two similar categories account for more than a quarter of all recreation counties. Both categories are relatively prosperous: Northeast counties had the highest level of earnings per job among all recreation types, and the Midwest category experienced sharp increases in household income during the 1990s. Both regions had rates of poverty among the lowest of all recreation categories.

Although almost every type of recreation county registered at least doubledigit population growth during the 1990s (the exception being the Northeast Mountain, Lake, and Second Home), Ski Resort counties grew the fastest (increasing 38 percent), continuing a trend from the 1980s. Other recreation categories in the West (West Mountain and Other Mountain) also experienced rapid population growth.

Ski Resort counties stand out in other ways, measuring substantially higher than other recreation counties on a number of economic variables, including ratio of employment to population, earnings per job, earnings per worker, per capita income, and median household income. Ski Resorts also had the lowest poverty rate among all recreation categories, but had substantially higher housing costs—nearly 40 percent higher than the average for other nonmetro counties—which grew rapidly during the 1990s.

Ski Resort counties also stand out in terms of social indicators, having the highest levels of educational attainment, the largest number of doctors, the lowest death rates, and the highest rate of crime among all recreation categories.

In contrast, Reservoir Lake counties and South Appalachian Mountain Resort counties are among the most economically challenged recreation county types. Reservoir Lake counties, which are mainly located in the Midwest and Great Plains regions, and South Appalachian Mountain Resort counties—in the upland areas of Georgia, North Carolina, Virginia, West Virginia, and Maryland—have among the lowest earnings per worker and lowest median household income levels. They also have among the lowest rents. Both of these regions have among the lowest levels of educational attainment. Further, they have higher-than-average age-adjusted death rates, but relatively low crime rates. The South Appalachian Mountain Resort category also has a significantly longer commute than other nonmetro counties, possibly a reflection of its mountainous topography.

Casino counties also have relatively low levels of economic development, with the highest rate of poverty—over 40 percent higher than for all recreation counties—as well as below-average levels of per capita income, median household income, and earnings per worker. Still, during the 1990s, Casino counties, which are mainly located in the Upper Midwest, the Dakotas, the Mississippi Delta region, and Nevada, collectively had sharp employment growth (a third faster than the average for all recreation counties).

Casino counties, which benefited from the establishment of gambling on Native American reservations during the 1990s, had a lower level of educational attainment, fewer physicians, a higher-than-average ageadjusted death rate, and a significantly higher rate of crime than most other recreation counties.

Conclusions

This study provides quantitative information on how tourism and recreation development affects socioeconomic conditions in rural areas. Specifically, we wanted to address economic issues related to employment, income, earnings, and cost of living, and social issues such as poverty, education, health, and crime. A summary follows of our main findings on the socioeconomic impacts of rural recreation and tourism development.

Employment. Our regression analysis found a positive and statistically significant association between recreation dependency and the percentage of working-age population with jobs. We also found that, with the exception of the older (65 and over) population, recreation dependency positively affected the change in this employment measure during the 1990s.

Earnings. We examined earnings per job and earnings per resident to measure the value of the jobs associated with rural recreation development. We found that the average earnings per job in recreation counties were not significantly different than in other nonmetro counties, and we found no direct (linear) relationship between local dependency on recreation and local earnings per job in our recreation counties.

However, our regression analysis found a positive relationship between recreation and growth in earnings per job during the 1990s. Thus, the trend seems to favor the pay levels for jobs in these recreation counties. These findings concern earnings of all who work in the county, including nonresidents. They report earnings per job, not per worker—an important distinction because workers may have more than one job, and the availability of second jobs (part-time and seasonal) may be greater in recreation counties than elsewhere. When we focused on total job earnings for residents of recreation counties, we found these earnings were significantly higher ($2,000 more per worker) than for residents of other rural counties. The regression analysis also found a significant positive relationship between recreation and resident-worker earnings. So the earnings picture for recreation counties appears positive for the average resident.

Cost of living. Our research suggests recreation development leads to higher living costs, at least with respect to housing. We found that the average rent was 23 percent higher in recreation counties, and it was positively and significantly associated with the degree of recreation dependency in our regression analysis. While this may reduce some of the economic advantages for residents of recreation counties, it does so only partially. Median household incomes, on average, were $3,185 higher in recreation counties than in other rural counties. Annual costs associated with rent were $1,080 higher in recreation counties, offsetting only about a third of the recreation county income advantage.

Growth strains. We found recreation led to significantly higher rates of population growth. In theory, this can aggravate social problems, such as school crowding, housing shortages, pollution, and loss of identification with the community. The one growth-related social problem we addressed was road congestion. Examining the time it takes to commute to work, we found little evidence that congestion was presenting undue problems for residents in recreation counties. Moreover, our regression analysis found that recreation was associated with smaller increases in average commute times in the 1990s than in other rural counties.

Poverty. Another social problem that appeared to be reduced in recreation counties was poverty. Our regression analysis found recreation was associated with lower poverty rates and with larger declines in the poverty rate during the 1990s.

Crime. There may be some cause for concern with regard to crime. We found crime rates (for serious crimes) were higher in recreation counties than in other rural counties, and our regression analysis also found a statistically significant positive relationship between crime rates and recreation dependency. However, crime statistics may be biased in recreation areas because crimes against tourists and seasonal residents are counted in the crime rate, while tourists and seasonal residents are not counted as part of the population base upon which the rate is calculated. Thus, even if people in recreation areas do not face a higher chance of becoming victims of crimes, the crime rates of these areas will appear higher than elsewhere. Nonetheless, one may still argue that recreation-related crime adds to the local cost of policing and incarcerating criminals, just as recreation-related traffic—even though it may not create congestion—adds to the cost of maintaining roads.

Education and health. Our analysis found that recreation is associated with a more educated population, particularly with a higher percentage of college-educated people. We also found relatively good health conditions (measured by age-adjusted death rates) in recreation counties. This might be expected from the higher numbers of physicians per 100,000 residents that we found in recreation counties. However, our regression analysis did not find a statistically significant relationship between recreation dependence and the local supply of physicians. So some other explanation must be posited for the general good health in recreation counties, such as greater opportunities for physical exercise or residents who are more health-conscious.

Variations by county type. Conditions vary significantly by recreation county type. For example, Ski Resort counties have among the wealthiest, best educated, and healthiest populations of all recreation county types. Ski Resort counties also have relatively high rates of crime. In contrast, Reservoir Lake counties and South Appalachian Mountain Resort counties have among the poorest and least educated residents of all recreation county types, along with relatively high ageadjusted death rates, but they have relatively low crime rates. Casino counties—which had among the highest rates of job growth and the largest absolute increases in earnings per job during the 1990s—also had among the highest rates of growth in employment per person for seniors, perhaps reflecting the greater need for jobs among those over age 65 in these relatively high-poverty communities.

Ideas for Future Research

We focused mainly on conditions facing residents of mature rural recreation counties, that is, places that already have a substantial amount of recreation. Additional insights may come from expanding the analysis to include emerging recreation areas and neighbouring places that may be affected by spillover impacts from recreation areas. Future research might also address issues related to specific population subgroups, such as low-paid workers, who may face more significant problems related to the high cost of housing in recreation areas. The analysis might also be expanded to examine recreation impacts on other aspects of community wellbeing, such as the environment, public services, institutions like churches and charitable foundations, and small business formation and entrepreneurial activity. Our knowledge of rural recreation impacts might also benefit from different formulations of the regression model. For example, models could be finetuned to focus on individual indicators, or they could be estimated separately for individual regions and types of recreation areas. Feedback effects might be incorporated into the model—for example, recreation can lead to higher housing costs, which in turn can lead to reduced tourism and recreation development. More sophisticated models may be able to separate out these two effects. The models might also be examined over different time periods to test for cyclical effects and robustness over time.

Research might also measure the effects of specific State and local policies, along with other factors thought to affect the level of rural recreation and tourism (such as the availability of natural amenities and proximity and access to nonmetro areas). This might help State and local officials assess their potential for recreation and tourism development and identify strategies to further this development.

Second Homes as a Part of New Rural Life Style

Second Homes-The Economic Impact on Rural Communities

There is concern in some quarters that second homes have a negative impact on the economy of rural communities. In some parts of the UK, local strength of feeling about this has occasionally erupted into arson, for example, with a number of second homes being burned down in Wales.

The main issues that create controversy are twofold. Firstly, there is the argument that second home owners drive up prices in rural areas, pushing them out of the reach of local people and exacerbating the problem that there is not enough affordable housing for low income local families. This is clearly an area that needs a balanced approach and well thought out strategy to help solve this very real issue.

The second common concern is that second houses are unoccupied for a large part of the year and this deprives local businesses of potential custom, sometimes badly affecting their viability. Another aspect of this is that local schools can become short of children, sometimes forcing local schools to close. Indeed, on some areas very popular with second home owners, the area can feel like a ghost town out of season, without the community vitality and vibrant local economy that characterises some other rural areas.

The problems seem to be focused on highly localised rural and coastal areas, the kind of attractive areas that are popular for second homes. For example, in North Cornwall, one in three properties is thought to be a second home or holiday home,

In general, the more remote rural areas have the greatest concentrations of second homes as a proportion of all the housing stock, intensifying the problem of creating a sustainable and robust local community with a thriving local economy.

Although second and holiday homes contribute to an uplift in property prices in rural areas, it is important not to view their economic impact in isolation from other factors contributing to changes within rural communities and especially pressures on local housing markets from other groups such as commuters, retirees, or people wanting a lifestyle change.

One way that second home owners can help avoid any negative economic impacts on the local community is to maximise the extent to which the second home does not stand empty.

By renting a second home out as a holiday home for part of the year, when it is not in use by the owner's family, it ensures that money is brought into the local economy as the family renting the holiday home will inevitably spend money in the local shops, restaurants and at local attractions. This is clearly a positive impact on the local economy and far better for the local community than having a second home stand empty. Yet many owners of second homes resist renting out their home to holidaymakers.

There are a wide variety of reasons for this. It is often not as simple as whether or not the owner of a second home would like to make a profitable return on their property.

Some second home owners simply do not want strangers in their home and this is a strongly felt emotion they are not likely to overcome.

Others do not want to get involved in what they see as complex property management issues, involving a lot of work and practical difficulty. For these owners, the answer is often to hire a holiday homes services specialist that can take away the hassle and arrange everything on their behalf, making the whole process of renting out a holiday home very straightforward. If a holiday homes services specialist is engaged, they can arrange all aspects of property management, cleaning services and key holder services as well as sometimes a holiday concierge service. This means that the second home owner can benefit from a stream of income from the property, all the gain without the pain. In addition, the impact on the local economy is positive as the holiday home rentals bring money into the local shops, restaurants and attractions as well as necessitating the employment of local trades people, such as plumbers, electricians, painters and carpenters.

The impacts, both positive and negative, of second homes and holiday homes touch on a diverse range of factors that affect the sustainability of rural communities. One thing is clear-renting out a second home as a holiday home has a more positive impact on the local economy than leaving it standing empty for long periods.

New Countryside, New Rural Life

Demonstrating the top leadership's ambition to build a "new socialist countryside", Chinese Premier Wen Jiabao presided over a State Council executive meeting on June 30, focusing on rural taxation reform and further relaxing farmers' financial burdens. A statement from the meeting promised to transfer more funds to the local governments after rural taxation reform cuts out a large chunk of their tax income, while proposing the establishment of a mechanism to monitor farmers' debts.

The meeting might sound too profound for housemaid Li Yuanyuan. Yet the chubby girl from Xiangyang County of Central China's Hubei Province believes that "the central government now is trying to help us peasants, who work very hard all the year round, but earn little. " Landing the job of housemaid in Beijing five years ago, Yuanyuan can earn 800 yuan (US$100) a month, compared to her family of five making about 10,000 yuan a year by growing rice and wheat in a small plot. "You see, I alone can make that much in Beijing," says the 20-year-old.

Bidding to bail out millions of peasants like Li Yuanyuan, China earlier this year set out the plan called "building a new socialist countryside" to redress the chasm dividing the country into two parts: the affluent urban east and the less developed or even underdeveloped rural west. The plan is believed to signify a grand shift in infrastructure and investment priorities from urban to rural areas.

Reorienting government investment to create a "new socialist countryside" was declared as a "major historic task" for China's 11th Five-Year Development Program (2006-2010) in Premier Wen Jiabao's government work report to the latest annual National People's Congress (NPC) session held in Beijing from March 5-13. The president of the School of Agro Economics and Rural Development at Beijing-based Renmin University of China saw the plan as a practical and realistic move "because the strategy is based on solid and extensive research in rural areas." "It's certainly one way to help raise farmers' incomes. Not until there is a substantial increase in their incomes can we possibly boost domestic consumption, which has already obstructed economic development as a whole," says Prof. Wen Tiejun, a noted expert on rural China. A recent survey on what peasants are expecting from the creation of the new countryside was conducted by the School of Journalism & Communication, and the Sociology Department, Nanjing University in East China.

The surveyors collected 940 questionnaires from 10 ordinary villages and 10 specially-chosen pilot ones across the country, plus 156 in-depth interviews. The findings indicated that 54.6 percent said the most important thing for them is to increase their incomes. And 19.5 percent planned to look for a job in the city. The survey also found 81. 9 percent said the annually agriculture taxations are not so heavy. Yet, their actual incomes are declining as the price of fertilizers, pesticides and seeds going up.

Although China is traditionally an agricultural power with more than half of the population still farming, industrialization and urbanization have overshadowed other sectors on the government agenda in the past decades. As a result, observes Prof. Wen, rural China has not kept pace with the development of urban areas. The new countryside plan indicates that the government is to pay equal, if not more, attention to the countryside as to the cities, and is to revitalize rural China through science and technology, Prof. Wen says. "Whether or not the countryside can get prosperous will have a great, far-reaching impact on the building of a harmonious society."

The official criteria for the new countryside, in Premier Wen's words, are "enhanced productive forces, higher living standards, civilized living style, an orderly and clean environment, and democratic administration." "This vision has defined the new countryside plan as a systematic and comprehensive policy, which clearly reflects the government's thinking on how to deal with the 'San Nong Wenti' – problems confronting China's agriculture, countryside and peasants," says Prof. Wen. But Li Changping, who served as the party chief of Qipan Township of Hubei for 17 years, does not see anything special in the strategy. "The new countryside is not just as simple as building new roads, new houses and new toilets," says Li, now a recognized rural development expert.

The 43-year-old Li earned his reputation as "China's Most Notable Party Secretary at Grassroots Level" after he wrote a letter to the former Premier Zhu Rongji in 2000, complaining that "peasants are too miserable, the countryside is too depressed and agriculture is too much in danger." Soon after that, Li had to resign from the post of township Party chief. He now works as a consultant for the charity Oxfam International, Hong Kong. Prof. Wen disagrees with Li. In his view, the new countryside plan has touched upon some "fundamental problems". One is the emphasis on a good interaction between urban and rural areas and on the construction of harmony in rural communities. For instance, while organic farming is encouraged, the countryside can supply cities with safe food and also keep its own development sustainable.

Second, the plan highlights the efforts to perfect social security systems in the countryside. There have been rural residents who became broke and impoverished once a family member got sick, or a child went to a higher learning institution. "You have to have a sound social security system to tackle these problems," Prof. Wen says. Third, the plan aims to build rural areas into desirable communities for comfortable living: not just attractive to conventional rural dwellers but also urbanites. Prof. Pan Wei, director of the China and World Research Centre at Beijing University, describes the new drive as China's "second rural revolution" since 1979, comparing it to the launch of the household-based system of contracted responsibility.

That reform of 27 years ago resulted in two significant changes in farmers' lives: increase in their incomes and growth in their purchasing power. That in turn led to township enterprises emerging as a new force where state companies failed to meet demand.

Rural development in the 1980s was designated to have industrialized the countryside. The three key elements of agriculture – land, labour and capital – were consumed to achieve that goal. Rural enterprises set up by peasants absorbed surplus farming manpower, shifting them into non-agricultural work without uprooting them from the countryside. Villagers who put money or technology became shareholders in village factories, and a group of peasant entrepreneurs came to the fore. An unprecedented increase in peasants' incomes helped narrow the urban-rural income gap. But only a small part of the rural communities, mainly in the east, sustained the momentum of development and remained affluent, experts say. The vast bulk of countryside had remained stagnant as urban expansion soared during the 1990s.

The central government has decided to spend 339.7 billion yuan on farmers this year, an increase of 14.2 percent on last year. Most of the money will be allocated to bettering rural schools, improving access to health care and public works like road construction and irrigation works. Rural infrastructure facilities lag far behind. Nearly seven percent of rural schoolhouses are in danger of collapsing, meaning more than one million pupils cannot go to school regularly, according to the Guangzhou-based Southern Weekend.

But while the increased spending must be welcomed, it's important to remember the base is low. Rural development forms 8.9 percent of China's entire budget, says Prof. Pan Wei of Beijing University. "It's a drop in the ocean. That is to say the new spending only amounts to an additional seven dollars per head a year." He suggests "developing peasants' own cooperative organizations and helping them get into profitable fields like buying and selling, financing and supermarkets."

Through their own organizations, peasants can negotiate effectively with other economic bodies and establish a stable contractual relationship. China has already set up 30 pilot cooperatives. Social services in the countryside are also in a precarious state. "You cannot deploy a doctor or a teacher to every single village. Therefore, we must prepare rural people with some necessary social skills to survive urban modernization, a must for a nation's modernization," says Prof. Ding Yuanzhu with the Macro-Economic Research Institute of the State Development and Reform Commission.

Building a new socialist countryside in the final analysis is all about building new cities in rural areas, or so believes the CCTV pundit Song Xiaojun. "The idea of a new countryside is about hope, materially and culturally. People mostly live on hope or expectation." "The city and the countryside both are children of the government. Now the government calls for rich urbanites to energetically support their long-overlooked rural brethren. That's a hope for the vast countryside." A vegetable vendor in north Beijing agrees with Song. Her home village, says Li Xiuli, is "boring and dull." Li, 27, had never been to a cinema before she came to Beijing from her home in North China's Inner Mongolia Autonomous Region five years ago. "The closest cinema was 30 kilometres away in downtown Ningcheng County. Here in Beijing, everything is entertaining. Supermarkets, malls, TV programs and the like. "However, Prof. Wen Tiejun says, international experience indicates that urbanization alone cannot save the countryside. Take a look at Japan's new countryside. The government spent 2 trillion yen on re-partitioning agricultural land during the course of its urbanization. Consequently, Japan's small-farmer economy lost its competitive ability and became dependent on increasing government subsidies to survive.

Therefore, privatizing agriculture land is not the solution. "The problem China really needs to solve now is the systematic contradiction: separation of the urban and rural regions," says

Ding Yunzhu, adding, "Again, the new countryside plan is the key to addressing the problem."

A New Rural Lifestyle-Keen Vendor, Make an Offer

Whether you want a large, new and modern family home or a quieter rural life with some income, 'SNOWHAVEN' will satisfy your needs. The home is on a 2.2 ha block and was designed and built to the highest standards with quality fixtures and fittings throughout.

The over-sized clay bricks have a sandstone appearance, the windows and doors are double-glazed, there is in-floor heating in the kitchen and bathrooms, granite bench-tops in the kitchen, a gas fire in the lounge room, reverse cycle air conditioning in the main bedroom, and both the external and internal walls are insulated. The home comprises a very large master bedroom with an adjacent bathroom and is quite separate from the rest of the house.

The second bedroom, with a kitchenette and disabled bathroom, and third bedroom are accessed from a large air-lock entrance and can be divided from the remainder of the house. The living and community areas are large and comprise a kitchen with walk-in pantry and views of the mountains. A breakfast bar divides the kitchen from the living/dining room, where the gas fire is located.

There is also a lounge room, formal dining room and laundry with a third toilet. The home is completed by a 2.4 metre wide covered veranda on all sides, which provides weather protection whilst not interrupting the 360 degree views. Outside there are two 9m x 7m sheds: a garage, with automatic doors, which includes an "artist's" studio and bathroom, and a steel shed with concrete floor, insulated roof, plumbing and power nearby. Water, a very important item in The Snowys, is collected in a huge 100,000 litre storage system from all roofs, and supplemented by a shared bore measured at 4,000 litres per day. Located on Glenrowan Estate, approximately midway between Jindabyne and Berridale and only 50 kilometres from Cooma and the NSW ski resorts of Thredbo Village and Perisher Blue, and sitting at nearly 1300 metres above sea level, this home has views of the Snowy Mountains to the west and the Monaro plains to the east. All in all, a very attractive rural package which has easy access to the ski fields, Jindabyne, Berridale and Cooma, with Canberra only 160 kilometres away. The bed and breakfast licence provides options and flexibility not usually found. Contact us for further information or to arrange an inspection.

Second Home Development in Nordic Countries

Together with the associations for local authorities in Sweden, Finland and Norway, Nordregio Academy will provide the research community as well as local and central authorities with an opportunity for experience transfer and learning. The seminar will summarize current research on second home development in Nordic countries, in particular research that helps us to better understand societal driving forces, to clarify the relations between recreational home ownership, tourism and local development and to identify the main similarities and differences between the Nordic countries in these issues.

The seminar will treat four major themes:

- New lifestyles have expanded the scope and geographic scale of living and working. Increasing mobility impacts how people interweave home, work, and leisure. Do new lifestyles really bring added value to rural areas?
- Recreational commodities or natural reserves: how should open areas be viewed, and how can development preserve desired traits while exploiting them? How can countryside homes be sustainable?
- Goods and services targeting the part-time population: the economic impact of second home development and local economic restructuring. What are the possibilities and what are the limitations? " Local development strategies: by accident or design: the characteristics of successful and less successful development strategies.

Cost of Living in Philippines, Rural Area, Rural Lifestyle

I believe, as I have said in the recent past, that the best place to find information on budget is in the archives. Of this List.I can live well in our island at about $900 to $1000 a month. We have cable, hot water, DSL, eat well and have an old car that is paid for. We owe nothing in credit cards and enjoy life here to the fullest. Originally when I got here, the peso traded 50 to a dollar. Then the rate went to 56 then down to as low as 40 to a dollar.

Prices within the local economy have also increased. Factor lower peso/dollar rations and domestic inflation and we see about 25% or so lose in the USD buying power. Yesterday I got a thousand pesos of diesel fuel for our old car. I waited as the attendant of the station raised the price one peso a litter. That is up about 9 cents a gallon by rough count. Someone with a calculator could correct me. But, the price of domestic fuel is increasing often. Poultry and pig feed are also up. Transportation costs are also up. In 2003 it cost me 4 pesos to take a tricycle or jeepney from my home to the buyan. Now that same ride costs me 10 pesos. Fuel is down from nearly 60 pesos a litter to about 33 pesos a litter on out island South of Luzon.

Tailors charge me more. Repair and replacement of a zipper was about 30 pesos a year ago. Now it is nearly 40 pesos to replace the same zipper. Shoes are about 500 to 700 pesos a pair. I plan to purchase 4 to 6 pairs before I return to Houston.

Clothing is still relatively cheap, but I see more ready made and less tailor made than when I first came her 38 years ago. Eggs in the market are 4.5 pesos each, a bit higher than in a supermarket, on sale in Texas. Milk is high and few purchase it on any regular basis. Tomatoes were 30 pesos a kilo or about 60 cents a pound. I saw roma tomatoes for 48 cents a pound in an ad that I used to teach ESL students before I left Texas. Carrots, cabbage and other fresh vegetables are cheap, but by standards here, the local populace has problems putting such fare on their tables. Beans, squash and okra are common and cheap, at least here. I bought roasted and salted peanuts yesterday, 60 pesos for 1/2 kilo. Good puluton. Labour, for a yard worker or laundry women is about p150 a day. Minimum wages are about p250 to p260 a day, but no one pays anywhere near that amt. Pork now sells at p110 live weight and about p190 dressed. Chicken is about the same. Beef, tough as hell and requiring steel teeth, is available for about p160 a kilo. Bovine and Carabobo beef are only killed once a week in our area. Correction, we get chicken for p150 as we resell it at the store. Regular price is about 180 a kilo. Chicken in Houston is as low as 48 cents a pound, whole fryer, on sale. I ordered 3 kilos of ground pork for next Saturday.

The sukie will also provide 3 liters of casings at no cost, cleaned of course, [the casings that is]. We will make sausage and then stuff the casings. I make so darn good sausage too. I expect to purchase vegetables at the flea market here on the island every week. We usually purchase charcoal for resale and because we have a car, we do not have to factor in transportation as we were going to the market after all. [Poor business logic, I know!] Overall a tank of gas is about p565. When we came here a few years ago the same tank was pressing 400 ps a tank. With the current economy, less dollars are coming into the country from abroad. Natives are encouraged to take any job possible regardless of returns on their efforts. Some are not listening and are returning to the islands of paradise and have no plans of returning to overseas employment.

I see various government projects in the works, but far less than in the past. There are a few sewers going in, but not nearly the projects that were in full swing a few years ago. Overall, we got about half a tank of LPG gas yesterday. That will last us about two weeks.

Our gas for cooking may last until we head home. We supplement with some charcoal that we purchased at the chungy market yesterday. Power is high and we spend about 4to 5 k a month. Water is about 350 pesos a month. We have a small ice business and use more than others might. The water is drinkable from the tap, but we still use filtered water for our usual consumption at our table. We spend about 200 a day on food. We could spend less but it is fiesta and we have relatives coming from the mainland and from abroad. Now lets get to the important things.

Beer is about 19 to 22 pesos a bottle, depending on the type you choose to swill down. Rum is 21 pesos for a 250 cc bottle. Pop cola is 7 pesos and coke about 10 pesos a small bottle. Ice is 2 pesos a block. We sell a lot of ice and have problems keeping up with the supply. We would add a second reifer, but then the supply would be above the need and the price may fall. We pay about $40 for health care, [USA], a month, we are giving up on vonage as the majic jack works so well for us. I am hoping to make a few faxes one way and return before doing away with vonage, but my mind is pretty well set.

Internet is about p1995 on our island, for unlimited use, DSL. We hear it is cheaper on other islands, but we have not gone out to compare prices prices on our island. We get good service and know the tech well. He is a presonal friend. We are grateful for our high quality internet, [while the power is on], and we enjoy internet at home. We could use a cafe for much less but then we would have to factor in the transportation. We own our home. We built the structure for about $7500 about 6 years ago. Prices are up about 100% since that time.

Imagining Rural Life: Schooling as a Sense of Place

In American and British education literature, "rural" designates an isolated region, often the now-fragmented remnants of a once flourishing farming community. Rural areas are characterized by low socioeconomic status (SES), disconnected from metropolitan areas and low in population density. Families have often lived in rural areas for several generations; newer families moving in are uncommon.

Research of the 1980s and 1990s tells us that members of rural communities frequently express concern for the continuation of their lifestyle, which is threatened not only by out-migration of young people to metropolitan areas, but also by declining economic opportunities and closure of local schools through consolidation.

The region discussed in this ethnographic study contradicts the above definition of rural. Rural in this case involves previously urban families migrating to homes surrounded by land undeveloped with buildings and industry other than farming. The families of this study, in contrast to other rural families, migrated to the area from more populated regions, including large cities. Some families moved to the region from across the continent.

Most importantly, many of these families represent a higher SES than "old-timers" and have chosen to live in the area not because of occupations in farming, mining, timber, or other historically rural occupations, but in search of a quality of life presumed to be found in the country. My purpose is to explore how these families construct their rural identity by building a small school.

Sense of Place

Significant scholarship has emerged in the arena of place and identity. Perin's (1977) seminal work on cities and suburbs in the United States provides scholars with a means of exploring those cultural values we take for granted. In her discussion of homeowners and renters, suburban sprawl and zoning regulations, she reveals cultural values of self, identity, and social relationships through our identification with place.

Hummon (1990) builds from Perin's work to consider how place exists within cultural notions of community. Through our place of residence, Hummon argues, we form our world view and our understanding of other persons as well as ourselves. Perin and Hummon consider the typically unobserved effect of place on ourselves and our world views; they seek to bring those effects to the surface. In his widely cited work, Orr (1992) argues for all persons, scholars and lay persons alike, to develop a more active understanding of place, including an intentional involvement with a place.

Attending to place and the interrelationship between all of its parts comprises the fundamental work of living "sustainably." Orr contrasts "good inhabitance" with mere "residency." The former requires "detailed knowledge of a place and a sense of care and rootedness," whereas the latter requires only "cash and a map".

He demonstrates that some people achieve a deep connection with a place, while others merely pass through (albeit potentially for a duration of many years). Those who establish a deep connection, in Hummon's (1990) and Perin's (1977) conceptions, may define their identity through that place.

Of the authors discussed, Orr may provide the strongest statement on place as he observes a moral necessity for actively engaging in one's place. Place, particularly a rural place, becomes more than an opportunity for learning-it is the central cohesion point of a life interconnected with other beings. He raises the philosophical question of what constitutes an ethical life. If a person has the financial resources to purchase a home and property, and that person chooses to have nothing to do with their neighbours (or the land itself), is that person merely fulfilling their right in the American dream? Or is that person living unethically? Orr makes his opinion abundantly clear: to live alone is a fiction. Our lives are inextricably interconnected, and to imagine otherwise demonstrates a lack of awareness of the wholeness of our world. Orr's philosophical and ethical concerns for place provide a potent backdrop for the people and region in the current study. To attune to wholeness and connectedness means, necessarily, to move beyond culturally prescient individualism in which parents make educational decisions only for the benefit of their own children, rather than for the benefit of all. Orr and other authors do not ignore the contested nature of place as people construct different meanings of place and themselves in it. According to Lutz and Merz (992), "different individuals in the same geographic place may have different views of or sense of community".

Lutz and Merz go on to ask whether "without rural schools can there be rural community?". Certainly the studies exploring the effects of school closure suggest the answer is negative. While these and other studies explore the impact of school closure (primarily as a result of consolidation), the current study considers the impact of a school opening. I explore whether the introduction of a school might have both constructed a new rural community as well as disrupted the existing rural community.

In the process, I consider the nature of our modern communities. In this postmodern society, our communities are made up largely of replaced persons who come from different backgrounds and experiences. They replace themselves in new locations where they feel they can live a particular desired lifestyle and seek connection there. In the process, what they share within their group—sameness-gets privileged over their differences. Between the group and outsiders, however, differences enable group members to put up walls to keep out those who hold different cultural values and practices.

Those walls limit possibilities for growth and change, but the walls do not resolutely hold. Supposed differences are illusory and often permeable. A "sense of community" emerges, therefore, not out of what a group of people share in common, but out of the common enemy, outsider, or other. It is a reactive sameness, rather than a shared constructive experience. My particular concern is with the cultural construction of rural community that has been deemed in jeopardy.

Reborn Rural Community

The American ideology of small towns and rural regions perceives these places to be simpler worlds that are slower paced, less prone to change, and more "direct, personal, and comprehensible" than urban locales). That ideology also includes images of rural decline such as the dust-bowl devastation of the 1930s, family farm foreclosures, and the gradual encroachment of suburbia onto former farmland.

All of these images suggest that rural places are not as up-to-date either technologically or culturally as urban centres. In addition, much rural literature suggests that small towns and rural centres are in danger of disappearing. The context of fear elicits an impulse for conservation rather than change, which accords with American cultural assumptions of rural regions as conservative and urban regions as progressive. A different construct emerges as some rural regions have begun to comprise an alternate ideology. From this perspective, such regions may be places of new possibility.

In reaction to perceived dangers, stresses, and the frenetic lifestyle of city life, middle and upper-middle class Americans have begun to look to small towns and rural regions. Exasperated with their city lives, these people have begun a reverse migration back to the land. With the influx of new money and energy, rural regions undergo a renaissance that is fuelled by families who believe and want to enact the "nostalgic and romantic image of rural living". While that image may be mythical for more traditionally rural families, its salience is evident in the migrations occurring today.

Significantly, not all rural regions share salient demographic, economic, and cultural features. To differentiate these regions, Gjelten (1982) proposes a typology of rural school settings that includes the concept of a "reborn" rural region. I "Disgruntled city dwellers" flock to a reborn rural region, bringing with them urban values.

These regions "are mostly in the scenic and tranquil rural spots, where there is much to attract a refugee population from the city". Urbanites admire the lower property values, lower crime rates, larger open spaces, and cleaner environment found in such rural areas. In addition, they expect to find a slower pace, less material lifestyle, and more personal interactions than they experience in cities.

Urbanites Grasp Nostalgically for a Putatively Lost Way of Life

Today's urbanites are missing something. We don't have the sense of community and perma-'The other rural regions Gjelten (1982) defines are stable rural, depressed rural, high growth rural, and isolated ruralnence our ancestors had. Qualities once taken for granted-trust and honesty, regional and ethnic heritage, clean air and friendly neighbours-are special treasures. As the news highlights the emerging global economy, many of us simply hunger for a supportive local network. We need to feel *connected.* When these urbanites move to the "outland", they bring with them economic resource-to purchase, for example, an ailing farmhouse and restore it. In the process of restoration, they infuse capital into the local economy through purchasing of the home, hiring carpenters, and other crafts people, and making purchases in hardware stores and other local shops. "The newcomers have money, and are using it to transform the rural town into a new suburb-better schools, paved roads, rising real estate values and property taxes to match". In a region of otherwise declining farm values or the loss of other industries such as mining, these urbanites may help keep local businesses alive.

These Transplants May also Take Advantage of Business Opportunities

The new people moving in (to the reborn rural community) have probably *chosen* the community and therefore are likely to bring with them a positive attitude and a level of enthusiasm that may easily overshadow the spirit of the long time residents. If this energy can be harnessed to work for the betterment of the school, and it often can be, amazing improvements can happen. Many of the newcomers have talents and skills that can be put to good use in the school, whether the people work as paid teachers or as unpaid volunteers. The newcomers bring new cultural values along with their money. Urban Americans prefer moving to a small town or rural region that is nevertheless close to an urban area where they can take advantage of a city's resources when they choose. Transplanted urban values include geographic mobility (the ability and the expectation of relocating one's residence), diverse financial resources (investments as well as occupations), culinary tastes, and expectations of privacy. Prospective migrants are cautioned to be aware of local values and to adjust themselves to local ways by working with established cultural norms, not against them. While urbanities may adapt their values to more closely fit the local customs, in the process they also change those customs, a point that will be developed more fully below.

Gjeiten (1982), however, suggests that urban transplants may hold a romanticized and nostalgic view of rural life which they then perpetuate. Nostalgia involves a "symbolic management of the present" that simplifies and ennobles particular practices and values while withholding others. In the region of this study, newcomers started school-based "traditions" which they felt expressed their conceptions of rural life. "Most bring their city ways with them, but they are also enchanted by the country, and as converts to the rural lifestyle, they are among the most zealous defenders of many traditional rural customs and institutions". Local parades, tree-lighting ceremonies, and crafts-making are only a few of the "rural traditions" practicedby relocated urbanities. Such practices suggest a culturally conservative and paternalistic attitude of newcomers towards the rural way of life. Newcomers institute their versions of rural traditions, rather than adapt to customs already established.

The changes brought by disgruntled urbanities are not necessarily positive. New landowners may disrupt generations-old hunting traditions when they post "no hunting" and "no trespassing" signs. Urbanities likely bring different religious traditions that clash with existing practices. Economic disruption can also result as urbanities purchase homes and land for premium prices and commence upgrades. When property values rise, "the next generation of natives can't afford to live in their hometowns". Newcomers are likely to sell their rural homes and move again, whereas rural families may remain on the same farm for generations.

For those who remain, property taxes rise with property values. "Urban" values can create problems in traditional rural communities. In some reborn rural communities, there may develop a schism between the natives and the newcomers. There may even be two separate communities, each with its own set of values and ideas. As conflict develops between the groups, communication may diminish, and people may associate only with each other. In his discussion of 15 "small places" around the United States, Rawls (1990) compares small town newcomers with weeds that, like dandelions, "tend to take over". Despite advice to adjust to local ways, "the intention today appears to be to improve small places rather than adapt to them". What constitutes improvement or imposition may well differ according to one's cultural perspective.

According to Perin (1977), newcomers prompt "status renegotiation" as their arrival affects the social position of old-timer residents. She observed how such renegotiation is carried out in zoning hearings and homeowners' associations.

Perin's study focused on urban movement to then-newly suburban environs in which the newcomers' arrival signified their own increased status. From the perspective of the "old-time" suburban dwellers, their status is threatened by newcomers. Similar renegotiation may occur in reborn rural regions. Established status hierarchies based on relationships, history, and age may be disrupted by income, profession, and education. Participant Observation in Oakleaf 2 My study in Oakleaf was conducted over 11/2 years as part of a study of the local school. During that time, I volunteered at the school 4 days a week, substitute taught, and visited school members in their homes and other sites in the region. I attended and participated in as many school and community events as possible, such as a Thanksgiving pageant, camp-out, and roadside cleanup day. Much of the data were collected in 21 semi-directed interviews with local residents, excerpts of which appear below. Interviews were conducted at the individual's home, workplace, or at the school, according to the interviewee's preference. Interviews lasted from 45 minutes to 21/2 hours. I used a prepared list of questions to prompt the interview, but followed each person's lead as they recounted stories and shared artifacts.

Oakleaf Country School Oakleaf is located in the Piedmont region of the southeastern United States. Oakleaf refers to a crossroads area marked by an elementary school, a post office, a grocery, and a doctor's office. It is located about 15 miles from Springfield, a university town of about 45,000 residents.

The Oakleaf area lies in a particularly picturesque part of the county, which covers about 750 square miles and about 75,000 residents. The school is situated on two and a half acres of gently sloping hillside donated by a local wealthy landowner.

Oakleaf Country School is a nondenominational independent school founded in 1984 by parents. At the time of the study, 55 students attended kindergarten through fifth grade, in addition to approximately 20 preschool students who attended on either a 2-or 3-day schedule. The school first occupied one room and building; it has been expanded as the enrolment has grown to the present four classrooms, library, director's office, kitchen, reception area, and two sets of bathrooms.

Depending on enrolment, the school employs four fulltime teachers as well as one half-time preschool assistant, and part-time art, physical education, music, and language teachers. The paid administration consists of a full-time director, an office and financial manager, and an administrative assistant. Parents and community members make up the nine-member volunteer Board of Trustees. The curriculum has been constructed by the teachers and parents over the years and may be characterized by a lack of textbooks and a proliferation of projects. Although the school day is scheduled according to subjects, the project-based curriculum often involves the integration of subject matter. Further, teachers frequently bring their multigrade classes together for joint projects. The overall mood is relaxed, but focused. Teachers and students frequently call class meetings to discuss issues of discipline, social interactions, or other misunderstandings.

They express the belief that time spent discussing and negotiating noncurricular concerns promotes a more positive and trusting environment for everyone. Instead of report cards, teachers write lengthy evaluations on individual students as well as the class as a whole. The concern is to evaluate each student's individual progress rather than to rank the class or the school. While the location of their homes contributes to Oakleafers' rural self-conception, the school provides a symbolic and experiential centre of the newcomer rural community.

The parents' motivation for founding the school rested on three concerns. First, public school redistricting announced in the 1983-1984 academic year required their elementary age children, including kindergartners, to ride the bus 45-60 minutes (one way) to school; the parents felt this distance too great for young children. Second, parents preferred their children to attend a smaller school than the new elementary school formed by redistricting. Third, parents wanted to playa greater role in their children's education than they believed was possible in the local public schools. They described feeling pushed out of the process of educational decision making because they were not education experts. For example, parents felt that the school board dismissed their desire to keep a small school because they could not prove that small schools were better.'

The physical setting of the school, school rituals, the school curriculum, and other school activities contribute to the rural construction of the school place. Newcomer families, whether they live in the nearby town, in a renovated farmhouse, or a subdivision, connect to a rural identity through the school. One family that lives in town their rural environment: You sense that different and unique.

The first time you set foot on the grounds you're looking at these log buildings that have been assembled. The whole atmosphere is a country school. And then you sort of associate the values of a country school as being solid and having a little more relaxed feeling about learning-relaxed in that it's not as dictated. I mean, those were all of the associations I had of a country school: being more connected to your place, your environment, and just the awareness of the trees, the fields and the views to the mountains.

Just that whole sweep of view. You want to believe that it will have some influence on the kids when they're out playing on the playground, they're hearing the cows. It's all that sort of pastoral, romantic notion of things. Set in that pastoral landscape, the country school focuses many family events throughout the year. Although no longer a parent-run school, parents continue to be closely involved with day-to-day events of the school.

Through parents' involvement, the school is not only a place for children, but also houses the activities and needs of adults as they work together. Some of the effect of the school emerges as a gestalt. Asked about the affective qualities of the school one parent commented, When you drive by and you see the little Fourth of July parades, or other things. It kind of adds to that. You think, "Oh, that's really nice." "Nice" because of opportunities for children and adults to socialize. In a statement reminiscent of distant prairie homes, one parent stated that her children rely on the school for social activities:

> *It's neat for the kids in this community to have a school that's here, because they are country kids and so it's hard to have playmates and things like that. They don't all have neighbours. So this is kind of their neighbourhood and I think that's really important for them.*

By overemphasizing the distances between homes, this parent justifies the role of the school as a "neighbourhood" locus. She reinforces the rural quality by *not* mentioning daily car trips between houses, after school soccer clubs and dance lessons, frequent sleep-overs, as well as activities in town that provide children opportunities to play together. According to residents, Oakleaf Country School provides a rural sense of place through its "character." The two original school rooms are log buildings, the driveway remains unpaved, and the playground is mostly open field. I think I ended up being comfortable with Oakleaf initially from just the atmosphere of the place. The whole character of the place. The scale, the log buildings, the big oak trees in the playground, the views all around, it was just wonderful that you could see all around at the views from the windows. We being architects, and being very tuned into how the setting is and how it affects you, I think that was probably what initially caught my attention first, was the whole atmosphere of the place. The scale of it.

Schools members reveal great pride in the log buildings, which visually distinguish the school from others in the area. In fall of 1998, school members decided the students should have a playhouse on the playground and tapped in to the nostalgic sentiment in their announcement to parents and friends: "15 years ago, parents themselves built a log schoolhouse. Come back to [Oakleaf] with tools (or not!) and help us 'bam-raise' a genuine old log playhouse for new fun on the playground". In the earliest years of the school, parents supplied most of the labour to build the school. This invitation to barn-raise reminds school members of that fact. While few families in the region ever participate in actual bam-raisings today, these families know the phrase and its connection to rural and older ways. Yet they do not wish to simply return to the past, as the "genuine old playhouse" will be used for "new fun."

Supported by the physical setting of the school, Oakleaf's rurality emerges in school rituals, curricula, and activities. At the fifth graders' graduation and other annual events, students sing the first two stanzas of the Shaker traditional song "Simple Gifts:"

'Tis the gift to be simple, 'tis the gift to be free 'Tis the gift to come down where we ought to be And when we find ourselves in the place just right 'Twill be in the valley of love and delight.

* When true simplicity is gained.
* To bow and to bend we shan't be ashamed.
* To tum, tum will be our delight.
* Til by turning, turning we come 'round right.

The song contrasts markedly with the substantial materialism of students' families. Whether they live in reno vated farmhouses or newly built homes, they enjoy wellequipped kitchens, computers, fancy cars, and landscaped gardens. The school provides a refuge of simplicity as many material and popular culture items are not allowed in the school. Teachers (and parents) do not allow students to bring fashionable toys and clothing, particularly logo-ed items, to school. For these replaced families, the enforced simplicity of the school symbolizes the imagined rural life as simple and uncomplicated.

The edict lies strongest against any forms of weapons including play guns and images of guns. One young boy in his first week at school drew a picture of a rifle, an image that is forbidden. His teacher allowed the image, however, not only because he was new and still learning the rules, but also because the drawing was of a hunting rifle and illustrated the boy's story about a hunting trip with his uncle.

Hunting, while not condoned, is tolerated reluctantly because of its prevalence in local rural culture. Founding and later families expressed some desire to tap into that culture: "We were coming to have our children just be a part of it and relish being a part of the community, to learn that this is their roots." "Their roots" does not refer to their particular family histories, but to a nostalgic remembrance of past generations' lives.

Other "rural activities" at the school include day hikes and overnight backpacking trips in the nearby mountains. Students keep a small vegetable garden on the school grounds. Once a year, students, teachers, and parents spend a day of fishing, painting, and crafts before camping out at a local 4H camp. The school hosts a May Day celebration in which students dance around a may pole festooned with flowers and garlands. These and other events link students to the local place through an emphasis on the outdoor environment and, at times, the daily life of the community. While the school serves as the locus of newcomers' rural lives, that school is situated in a larger landscape. A few families moved to Oakleaf specifically because of the school's reputation, but most school families moved to the area before choosing the small school. Replaced urbanities name many reasons why they move to the Oakleaf region, including privacy, safety, a slower lifestyle, the physical setting, a "positive place" in which to raise children, and, in general, a desire to live in the country.

They seek an improved quality of life that represents a retreat and a contrast from urban life. As one couple said, "We wanted to live in the country after living in the city for so long." A move to Oakleaf is a move to a better quality of life, according to these parents. They purchase larger homes and more property than they could afford in most cities. Notably, these newcomers have "picked" Oakleaf and its neighbouring town Springfield. They have the financial means to choose a particular location and a lifestyle of retreat.

The region these families chose is one of the more affluent in the county. While the median value of a singlefamily home in the county is $111,200, within the Oakleaf census block the average house value is $229,300 (1990 Census). Throughout the county, but especially in Oakleaf, local residents, newcomers as well as old-timers, report a significant rise in home values during the past 10 years. They "read" the economic status not only in their tax bills, but also in material goods. Residents observe a rise in family incomes evidenced by the higher quality of vehicles parked in the school lot. One parent commented that "there are more BMWs now."

Although many Oakleafers purchase homes in subdivisions, they consider their lifestyle to be rural, not suburban. House designs mimic subdivision homes built around Washington, DC and San Francisco suburbs to the extent that the same developer may have built the homes. Home lots, however, are larger than typical subdivisions surrounding cities. In addition, Oakleaf subdivisions lie adjacent to farms and estates, not on the edges of cities. In their more remote locations, former urbanities enjoy a degree of privacy hitherto unknown, while benefiting from positive interpersonal relations with neighbours.

My husband wanted to be somewhere he could run up a power saw at midnight and no neighbours would complain. And I wanted to be someplace the kids could walk to neighbours' houses. And there would be people wanting them to be visiting. (A parent) Many newcomers share this parent's desire to be a part of a community, which she expresses as a place that provides both privacy and cooperation. Privacy results not from a lack of interaction with others, but in a quantity of physical space separating one home from the next.

In sharp contrast to the close proximity of urban neighbours, the low population density in Oakleaf ensures a buffer between houses. Yet the distances are not so great that a child could not walk to a neighbor's home to play. Significantly, this parent notes that her children would be welcome as "there would be people wanting them to be visiting," a further allusive contrast to an impersonal city in which neighbours may not know others on their block, or in their apartment building.

These relocated urbanities express the desire to "get away" and "escape," yet they are not seeking lives of solitude. They seek a community of active engagement with others, and report that they have found it in the rural lifestyle of Oakleaf. Newcomers seek to escape the city without giving up all city conveniences. Oakleaf's particular location suitsthese families well. Although a family may live on 20 acres that backs up against a wilderness area, they are only 20 minutes from Springfield. Cultural events such as restaurants and the arts, as well as professional opportunities, are readily available in Springfield. Many families also work in town, enjoying an easy commute along two-lane country roads. Oakleaf seems to offer the best of both worlds, as one newcomer couple explains:

> *Although the school's role as the locus of rural culture imagines rural life as simple and romantic, this representation satisfies transplanted urbanities. Oakleaf newcomers embrace the school as an idealized rural setting in which everyone works together to construct*

> *buildings and enact rituals according to the seasons. Yet this nostalgic rural image does not speak to the lived experiences of rural oldtimers who have experienced crop failure, mining accidents, and loss of farm land in this and other rural regions. As newcomers construct their imagined rural lives, they displace the rural lives of old-timers. An Oakleaf parent who married into an old-timer family describes the older way of life through vignettes: 'Who walk into the store and don't expect you to drop everything and wait on them immediately, or come out to the gas pump when you're in the middle of waiting on five people. These folks have the respect to know they have to wait their tum, that it's all going to be there in the end.*

There's an influx of middle class, upper middle class people that build $400,000 houses and have two cars. Twenty years ago Oakleaf was a town where lower middle class and probably 40% or 50% of the people at that time, their parents were born here. And 30% of the people still farmed on a part-time basis. You know, raised cows or had a huge garden or even a field that they cultivated. So that's been lost.

Old-timers in Oakleaf shop at the local grocery and deer check station that is stocked with bare necessities, defined by one old-timer as beer, ammunition, baby diapers, and feed for cows. The dark, overstocked store contrasts with the well-lit, clean school next door. These two buildings represent the two communities which live intertwined.

The school is the centre of the newcomer rural life, and the store is the centre of the old-timer rural life. While some newcomers may stop by the store, they are not wholly welcome as they don't "take their time" and "wait their tum." Likewise, some old-timers may send their children to the country school (about 5% of the annual enrolment), but usually withdraw them at the end of preschool in favor of the bus trip to the public and free kindergarten.

While the buildings symbolize the community rift, economics appears to be the underlying cause of the strain. With the influx of newcomers, a higher economic standard of living has been introduced. At one time, many locals were employed in farming. Today, newcomer residents enjoy business, law, and other professions. They do not work their land, but work in an office.

Newcomers recognize the economic shift: Some old-timers may have been considered well-off financially, but they were not considered different from "regular folk." As one Oakleaf parent who married into an old-timer family recounts, old-timers who were well-off financially were also integrated into community life: "grandfather owned a big farm. He was the affluent member of the community. A 300 acre farm. He was just a regular guy 'How many groundhogs did you shoot this year?'"

Attracted to the area, the number of newcomers has risen each year, causing property values to rise. Significantly, newcomers benefit in this environment. In comparison to the metropolitan area we came from, and grew up in, this is heaven. Plus we have the advantages here of having, because of the university, cultural things and-Good medical facilities-perfect advantages because of the great outdoors, and, you know, the city is not too far.

Oakleaf newcomers usually buy small farms or homes situated on several acres of land. Some families buy old farm houses that they refurbish; others purchase newly built homes, often custom-designed. While they may keep a few cows or horses, or pasture the land to qualify as a farm for tax purposes, no newcomer family considers itself a farming family.

Tending a garden or keeping a horse are pasttimes, not careers, as primarily white-collar professional occupations provide their primary income. In Oakleaf, newcomers continue their professional occupations such as health care providers, architects, university professors, investment bankers, designers, and engineers. However, while Oakleaf newcomers do not consider themselves farmers, they did move to the area to live what they consider to be rural lives.

It sounds pretty crass, but one thing that I like about the school being here is it does put a very good light on this community, and my property value just zooms right on up there. I mean, we bought the piece of land we have for $30,000-25 acresand the bank tells us that with our $75,000 house on it that it's now worth close to $300,000. Well, I think that this school is one of the factors that makes the property values go up.

This newcomer parent enjoys the rising property values because she, like other newcomers, expects to sell her property and move in several years. At that time she will enjoy a strong return on her property investment. Old-timers who have lived in the region for generations do not expect to move on. Rising property values for them signify increased property taxes. The same parent observes that, "a lot of the old-timers don't like that because their property values are also going up and they haven't done anything.

It's not their fault that all these old hippies and nouveau riche or whatever are moving out here. If you're just standing there, then your taxes are going up." Because of rising property values, younger generations of old-timers can no longer buy land. "Foothill county is no longer the place to go if you want to homestead." Higher land prices are less of an issue for newcomer families who typically arrive in the area after establishing a successful career and a healthy bank account elsewhere.

Throughout these economic changes, the culture has shifted as well. "I'd say it's kind of a rural area but it's changed, is slowly changing into a semi-rural, gentrified suburb." A suburb, with its closer connections to city than country implies busyness and hurriedness, qualities which are not valued among the rural old-timers. Furthermore, suburbs imply shopping malls and national chains of stores, rather than locally-owned businesses such as Jaeger's Store.

While the school founders were still planning the building, some locals expressed concern that the school would trigger a process of gentrification and development, and that a "McDonald's" was sure to follow. One parent remembered those early days: [There was a zoning hearing] to allow a school on this property, which had just been a cow pasture. And there was opposition. Some of the neighbours complained that traffic would be increasing in the area, that it would change the rural area, or the rural character of the community that allows the school, and a lot of other things would come in. The rural lifestyle may become "lost." [A parent] wrote to a Bob Dylan tune, some funny song about how people are moving, you know people are moving and it's changing. I think [Oakleaf is] becoming a much more affluent area than it was when the school started. Newcomers' greater economic power puts old-timers at a disadvantage. The strongest objections raised to newcomers may echo the sentiments of a colonized people.

My husband and his family moved into a Black neighbourhood on a road where there was no traffic. They used to sit on the porch and watch the seldom-seen cars go by. Now it's a highway and their Black neighbours are clearly in the minority. Or at least, the farmers are in the minority. There is, it's not an animosity, but there is a feeling among the natives of this area that they have been put on a reservation.

Disrupting and Excluding Rural Ways Oakleaf newcomers construct their rural identity through the local independent school. The school place symbolizes those rural qualities desired by newcomers: beautiful and peaceful open land, hand-constructed buildings, and land-focused rituals such as May Poles. Yet rurality is romanticized and nostalgic, in which families enjoy open pasture but few rise before dawn to milk a cow. The imagined rurality is not wholly naive as newcomers are fully aware that their reborn rural region has many elements of suburban or even urban life.

It really has a suburban flavor in that a lot of the people, most of the people that live out here do not make their living off the land. And that's the difference. There are a lot of big farms but principally the owners do something else. So that feels different to me than the rural which I really grew up in. We had a dairy farm and we worked the land, and so I felt like that was rural. But again, here, since most of the people that live here don't use the land to earn a living, it doesn't feel rural, like I'm used to. The kids get very upset when somebody says they live on a farm.

Despite the apparent disjunction between newcomers and old-timers, newcomers assert their construction of a rural identity is in solidarity with old-timers. While newcomers could have brought in shopping malls, modem construction, and other indicators of nonrural life, they chose to adapt their lifestyle to be more in accordance with existing rural values. They contrast their adopted lifestyle against the long-established rural gentry who send their childrento elite private day and boarding schools. However, the reborn rural community presumes the perspective of the newcomer and implies that changes are good. Progress and growth become the normative assumptions of rural place.

What happens to those residents who are not part of the new community? Old timers are not a part of redefining the rural region; they are excluded from the process. While each year two or three old-timer families send their children to the school, they assert that they are not part of the school community. Their exclusion is partly by their own choice, partly because they don't feel as welcome, and partly as they don't have the income to support private school tuition. These families usually leave Oakleaf Country School at the end of preschool. In several ways, oldtimers' lifestyles have been disrupted and they lack the economic and political ability to assert themselves. Their way of life is changing without their input or consent.

The people where I live put up "no hunting" signs. My road was prime hunting grounds for the old people who were hunters. The whole hunting shelter area is shot [because of no-hunting signs]... I think there were more deer killed on our road last year by cars than by hunters. So the older families either are finding that they cannot build here because it's so expensive, or they cannot hunt where they used to hunt, or something. Some way that they had is being disturbed.

Conclusion

Throughout the newcomers' construction of a rural way of life, they develop a community which, by its nature, excludes old-timers. In education literature, as well as everyday discourse, community typically refers to culturally prevalent notions of positivism and simplicity: "In ordinary speech for most people in the United States, the term *community* refers to the people with whom I identify in a locale a community is a group that shares a specific heritage, a common self-identification, a common culture and set of norms".

However, Young also provides us with the necessary counterpart to a group banding together. She continues: In the United States today, identification as a member of such a community also often occurs as an oppositional differentiation from other groups, who are feared or at best devalued. Persons identify only with some other persons, feel in community only with those, and fear the difference others confront them with because they identify with a different culture, history, and point of view on the world. Oakleaf newcomers gain *within* their own group through the construction of a rural community. At the same time, their actions negatively impact old-timers who are, by definition, excluded.

Aware of this exclusion, the Oakleaf Country School and its newcomer families have been and continue to be concerned to establish links with the old-timer community.

Their efforts are emblematic of wanting to dispel their own outsider status and provide value, not merely hegemony. The results of their efforts have been mixed. "I think that most of the community has accepted the school. I wouldn't say that the older faction of this community has embraced it. But accepted it." A sigh of fatigue and powerlessness may be heard in the old-timers' acceptance of a new rural identity of which they are not a part. The effect of Oakleaf Country School on the old-timer community may resemble efforts to construct charter schools in both rural and urban areas. Our nation's history has been one of internal migration, as well as immigration, and we are therefore familiar with cultural clashes between those who came before and those who have just arrived.

These communities change as economic bases shift and bring in new populations. While much of rural school literature has explored the effects of school consolidation and closure, the impact of a new school opening does not appear to have garnered much study. Such an omission is understandable given the lengthy and extensive history of communities losing their local schools. However, given the conjunction of a back to the land movement, charter school legislation, and an economy that increasingly allows whitecollar professionals to work in rural areas rather than urban areas, the cultural tension between newcomers and old-timers is unlikely to go away and may instead increase.

Rural identity may be increasingly constructed in local schools, as Oakleaf newcomers built their own elementary school to symbolize and centralize their cultural notions of community. Rural school researchers, like their urban counterparts, need to attend to the cultural shifts and tensions which frequently accompany population changes. Who will control these new schools? In the case of rural schools (and, thereby, rural identity), they may be taken over by newcomers with more financial resources than those folks who have lived in the regions for generations.

In the meantime, newcomer rural identity in Oakleaf is not about conservation, but about expansion. It concerns a selective retreat from urban bustle to a nostalgic and romanticized lifestyle. The newcomers' rural lifestyle appropriates rituals and visual trappings of rural life, without the less savory (in their eyes) aspects such as shooting groundhogs, chopping firewood, or milking a cow. In their designer homes, these newcomers look out on the rural landscape and simply enjoy the view.

Advantages of Rural Life

When considering living in a rural community there are several things that come to mind. You must understand that jobs are limited so it is best if you are lucky enough to have a job that doesn't require you be in the office everyday. Being a consultant is business that requires travel is good. You are on the road most of the time going from client to client, as a rule of thumb.

With the internet playing a large part in today's business world it is more feasible to live in a rural community. Most of your work can be done online; however, from time to time you will have to make an appearance in the home office. There are also more jobs becoming available online that do not require travel. The biggest set back of these type of jobs is you must be disciplined and a self starter.

More companies are hiring data entry persons that can work exclusively from home online. The medical field is more open to outsourcing their billing so that is a real possibility. Once you understand that living in a rural area you will have to find a job that allows you to do most, if not all, of your work from home.

The advantages of rural life can be wonderful. In a small town most everybody knows everybody and believe me that has some tremendous advantages. The schools tend not to be overcrowded so your children get more one on one help due to smaller classes. There is a lot to be said for smaller classrooms. I speak from personal experience. My three children have all gone to a small school all their lives and I must say it has helped them excel. My oldest graduated second in her class last year and received enough scholarships to pay for her school totally, with five dollars left over. My second oldest is a senior this year and he will graduate first in his class and he is being recruited by some of the best schools in the country, not just a couple of them, many top schools are trying their best to get him to go to their school.

My family likes very much the small town life. We have good friends here and it is a tight community. One advantage is if you forget to lock your doors at night you probably won't have a problem with someone breaking into your home. We tend to watch out for each other. I am not saying this is Mayberry by any means, but it is peaceful and we do not have to deal with traffic and pollution.

It is not all roses by any means. For example, the grocery store is 35 miles away so you learn to make a list, and with gas prices what they are, you try your best to limit those trips to town. We have very few fast food restaurants around close by, which I consider a blessing, home cooking is always better.

The Green Party believes that the pressure for one-off rural housing has become more acute during the last decade because of the rapid escalation in house prices. In Government, with the introduction of our new housing policies, we anticipate that this pressure will gradually abate as housing becomes affordable again.

We believe that the best way to maintain and increase population numbers in rural areas ? based on the evidence of the recent census results-is to support villages, as villages have held their population better than scattered communities in the open countryside. Areas of population loss as indicated by CLAR maps match areas with poor or nonexistent village and town structure.

This lack of village structure, which could have been the focus for new service jobs or small industries, is the main reason these areas suffered more population loss than others. Therefore, we believe that the best way to address population loss in weak areas is to create new villages or village clusters and to actively prevent further dispersal of settlement.

We believe that whatever perceptions exist concerning the lower quality of life in villages and towns as compared to the countryside, is not because of their ?alien? form or higher density, but because of their growing association with decline, disadvantage and poverty. Not long ago, villages were highly valued as centres of trade and enterprise and recognised as important contributors to Irish nation building. Since the 1980s, as the percentage of social housing relative to private being built grew higher in villages and towns than the average for the county, so negative perception grew. This perception has led to the low take-up of both local authority housing and affordable services sites in many villages.

In Government the Green Party will do the following:

- We will support rural housing being concentrated in clusters around existing village settlements so as to ensure sustainability. We will ensure that shops, schools and other services will be located within walking distance of everybody so that we can cut down on car usage.
- In order to encourage sustainable development in rural areas we will encourage local authorities to buy or to Compulsorily Purchase land-banks around villages and to provide serviced sites at cost to residents of the area and to people who wish to work in the area.
- As stated elsewhere in our policy we will discourage the building of holiday homes in rural areas by the introduction of an Annual Site Value Tax on second homes.

  We will support the preparation of village framework designs or Strategic Development Zones draft planning schemes for small rural villages. The Green Party believes that many small rural villages are a very low priority for Area Development Plans because of their small size, their very specific needs and the necessity to plan larger settlements under greater development pressure. But, if small villages are to play their allotted role in the National

Spatial Strategy (NSS) to provide housing with rural quality of life for locals and non-locals, action cannot wait until other priorities are met.

Most small villages in Ireland comprise one main street or a set of crossroads. With the rise in private car use, many of these approach roads are now major traffic routes and are unattractive or even dangerous roads on which to site further houses. The other development pattern seen in villages is the suburban cul-de-sac estate in a single field, unrelated and disconnected from the existing village. We believe that it is vital if we wish to provide an alternative to scattered housing in these areas, that existing small settlements, however modest, expand to provide pedestrian accessible, high quality and affordable houses while retaining and improving their distinctive rural character.

We support three-dimensional, costed Framework Designs for modestly-sized development schemes being prepared and submitted for Outline Planning Permission in the normal way. This might require an agreement to amend or vary the County Development Plan if the villages have no prior designation for development. The Framework Design should have a simple and limited brief that does not require elaborate statistical information or research-that is to lay out new access roads, public spaces and sites for services, buildings and utilities.

Alternatively, Part IX of the 2000 Act for Strategic Development Zones should be used specifying the economic, social and environmental importance of the development of small villages for rural housing provision. In that case, the Framework Design would correspond to the Draft Planning Scheme outlined in Section 168 and would be processed under the relevant sections.

More rigour would be called for in the development of the Framework Design (or Draft Planning Schemes as they would become) under these circumstances as appeals to an Bord Pleanala are precluded under Part IX. Funding for the preparation of Framework Design or Draft Planning Schemes can be recouped under the development levy system. The local authority need not carry out or commission the Framework Design directly. A number of agents are capable of this task including the local Leader or

Partnership Company, a good local development association or a Community Land Trust. Planning and Engineering advice should be provided by the local authority, and it should monitor the entire process closely to ensure statutory and local development requirements are met.

We will promote a number of new sustainable settlement pilot projects in areas of weak settlement structure. We will provide a revolving development fund for this purpose, available to a range of potential development agencies including local authorities, Partnership and Leader Companies, Housing Associations or other not-for-profit Companies such as Community Land Trusts.

An example of a sustainable and innovative new model of village renewal is the 'Farm Village' model developed by Sustainable Communities Ireland and currently being developed at Cloughjordan village in Co Tipperary and also similar initiatives by Blackwater Resource Agency in North Cork, a Leader Company and Freshford 20/20, a partnership of local orgnaisation and Kilkenny Co. Co. This model includes the provision of on-site sewerage and water treatment infrastructure, on-site generation of renewable energy to provide at least 50% of the energy needs of community facilities, employment and enterprise units, community transport vehicles, community gardens and open spaces.

This approach will see the model 'farm village' being integrated with the existing village as part of a carefully planned extension that will reinvigorate the entire area. We are completely opposed to the current trend of developing large, sprawling, surburban-style estates on the outskirts of rural villages which often do not have the level of services or infrastructure to cope with a significant increase in population.

We believe that Ireland is at a critical period of development at present and that if the wrong policies on rural housing are adopted now, major problems will arise in the future. It has been claimed that scattered rural housing is part of our heritage and should be facilitated, not restricted. Before the famine, in 1841, census figures show that about 90% of the population lived in rural areas.

However, the first ordnance survey map dating from the time, shows people did not live in scattered single rural houses but in 'farm villages' or clachans, consisting of clusters of 15-20 houses with open countryside around them. After the famine, the Congested Districts Board, and its successor, the Land Commission, moved people out of these villages into single houses as it was felt disease spread more quickly in crowded conditions. The splitting up of the big estates under the land acts continued this pattern of scattered housing.

Irish society has changed considerably since then. We are now an industrial nation with tourism a major employer, and farming is no longer the mainstay of the local economy. We believe that any settlement strategy for the 21st century must take into account the fact that modern living requires external services including piped water, electricity, and telephones. As these services are normally provided next to the public road, that is where the majority of new one-off rural houses are sited.

The result is ribbon development along rural roads, especially those leading out of towns. People also want to live where they can have a good quality of life and ready access to work, shops, schools and other services. Rural houses are in demand to a large extent because of the lower site prices but this does not take into account the higher long-term costs of commuting to work, schools etc. usually requiring a second family car. There are other costs that are not so obvious. An Foras Forbartha, in a study carried out in the mid 1970?s showed that it is more expensive to provide services to rural houses but the extra cost is often borne by the community, not by the individual.

In relation to the issue of one-off houses in the countryside, we wish to see the current social imbalance of housing development in villages versus the countryside being addressed.

In Government the Green Party will:

- Ensure the provision of affordable rural housing that is rural-generated as opposed to urban-generated. Urban-generated rural housing is housing that is built in rural areas for people who are working in towns or cities many miles away. This kind of development tries to get around the unaffordable cost of housing in urban areas but pushes the price of rural housing up for everybody. In contrast, rural-generated development meets the real development needs of rural areas.

- Promote rural planning policies that give preference to those who make an economic contribution to the rural community in which they wish to live, and who will participate in, and contribute to, the life of the local community. We will actively encourage a range of alternative rural enterprise through the planning process including organic agriculture, renewable energy projects, cottage industries, local specialty food production etc. We support the right of individuals who wish to establish new rural-based enterprises or businesses to be treated favourably within the planning process, subject to sustainability criteria.
- We will ensure the inclusion of a category of individual entitlement to planning permission in the open countryside based on functional or social need within sections of County Development Plans dealing with settlement strategy in rural areas. Functional need will relate to where proposed householders need to live in a rural area because their work requires proximity to it-for example in the case of guards, nurses or schoolteachers-and where there is no existing suitable accommodation available. Social need will cover where proposed householders are caregivers of established rural residents and where there is no existing suitable accommodation available. New holiday homes will only be permitted in existing or new sustainable settlements.
- Conditions will be attached to planning permissions for a new house (subject to the criterion of functional and social need) on an existing farm so as to minimize environmental impact, that it be sited near the farmhouse and that, in as far as possible, it share one upgraded sewerage treatment system and one road access point. This measure would reduce applications from landowners

purporting to need a new house for a family member but which is built at some distance from the existing family home and all too frequently sold soon afterwards. (Informal research by planners in co Meath showed that 50% of permissions granted for family members are being lived in by unrelated people 5 years later).

- We will support the widespread use of Section 47s by local authorities in relation to one-off rural housing in order to control resale within a 10-15 year period, and the use of planning conditions for local occupancy. We will introduce a form of Capital Gains Tax for houses built under family/social need that are resold within this period, to discourage speculation or abuse of this planning opportunity.
- We will ensure that rural planning decisions focus to a much greater extent on the environmental impacts of a dwelling, rather than purely on its visual impact. We will ensure that planning conditions ensure the maximum use of the most environmentally sustainable building materials. New homes will, in as far as possible, be constructed using sustainable natural materials and will use timber frame construction and natural cellulose or wool insulation in order to ensure better standards of insulation. New houses will be encouraged, through tax incentives, to take advantage of passive or active solar energy or wind power. Measures including conserving the use of fresh water by recycling surface water runoff, that is grey water for uses where fully treated water is not necessary. Where houses are to be located in rural areas, a landscaping planting plan based on native species will be required, rather than the typical quick-fill screening.
- We will introduce an Annual Septic Tank levy to cover the costs of monitoring and inspecting septic tanks. Although the one-off house owner provides his/her own sewerage treatment, this does not relieve the local authority of the considerable costs in monitoring and servicing the facility. Sewerage sludge must be collected once a year and treated

in licensed facilities but this is not happening at present because of a combination of lack of awareness and the lack of suitable facilities. This neglect has had a negative impact on water quality. The government is upgrading and chemically treating Group Water Schemes, which have consistently failed to meet minimum EU drinking water standards, because of agricultural and septic tank contamination in rural areas. In Government, we will require that septic tanks and percolation areas should be in accordance with the most up-to-date European and national guidelines available. Tax relief will be provided on the installation of alternative wastewater treatment systems such as reed-bed systems.

- Planning permission conditions for new homes in rural areas will require that each householder minimises and manages waste, including creating a composting facility and organising the separation and collection of individual waste streams.
- We will ensure that local authorities make schemes available such as exist in other countries whereby grants are provided for new or older converted houses to assist in making them more sustainable and minimising their resource use.
- We will address the current imbalance of investments in land and property in Ireland that is fuelling an asset price bubble in housing and in farmland. We will provide incentives for Irish people, both on an individual basis and in companies and communities, to invest in alternative productive assets. In the light of coming fossil fuel scarcity, the most productive assets are likely to be renewable energy generators. As our best renewable energy resources are in rural areas, hydro, wind, biomass, slurry and eventually tidal power, this policy will diversify investment from the larger cities and towns.

The Government's own policy framework for renewable energies, published in the Green Paper on Sustainable Energy in 1999, gave a strong endorsement for the community ownership of wind farms, but despite the establishment of a Renewable Energy Strategy Group in 2000 to develop strategies for the increased deployment of wind energy, little has been done since to increase community participation. In Government the Green Party would act to remove the barriers to the fulfilment of this policy. Other renewable energy resources, in particular biogas digestion in the midlands of the country, have great potential for community ownership and investment. We believe that Community Land Trusts as outlined earlier in this document could manage the collective investment of communities in natural renewable energy resource built up through goodwill royalties as in Scotland or through individual Credit Union savings and borrowings the main reason we moved here, and I think you may agree. We lived in Austin Texas and the year before my oldest was to start school a third grade kid shot and killed another kid in the very school that my children were going to be in. Don't get me wrong violence is everywhere but in our little town there has never been a school shooting. Call me crazy if you like, but I didn't have children to send them to school only to be in danger of possibly being shot.

Rural life isn't for everyone, and for that we are glad. If everyone moved here then we would have all the problems associated with living in a large city. However if you are looking for a peaceful place to raise a family I highly recommend the small town life. It has been very good to us and I don't see myself ever living in a large city again.

6

Destination Image of Nature-Based Tourism

Background and Context

As the world has entered the new millennium, tourism has been seen as one of the fundamental sectors vital to economic wellbeing in the Pacific region. Despite international catastrophes, such as terrorist attacks, local communities have to find ways to sustain themselves even if there is a decline in tourism travel. The Pacific region is unique and dynamic as a social and cultural environment, and many local communities in Pacific Island countries have seen the benefits from tourism. This makes South Pacific culture a major asset for the tourism industry of each country, but raises the question of how to sustain it and do justice to the people in the far scattered islands of the Pacific Ocean.

The Maori are one group who shares the rich and varied past of the Pacific region. They are Polynesian people who can be considered indigenous to such areas as Aotearoa, New Zealand. The unique cultural heritage of the Maori has generated strong international interest in recent years, thus encouraging cultural tourism.

The Growth of Culture in Tourism

There is no doubt that cultural tourism has been a major factor accounting for the positive rates of growth in most Pacific island countries. Recently, this has lead local people to have a new-found pride and respect for their ethnic background, values, beliefs, food arts, crafts and so forth. For over 100 years, the indigenous Pacific image has been used as a marketing tool for promoting tourism. Images of Pacific island people have been stereotyped as guides, entertainers, carvers, weavers and elements of the natural scenery. The indigenous people were seldom consulted, despite their major role in advertising and marketing for tourism.

Once people realized that their image had commercial value for tourism, they began to take increasing control over that image. In so doing, the people have built a viable cultural dimension into their local communities.

This has lead to an increase in the number of people wanting to gain a foothold and gain more responsibilities in the cottage industry of community tourism. The Maori have done this through joint ventures with non-Maori and Pacific island organizations setting up cooperative partnerships to tap into various markets. In the process, the Maori have decided to ask whether all of their people have awareness about the necessary skills, training and business opportunities that are available in order to establish and develop future-oriented, community-based tourism ventures to provide for their own people.

A number of criteria were set up in order to have a clearer picture of what the Maori want to achieve and gain as benefits from community-based tourism:

1. Tourism development for Maori and Pacific island people must support the revival and maintenance of the culture and society.
2. The definition and use of the term "culture" in the tourism industry and the community must be the responsibility of the local people.
3. Maintain the culture by establishing and working with organizations dedicated to preserving and teaching language, culture, history, social structure and performing arts.
4. Let the people achieve a visible and authoritative presence in the tourism industry with full, unconditional recognition.

Several actions can support the achievement of a visible, authoritative presence and recognition for the Maori in community-based tourism. First, invest in significant capital assets in the accommodation sector (home stays, lodges, farms, hotels and hotels).

This is where most of the permanent career employment in hospitality can be found. Second, give access to and acquire a measure of control over marketing and distribution channels to build autonomy and security for the indigenous presence in New Zealand's community-based tourism. Third, develop viable commercial ventures of heritage trails with the perspective that is cultural and historical for the Maori interpretation of local experiences. Fourth, create a symbol or brand identity representing the cultures of the Pacific that will be seen as supporting the quality of products and services within the larger tourism industry.

Community-based Tourism

One starting point for community-based tourism is to focus on strategic planning in order to maximize the long-term benefits that communities could gain from international tourism. At the same time, people at the local and community levels should be empowered through their boards, local governments and enterprise bodies through capacity building and identification of their strengths in sociocultural and environmental preservation.

This can serve as a precondition to making basic changes and aiming at the growth in commercial development. In New Zealand, there are key sections of the Resource Management Act of New Zealand that recognize the impact of culture and traditions of the Maori, as well as the heritage value of sites, buildings, places and areas.

The Maori Tourism Development Board was set up as an NGO that provides liaison, information, education and networking opportunities to foster a growing empowerment role for indigenous people in community-based travel and tourism. The aim is to develop closer economic relations in promoting cultural tourism worldwide and exchange cultural understanding among groups from all nations. The Maori Tourism Development Board works to establish positive tourism business relationships with regional and international tourism bodies, rural communities, Maori villages and Marae, Pacific island groups in Auckland, universities, other educational institutions, international organizations and businesses.

The awareness about the strength of culture and identity for the Maori derives in part from the general lack of support from the mainstream New Zealand tourism industry. In fact, even at the local political level there is a division in New Zealand where regional community councils acknowledge that the local village or town is a community, but a Maori village or Marae in the same area is a Maori group (*runanga*), and not subject to the same funding.

Maori find that they must look for other ways to sustain their communities, despite the fact they contribute to what might be termed the "mainstream communities" in rural areas. Although many Maori have been invited to be on rural community tourism boards or organizations, they have the general impression of feeling they are token members.

As a result, Maori have been developing their own Marae and cottage industry for community-based tourism. The Maori Tourism Development Board networks and supports such initiatives with advice and consultation based on the growth of the indigenous perspective. There have been suggestions that networking should extend regionally to the South Pacific Tourism Organization. This could help strengthen the role, funding and policy development from Aotearoa and the collective of Maori *hapu* (sub-tribes) and *iwi* (tribes); thus uniting Maori (people) as Polynesians with cousins in the Pacific islands.

Concluding Points

There are a number of community environmental issues that relate to the social and economic aspects of community-based tourism. For the issue of ecosystems, it is important to maintain native plants, animal and their habitats. This means designing cultural tourism development and overall tourism strategies that are relevant for the village, district or region.

Indigenous people need to be recognized and incorporated into cultural tourism development with a focus on their issues. Likewise, it is important to take pup the issue of the community and how to ensure that cultural tourism has a positive social and economic impact on community values.

The issue of heritage relates to ensuring the long-term protection of the cultural values, including their importance as a resource to provide a positive visitor experience.

The important environmental issues related to community-based tourism include concerns about coastal areas. The main issue is to preserve the natural character of the costal environment when designing cultural tourism products. Another issue concerns managing the landscape and visual amenities that provide local communities with their lifestyle choices and the visitor with a unique cultural and environmental experience. The issue about water is how to maintain or improve the quality of water through local planning services that address soil disturbances, run-offs and any discharge of contaminants. Noise is another environmental issue for community-based tourism and noise management as an effect of tourism relates to the product, people and traffic involved.

The final point to consider is that the development and management of community-based tourism is vitally important and deserves more serious consideration. Where indigenous people are involved, this means that the more affluent tourism players and stakeholders should not give exclusive concern to what works and what they do not want to change. Anyone involved in the tourism business should investigate the local community who live at a tourist site in order to give tourists exposure to the grass roots and the cultural dimension of local society. Otherwise, most tourists never see the cultural dimension of a tourist site or the way of life experienced by local communities.

Environmental Management of Ecotourism

Background and Concepts

Ecotourism can be contrasted to tourism in the general sense of the two terms, and this allows a more focused examination of issues related to environmental management. The first difference is that ecotourism is a non-extractive use of biodiversity. This means that it complements nature conservation. Where it is economically feasible, ecotourism reinforces conservation objectives. It also provides local communities and tour operators with a strong incentive to preserve natural features of the local environment. Nature is thus the basis for ecotourism and conservation is prerequisite for the sustainability of ecotourism. Further, nature or biodiversity conservation is an integral and inseparable part of sustainable development.

Therefore, it should not be viewed as anti-development. Any discussion about the environmental management of ecotourism must have a definition of ecotourism. At least two definitions are generally accepted worldwide. First is the definition from the International Union for the Conservation of Nature (IUCN) as cited by UNEP in 2001. Ecotourism is defined as environmentally responsible travel and visitation to relatively undisturbed natural areas in order to enjoy and appreciate nature (and any accompanying cultural features-both past and present) that promotes conservation, has low negative impact and provides for beneficial and active socioeconomic involvement of the local population.

The second definition is from the International Ecotourism Society. Ecotourism is defined as responsible travel to natural areas that conserves the environment and sustains the wellbeing of local people. From both definitions it can be observed that the ideal ecotourism is environmentally friendly and sustainable. It assumes a class of traveller who is well-educated, enlightened about the environment and committed to the conservation of nature.

Observations About the Ideal and the Reality

However, ecotourism as practiced in many Pacific island countries verges on being unsustainable. It thus requires close monitoring and continuous efforts to mitigate the negative impacts. With these considerations in mind, it is useful to see at what point does the reality in Pacific island countries depart from the ideal of ecotourism. One point of departure is the fact that less discriminating visitors grossly outnumber the number of ecotourists. It is often not easy to tell the difference between the two groups of tourists and the result is that some Pacific island countries are too eager to attract visitors, but are inexperienced in assessing the extent of ethics and etiquette among tourists about ecology, conservation and ecotourism.

A second point of departure is that ecotourism is considered first and foremost as a business enterprise where profits depend on numbers of tourists. Operators are under pressure to satisfy customers who are willing to pay. The result is that the line between environmentally sustainable numbers of tourists (carrying capacity) and levels of visitation considered to be profitable are difficult to define. Many kinds of impact are often less visible and not immediately discernable; the full consequences of these impacts are manifested at a later time. At the same time, there is the tyranny of small numbers. This is many small negative impacts accumulate over time and contribute to a significant, perhaps irreversible, negative trend or outcome. A third point of departure arises from the poor design and inadequate management of ecotourism activities and related infrastructure. One example is the noncompliance with design and building guidelines. Another example is the absence of proper environmental impact assessments.

Impacts and their Management

There are at least four types of direct impacts on the environments of Pacific island countries: (a) waste accumulation and littering; (b) altered natural features (such as reef/coral damage, vegetation damage, soil erosion, vandalism); (c) introduction of non-native plants and animals; and (d) excessive disturbance to wildlife. In order to manage such direct impacts, three different targets for improvement have been identified: tourist behaviour, facilities design and construction and activities design and implementation. In 1993, the Ecotourism Society listed more specific policies, regulations and actions.

A number of related actions can also be taken to manage direct impacts. There can be awareness raising activities, including greater availability of information and guidelines so that tourists have access to the information and clear instructions. Tour guiding that is good and responsible is also important. Any guidelines must include effective application and compliance in order to have sound ecotourism practices. All varieties of stakeholders should be involved: tour operators, tour guide trainers, eco-travel agencies, environmental agencies, environmental NGOs, schools, retail suppliers of outdoor equipment, hiking clubs and consumer societies. In Pacific island countries, there is also a need for awareness that some impacts are indirect. Many environmental impacts are less visible, but have lasting consequences and are often irreversible. Examples include the changing composition of a forest as a result of invasive plant species, declining wildlife population over time, and infrequent or irregular visits by migratory species.

General Picture of the Pacific Environment

Looking at the area of the South Pacific Ocean from a big picture perspective can give a clear view of how the environment is at risk and the extent to which tourism is part of the threat to the environment. The area is comprised of 38 million square kilometres of ocean, with land being less than 2 per cent of that area. The small land area is divided into 22 nations and territories with a great diversity of traditional cultures. There is also a great diversity of species and endemism as a result of species evolution over millions of years in isolation from continental landmasses. In many Pacific islands, up to 80 per cent of the species are native.

The area of the Pacific islands has the most extensive and diverse coral reef system in the world. It is also the location of the healthiest remaining populations of many species that are endangered globally. The high islands have large areas of original, intact forests that include many species found nowhere else in the world. As of 1998, about 233 areas were under some form of protection, and this is only about 4.5 per cent of the total Pacific land area. The total marine area under protection is unknown. Among various countries, 99 per Easter Island was under protection; 32 per cent of Tuvalu; 15 per cent of the Federated States of Micronesia, 7 per cent of Tonga, 6 per cent of Palau, 4 per cent of Samoa and 2 per cent of Fiji.

It must be noted that at least 50 per cent of the region's biodiversity is at risk. Island ecosystems and certain species are particularly vulnerable. Islands are the location where birds have the highest extinction rate. Human activities that are direct threats include over-harvesting, habitat destruction, uncontrolled waste disposal, proliferation of invasive species, illegal bio-prospecting and destructive trade in live reef fish. In addition, tourism is a significant threat to the environment in island developing countries. According to the world Conservation Union, development is the third major cause of habitat loss. Within the category of development, the top three causes of habitat destruction are industry, human settlements and tourism. Among the indirect effects on the environment, tourism/recreation was the number one threat to the environment.

In the mid-1980s, there were 30 land and marine sites of regional and international significance that were not under any form of protection. However, for the last five years, many Pacific island countries have taken a conservation area approach. At least 12 Pacific island countries, including Samoa and Tonga, have established conservation areas with support from SPREP, the World Wildlife Fund, the Nature Conservancy and Conservation International. A number of Pacific island countries and NGOs have also taken a joint initiative in conservancy to propose a South Pacific Whale Sanctuary, which would be re-submitted to the International Whaling Commission.

Among the future possibilities for conservation and environmental management is the recommendation that Pacific island countries sign the World Heritage Convention so that important cultural and nature areas can be included on the World Heritage List. There is considerable international interest in protecting marine areas of the Pacific region. It could be worthwhile for all Pacific island nations to consider signing the World Heritage Convention. In addition to protecting the environment and cultural heritage, World Heritage listing can be used as a marketing tool.

The Pacific island environment is the foundation for successful ecotourism, but that environment is highly vulnerable and under threat. In order for ecotourism to succeed, it is important to highlight three major implications. First, the natural environment is a total package in which all elements must be maintained and protected, not just small areas or enclaves that are tourist attractions. Second, effective protection can only be achieved in large areas covering entire ecosystems, not just particular species or habitats. Third, ecosystem-based management would cover large areas and require public and local community involvement, especially the integration of economic, social and cultural considerations.

Strategies for Developing Ecotourism

The International Year of Ecotourism 2002 has helped heighten the profile of ecotourism, especially with an increase in the number of international meetings and seminars. However, it might be difficult to formulate or implement policies that are attractive for ecotourism and for the strategies needed to implement tourism projects and policies that are ecologically based and sustainable. One difficulty is to know precisely what ecotourism is in order to prepare strategies.

It is clear that ecotourism is a subset of tourism and that it refers to sue of natural/ecological resources and usually entry into sensitive and fragile environments. Many might think ecotourism is the same as nature-based tourism, while others consider that an objective, value free definition is needed. Ultimately, it is the case that people who use the term determine the meaning of the term ecotourism as they intend it.

Ecotourism is, in fact, a very complex tourism product as some agencies and entrepreneurs have discovered. First, not all natural environments are suitable for tourism; second, ecotourists are a special group among the general category of tourists, and some tourists might not adopt an ecological frame of mind for only a small period during their tourist visit. Third, there are basic principles about a tourism attraction that apply even if the tourism resources are not environmentally based. Fourth, the management of ecotourism facilities and locations could become quite demanding and may become isolated geographically in the form of an enclave. Representatives from tourism organizations throughout the South Pacific subregion are probably already aware that commitments to any form of tourism are uneven with considerable variations in the international tourism profile of their country.

For the most part, the Pacific islands have a profile described as leisure and recreation based. However, other Pacific island countries do not yet have tourism products that would appeal to tourists from the major source markets. Even in countries where tourism is not well known, some of the critical issues related to ecotourism and the process of strategic planning can be viewed in light of the special circumstances of Pacific island countries. This should assist policy makers who are considering whether ecotourism could be an important component in their set of tourism resources and whether tourism development might be made more sustainable.

Strategic Questions about Ecotourism

It has already been recognized at the global level that just having the requisite resources might not be sufficient to sustain viable experiences or businesses based on ecotourism. There is a range of prerequisite criteria that must be met, and some strategic questions help identify these criteria. The following questions have been identified as important: (a) What has motivated the interest and commitment to developing a strategy for ecotourism? (b) What have been the strongest influences affecting the interest and commitment? (c) Who are the principal participants in ecotourism? (d) Should ecotourism be an independent strategy, or should it be integrated as a component of a broad-based tourism strategy?

Policy makers would have their own set of purposes or motivations in each country that accepts a strategy of ecotourism development. It is necessary to clarify what is being planned and why before the overall strategic exercise reaches an advance stage. The purpose that policy makers establish for ecotourism development would directly influence the process and outcomes.

To a great extent, the purpose for a strategy of ecotourism development has been derived from many discussions about the potential of ecotourism. Discussions at international meetings have asserted that small island countries, which may be unable to meet the challenges of conventional mass tourism, might be better suited to ecotourism as a specialized niche market. This message helped create the potential of ecotourism for policy makers concerned abut the negative social effects of mass tourism, the concern about the fragility of ecological resources and a willingness to share cultural and natural resources with discerning visitors who were environmentally and culturally sensitive.

The potential of ecotourism has several additional assumptions to keep in mind. A commitment to ecotourism requires the recognition that the outcome may not give many economic advantages, because the strategy is ecologically-driven, not economically-driven. In addition, ecotourism development presumes a need to involve the local population in the planning and the management. Community-based planning is thus an important component, and perhaps a prerequisite. From an early point in the process, it is also necessary to ask and answer whether ecotourism should be a stand-alone strategy or a sub-strategy within a broad-based tourism strategy. The opinion on balance is that an ecotourism strategy would be a subset of a broad-based tourism strategy, because it is dependent on many components of a general tourism strategy.

Strategic Planning Process

Whether a component of the general tourism strategy or a stand-alone specific ecotourism strategy, there would need to be a systematic process of formulating strategy based on clearly articulated objects, thorough assessment of available resources, an estimation of market demand and the creation of an appropriate quantitative, qualitative and geographical strategy.

Regardless of the scope and scale of the strategic planning process, there are basic similarities based on a thorough step-by-step approach. This approach could be the significant factor for determining how appropriate is the choice of a strategy. Creating a purpose-designed strategic planning process has become fairly standardized, but the key issue is to fine tune and balance the components to fit the circumstances of the agency and the community and address critical issues.

The critical elements of the strategic planning process are prepare the study; do the survey; conduct analysis, synthesis, projections and predictions; formulate the policy and plan; and specify what is the output and the expected outcomes. It is important to keep in mind that no matter how broad or narrow the focus of the plan, it must be integrated with other sectors on the national agenda.

The main steps in the strategic planning process start with setting the objectives and how this is done. The objectives set the vision and often the operational targets for the plan. Equally important is the consultative process involving various stakeholders that should lead up to statements about what everyone expects to accomplish along with statements about the purpose of activities. Since various stakeholders will have different expectations, it is important that objectives be categorized as (a) essential or optional, (b) independent or dependent on achieving other objectives, (c) statements of what is intended, and (d) statements of implementation.

Methods of Resource Assessment

There are many methods and techniques used to assess capabilities and what is suitable from a wide spectrum of resources needed to support tourism development. Simple methods would involve building an information base that includes inventory, categorizing, simple assessment and identification of patterns and linkages.

Assessment of carrying capacity can involve analysis and projections in the early phases of plan formulation as long as the limits and suitability of this method are understood. In recent years, various types of opportunity spectrum methods have been used to assess resources. The eight factors used in the Ecotourism Opportunity Spectrum (ECOS). The significance of each factor will depend on the circumstances of where the ecotourism region and site are located. The intensity of existing or proposed ecotourism development and the nature of the development, whether by an eco-specialist or eco-generalist, would also have an impact on any opportunity for ecotourism development.

The ECOS assessment could be further refined to include other features and criteria, such as: landscape assessments, attractiveness indices, resource status

Frameworks for Geographical Arrangements

Any framework for the geographical arrangements of ecotourism development must be derived systematically in order to protect ecotourism resources, have a balance between development and conservation, concentrate the touristic experience, integrate ecotourism with appropriate related tourism activities, create special enclaves suited to the particular needs of ecotourism, maintain capacity limits for development and access, provide services for ecotourists and create investment confidence. In order to meet all of these criteria, three basic points should serve as the guideline: (a) only certain areas within a tourist region are absolutely necessary for tourism development; (b) strategic planning for tourism goes beyond and rejects the popular belief that all land has equal potential for tourism development (if promoted heavily); and (c) any examples of unstructured tourism development located anywhere have inherent social and ecological problems due to one-dimensional tourism development approaches. Using a systematic framework for geographical arrangements will show that social and ecological problems could be avoided or reduced; they are not inherent or unavoidable for ecotourism development. There are three basic frameworks or models for the geographical arrangements of an ecotourism region and destination.

Destination Region Model

The destination region model is a simple model for an ecotourism destination. It allows for separating on a geographic basis those areas to be used intensively for tourism activity, regardless of scale. It includes circulation routes, service centres, all of which are separated from the natural environmental resources that need protection or preservation. The natural environmental resources keep their attractiveness for ecotourism, and it is possible to manage and sustain these resources. The four major components of the destination region model.

The Corridor model is characterized by route systems through the ecotourism region in order to provide access to ecotourism resources. While there are many variants to the model, it is best used for conservation areas, wilderness regions and hill country zones. The model has its origin in the principles of the conservation movement. These principles include providing limited access to environmentally sensitive areas, surrounding core areas with buffer zones to provide limited access and restricted support development, nodal points that represent small excised support services, and conserved areas with controlled circulation.

A network of principal routes with supporting secondary routes and trails characterizes the model. The network patterns can include corridor access through the protected region with no detours; targeted trail heads and significant sites as detours from the principal route; and secondary loops through subregions with particular tourist experiences or access to selected sites. The model has geographical referencing for differentiated zones of access. There is controlled access through a series of sub-zones designed to protect the ecology of the core environmental ecotourism zone. In wilderness areas where planners are concerned with both conservation and tourism development, they may differentiate the trail systems according to various criteria.

The Twin Model

The twin model is a hybrid combination of the first two models. Its main characteristic is to provide a base camp at the outer perimeter of the ecotourism region along with most, if not all, essential support services. The idea of "twinning" comes from the match between two components –the base camp and the ecotourism attraction. In some circumstances, the base camp could be an ecotourism attraction in its own right.

Management Regimes

Resources have to be managed in a way that achieves sustainability in order to make ecotourism a realistic development possibility. Various types of management regimes have been developed and advocated. For example, there are protocols and agendas from international organizations such as UNEP and

UNCSD; the Rio Agenda 21; the SIDS agenda and United Nations and NGO guidelines. Tourism industry groups such as WTTC and PATA have developed and advocated management regimes as have national tourism organizations and regional tourism organizations. At the same time, research institutes and tourism interest groups have developed and/or advocated systems, principles, values, norms and procedures for management of ecotourism.

Among the management tools and mechanisms that have been developed and advocated are:

- Industry self-regulation as an alternative to government-imposed regulations
- Technical assistance packages from the government
- Industry-based codes of practice for ecotourism operators
- Reward systems for good practices
- Accreditation programmes – whether by government or industry
- Rapid assessment models
- Financial assistance programmes when preferred styles and forms of ecotourism are developed
- Partnership programmes
- Community-based programmes
- Codes of practice for ecotourists about appropriate behaviour.

Each of these management tools and forms has its own characteristic approach and depends on supporting structures and resource requirements. Circumstances may determine which forms are appropriate and whether a combination of forms can be implemented concurrently. Local factors such as politics, culture and economics will have an effect on choice of management regimes and related mechanisms, and this means that tools and mechanisms that work in one case of ecotourism development might not be easily transferred or copied for another case. The main point, therefore, is that a specific purpose-designed management regime would be needed for each new case of ecotourism development.

Concluding Points and Some Questions to Consider

The special circumstances of the island developing countries in the Pacific region raise a set of three questions. First, is ecotourism a viable strategy everywhere in the region? Second, Will national ecotourism strategies be independent and competitive with neighbouring island countries, or will ecotourism strategies be integrated and cooperative across the region? Third, what strategic capacities are needed to support the creation, development and implementation of sustainable strategies for ecotourism development?

Assuming the suitable ecotourism resources are available, there are three important strategic linkages to consider, because they will influence the viability of ecotourism in any region. The three linkages are: (a) between ecotourism resource regions and the ecotourists' country of origin; (b) between ecotourism as a principal attraction and as a companion attraction; and (c) between the prerequisites of tourism and ecotourism.

In terms of ecotourism resource regions, the prevailing evidence is that the most desirable locations are often in developing countries. The ecotourist visitors will be from the main developed countries in North America and Europe, plus Japan. In the countries of the ecotourism resource region, such as the Pacific subregion, targeted areas exploiting ecotourism can create a competitive market edge in the international tourism market, whether or not ecotourism is the main attraction.

Moreover, there is evidence that ecotourism is a special form of tourism that depends on the basic requirements of general tourism, including infrastructure, accommodation, transport, support services, information, marketing and trained human resources.

If these three kinds of linkages are kept in mind, then ecotourism might also benefit from being viewed at a regional level. Once attention is at the regional level, another set of questions would have to be addressed: (a) How comparable, competitive and complementary are the ecotourism resources in the Pacific island subregion? (b) How sustainable are the ecotourism resources? (c) How adequate are the support resources? (d) Could there be cooperative, mutual support strategies within and across the region?

If policy makers start thinking about the answers to these four questions, then it would be possible to address the overriding strategic question about the future of ecotourism in the Pacific island subregion. That is, would some type of cooperative ecotourism strategic structure be worthwhile, could it be created and could it be sustained? While the Pacific island countries generally face difficulties of location and logistics, they do have unique natural and cultural resources and the mystique of the south Pacific. This is the starting point for opportunities to bring together and strengthen the resources needed to create ecotourism at the national and regional level.

Development and Management of Community-Based Tourism

Introduction

In early 2001, a team that included the author as a community development specialist had reviewed New Zealand's assistance to Fiji in support of two community-based ecotourism projects. The projects supported by New Zealand were considered as best practices in ecotourism in Fiji and provide the case study for this presentation.

Tourism is the major industry for Fiji and it is a major tourism destination in the Pacific, second only to Hawaii. In 1998, a record number of tourists, about 372,000 people, visited Fiji. The tourism industry has made Fiji a major destination and it is also the largest sector of the economy. However, an average Fijian family gets very limited direct economic benefits from mainstream tourism development. The economic benefits from resort-style tourism development are unevenly distributed. Ecotourism, nature-based and culture-based tourism in rural districts has been seen in terms of the potential to bring economic benefits of tourism to local communities in rural areas.

Ecotourism is considered to have the potential of contributing to protection of natural and cultural values and poverty alleviation in rural areas accessible to main tourist centres; and this is how ecotourism fits into the integrated development strategy. The government of Fiji supports ecotourism ventures that are carefully targeted to maximize economic benefits and minimize negative social impacts.

The government's overall guiding policy document is the *Fiji Tourism Development Plan 1998-2005*, which gives an important role to ecotourism in terms of environmental protection and rural job creation. In 1999, the government approved the *Ecotourism and Village Based Tourism Policy and Strategy for Fiji*. This document defines ecotourism and adds to the definition by mentioning the activities and characteristics considered to be ecotourism ventures.

These include: small scale, low capital ventures; provide activities that let tourists experience nature and indigenous culture; are likely to be owned by local people; ventures likely to be owned and operated by local people; activities based in the village or involving transportation by land or sea; and projects with fewer leakages that large-scale tourism projects.

Over the last ten years, over 70 ecotourism attractions have been developed and ecotourism has become the most important segment of Fiji's tourist industry. At the same time, the Ministry of Tourism (MOT) has become the lead government agency by implementing the policy, plus gaining more attention for taking a greater role in local rural communities.

The Ministry of Tourism has also strengthened its capacity to promote community-based ecotourism and conservation projects. Equally significant, at the regional level the 1998 SPREP Ministerial Meeting endorsed the Action Strategy for Nature Conservation in the Pacific Region 1999-2002, based on the experiences with rural ecotourism development built up in Fiji, as well as other island developing countries.

Case Studies of Fijian Ecotourism Projects Supported by NZODA

The NZODA Fiji Ecotourism Programme started in the late 1980s as an investigation of the remaining important natural forest areas in Fiji. NZODA had become the major supporter of ecotourism development activities as part of piloting integrated projects in two areas: one is the Bouma National Heritage Park on Taveuni, an island just off Vanua Levu, a second is the Koroyanitu National Heritage Park near Lautoka on Viti Levu.

The aim of NZODA assistance has been to provide communities in the project with the means to protect their natural environment within the national heritage parks, while achieving sustainable livelihoods based on conserving natural resources and the cultural heritage.

The villagers chose ecotourism as the income-generating activity, with a community-based project to be established in each village. The objectives of the projects are: (a) conserve, protect and enhance the area's natural and cultural heritage; (b) develop and maintain first class recreation and tourism assets for local people and overseas visitors to enjoy and create a benefit for Fiji's international tourism image; (c) create local employment and income opportunities for women and men in the local communities; (d) facilitate and strengthen capacity building in the project communities in order to sustain project activities, especially ecotourism management, enterprise management, natural resource conservation, cultural protection and community self-development; and (e) facilitate development and consolidation of linkages from communities to organizations at all levels in order to sustain community projects in the medium-and long-term.

One objective of the team when reviewing New Zealand's assistance to the two projects was to bring a clear vision of market reality to the projects in terms of the ecotourism products being developed and to facilitate the development of community-based tourism enterprises.

The team brought skills that could be transferred to counterparts in Fiji, including a clear understanding of the strong link between nature/heritage conservation and the components of ecotourism.

Tourism Product Development

The two projects in Fiji that have been supported by New Zealand covered six villages. Unique ecotourism products were developed in each village.

(1) At Abaca village, visitors can stay at a lodge or with families. Guides are available for day trekking and there are also self-guided trails to waterfalls and a mountaintop. A visitor centre in the park supports management, provides information and sells souvenir items and handicrafts. Ecotourism at this village has won a number of regional awards.

(2) A new overnight trek operation is run by Navilawa village in partnership with Abaca village and a transport company in Nadi. The village provides accommodation and food, and then visitors take a two-day, one evening trek.

(3) Waitabu village provides a guided snorkelling tour of the marine reserve, Waitabu Marine Park, using traditional bamboo rafts. A travel company acts as a partner. Ecotourism in this park has been added to the Bouma National Heritage Park ecotourism activities.

(4) Vidawa village organizes a guided day-long forest hike through Bouma National Heritage Park, which includes a traditional meal at midday.

(5) The Tavoro Waterfalls is the most well-established and popular ecotourism activity at Bouma National Heritage Park. Visitors can enter the area at their own leisure and use the other available tourist services.

(6) The Lavena coastal walk is the second oldest ecotourism activity at Bouma National Heritage Park. The area involves a walk along the coast to the waterfalls nearby. The community raised funds to build a lodge, which includes accommodation, a restaurant, a handicraft shop and visitor's centre.

Building the Community

The project has focused on building capacity and capability in the areas of ecotour operations and enterprise management. At the time of the review, all communities had the capacity and were successfully operating their ecotourism activities. It was found that some additional assistance would be needed to build greater depth to their capacity, thus enabling the local people to sustain the activities over a longer term. A second focus was developing the communities' capacity to manage their ecotourism activities as business enterprises.

This would increase direct employment and income within the communities and expand the range of options for new locally based livelihoods. The people have already had some training and experience in business operations, but more assistance could build business enterprise capacity further. The extent of the need and the priorities for attention varied among the different communities.

It was observed that the project had strengthened social cohesion and improved the well being of individuals and the community as a whole, although there is variation among the villages. Individuals with particular skills and interests, especially women and youth, have been able to develop non-traditional roles with the support of the community. Ecotourism has provided all of the communities with a new steam of income and this is an incentive for people to stay in the village and manage their own enterprise. Local people have recognized and valued the preservation of their culture and heritage. There is increased awareness of conservation and management of natural resources along with environmental protection. The main challenge is to see how community development can ensure the long-term sustainability of the projects and the communities.

Areas for Building Greater Capacity

Work plans are needed and additional capacity has to be created in some communities to manage the ecotourism activities as well as carry out daily activities and have some spare time. This has been a challenge for the smaller communities in particular. Another challenge for community-based tourism was the conflict between traditional practices and business practices, because this could determine the success or failure of a particular local enterprise. Outside support agencies could help in this area and build linkages with the community enterprise management people.

The communities were in need of more support from and linkages to provincial and national agencies that could act as partners. To meet this challenge, the government needed to improve its capacity by having one national agency with a mandate and capacity to guide participatory community development. At the same time, parts of the government with technical expertise in ecotourism, small business enterprise and environmental management, for example, should be identified and encouraged to help local communities.

Development impacts

The project has had a major positive impact on the natural environment by establishing protected areas. The communities are committed to protection and the provincial authority has received assurances from landowners and the wider community that they would support environmental protection. There have also been direct gains in biodiversity, especially since creation of Koroyanitu National Heritage Park has prevented the spread of commercial logging.

The understanding is now broader, with a stronger commitment to environmental sustainability, especially since communities are aware of the benefits already realized. People have realized that environmental protection is good not only for the tourists, but for the community as well. There is also a national agency to support land conservation and assist landowners to give long-term protection to their land and not open their land to commercial logging. Some physical infrastructure has been upgraded and replaced.

The economic and financial impact can be considered as successful. A new form of income generation has been developed and sustained thus far. New or expanded income generating enterprises based on ecotourism have been established and are operating. There are still some contradictions between the traditional reciprocal economy and the sustainable enterprise management model based on the cash economy. Where the previous cash economy was extractive and degraded or destroyed the environment, the sustainable enterprise management of ecotourism might fit more appropriately with the traditional economy. However, this aspect needs more careful study and community participation to improve understanding.

The aim of creating self-sustaining, community-based ecotourism enterprises is to have a local business activity that can sustain recurrent costs. In some villages, this has occurred and ecotourism has even supported other non-related development activities. Careful monitoring is needed to be sure this will eventually occur in other villages without economic or social complications.

The social impact of the projects relates to the impact of the financial benefits from the projects. Ecotourism has introduced different ways of doing many activities in daily life, as well as added new experiences when ecotourists come to villages. Operating an ecotourism enterprise has crated new roles and challenged existing roles, especially traditional gender roles. Women have gained socially in many ways, but this has also created some conflict in the household.

Visitors can disrupt family life as well as community commitments and obligations. The social development process has created both cohesion and conflict, and this is a challenge to traditional village decision-making and dispute settlement. At the same time, the projects have helped to save indigenous knowledge, and the government is documenting this.

Technical assistance in community development would enable local communities to have dialogues, articulate viewpoints and reflect together on what has been changing in the life of the community when a business culture and ecotourism operations are introduced. Training in facilitation and social group interactions can help address the challenges to how the community is organized, leadership issues and governance issues.

Key Issues

The review team noted the achievements in all six villages and ongoing training to strengthen people's capacities for managing and operating ecotourism enterprises. The priority at this stage would be to secure these achievements and make the ecotourism activities self-sustaining in ways appropriate for the local level. The emphasis is now shifting to capacity building of village communities for sustained management and implementation.

While ecotourism training would still be included, training that is ecotourism-related would cover community development, sustainable resource management and development and maintenance of ecotourism products.

Financial sustainability is a component in the ultimate aim of self-sustainability, but this also involves long-term financing and management of the system at the national level. Therefore, self-sustainability involves a more complex set of issues relating to localization of management at the local community level, building productive partnerships from the local to the provincial level and establishing supportive links from the local level to the provincial and national level.

At the national level the various tourism entities in the government need to establish clear roles and maintain national level partnerships that can assist communities and projects at the local level. Assistance from the national and provincial levels can also help to better establish village ecotourism activities in the cultural context in ways that community enterprises could achieve long-term sustainability. Likewise, the national level is able to set up the legal base and the mechanisms to support communities determined to manage their own lands for conservation of the environment and for protection of the cultural heritage.

Agencies at all levels should be able to work together with communities to manage and monitor the natural and cultural heritage resources. Participatory community development and managing change in communities have been difficult to achieve since ecotourism brings many new concepts, practices and influences to rural communities.

Building community awareness and establishing linkages from the local to the provincial and national levels can provide expertise that might intervene to help those who see traditional roles and norms being challenged. Building capacity is the cornerstone of all aspects of the project, and this includes ecotourism operations as well as protection of the environment and cultural heritage; building on enterprise management skills; managing community development dynamics and building confidence in local partnerships.

Lessons Learned

The lessons learned from the review by the team from New Zealand covered five areas.

First, community lessons showed that problems occur when there are conflicts between traditional institutions and the requirements of business management. It is important to be aware that community and landholder interests are often not the same. Working with communities is time consuming, especially because there is a wide range of stakeholders and interested parties concerned with ecotourism.

Second, lessons learned in the area of business management show that often ecotourism projects have not been commercially realistic, so management models have to be more flexible and adaptive to each ecotourism business activity. Ecotourism income is often based on a narrow range of products and services, but there are still many opportunities to expand. Transport and road conditions often limit ecotourism development. There are some regulations that limit certain aspects of ecotourism development.

Third, lessons in conservation show that ecotourism has brought gains in terms of areas that are protected. At the least, ecotourism can highlight the need for conservation and the nature of the benefits that occur.

Fourth, exercises designed to encourage participation by all stakeholders are essential at the start of the project. Gender issues have not been fully addressed and they need to be. Projects will work out satisfactorily when people have common interests.

Fifth, the lessons for donors are as follows: (a) a long time horizon is need for community and business development and financial handouts may send the wrong message to community entrepreneurs. Donors should separate their support for park and ecotourism development from business development.

Conclusions

Global Codes of Ethics for Tourism

Tourism's contribution to mutual understanding and respect between peoples and societies

1. The understanding and promotion of the ethical values common to humanity, with an attitude of tolerance and respect for the diversity of religious, philosophical and moral beliefs, are both the foundation and the consequence of responsible tourism; stakeholders in tourism development and tourists themselves should observe the social and cultural traditions and practices of all peoples, including those of minorities and indigenous peoples and to recognize their worth;
2. Tourism activities should be conducted in harmony with the attributes and traditions of the host regions and countries and in respect for their laws, practices and customs;
3. The host communities, on the one hand, and local professionals, on the other, should acquaint themselves with and respect the tourists who visit them and find out about their lifestyles, tastes and expectations; the education and training imparted to professionals contribute to a hospitable welcome;
4. It is the task of the public authorities to provide protection for tourists and visitors and their belongings; they must pay particular attention to the safety of foreign tourists owing to the particular vulnerability they may have; they should facilitate the introduction of specific means of information, prevention, security, insurance and assistance consistent with their needs; any attacks, assaults, kidnappings or threats against tourists or workers in the tourism industry, as well as the wilful destruction of tourism facilities or of elements of cultural or natural heritage should be severely condemned and punished in accordance with their respective national laws;
5. When travelling, tourists and visitors should not commit any criminal act or any act considered criminal by the laws of the country visited and abstain from any conduct felt to be offensive or injurious by the local populations, or likely to damage the local environment; they should refrain from all trafficking in illicit drugs, arms, antiques,

protected species and products and substances that are dangerous or prohibited by national regulations;

6. Tourists and visitors have the responsibility to acquaint themselves, even before their departure, with the characteristics of the countries they are preparing to visit; they must be aware of the health and security risks inherent in any travel outside their usual environment and behave in such a way as to minimize those risks;

Tourism as a Vehicle for Individual and Collective Fulfilment

1. Tourism, the activity most frequently associated with rest and relaxation, sport and access to culture and nature, should be planned and practised as a privileged means of individual and collective fulfilment; when practised with a sufficiently open mind, it is an irreplaceable factor of self-education, mutual tolerance and for learning about the legitimate differences between peoples and cultures and their diversity;
2. Tourism activities should respect the equality of men and women; they should promote human rights and, more particularly, the individual rights of the most vulnerable groups, notably children, the elderly, the handicapped, ethnic minorities and indigenous peoples;
3. The exploitation of human beings in any form, particularly sexual, especially when applied to children, conflicts with the fundamental aims of tourism and is the negation of tourism; as such, in accordance with international law, it should be energetically combatted with the cooperation of all the States concerned and penalized without concession by the national legislation of both the countries visited and the countries of the perpetrators of these acts, even when they are carried out abroad;
4. Travel for purposes of religion, health, education and cultural or linguistic exchanges are particularly beneficial forms of tourism, which deserve encouragement;
5. The introduction into curricula of education about the value of tourist exchanges, their economic, social and

cultural benefits, and also their risks, should be encouraged;

Tourism, a Factor of Sustainable Development

1. All the stakeholders in tourism development should safeguard the natural environment with a view to achieving sound, continuous and sustainable economic growth geared to satisfying equitably the needs and aspirations of present and future generations;
2. All forms of tourism development that are conducive to saving rare and precious resources, in particular water and energy, as well as avoiding so far as possible waste production, should be given priority and encouraged by national, regional and local public authorities;
3. The staggering in time and space of tourist and visitor flows, particularly those resulting from paid leave and school holidays, and a more even distribution of holidays should be sought so as to reduce the pressure of tourism activity on the environment and enhance its beneficial impact on the tourism industry and the local economy;
4. Tourism infrastructure should be designed and tourism activities programmed in such a way as to protect the natural heritage composed of ecosystems and biodiversity and to preserve endangered species of wildlife; the stakeholders in tourism development, and especially professionals, should agree to the imposition of limitations or constraints on their activities when these are exercised in particularly sensitive areas: desert, polar or high mountain regions, coastal areas, tropical forests or wetlands, propitious to the creation of nature reserves or protected areas;
5. Nature tourism and ecotourism are recognized as being particularly conducive to enriching and enhancing the standing of tourism, provided they respect the natural heritage and local populations and are in keeping with the carrying capacity of the sites;

Tourism, a User of the Cultural Heritage of Mankind and Contributor to its Enhancement

1. Tourism resources belong to the common heritage of mankind; the communities in whose territories they are situated have particular rights and obligations to them;
2. Tourism policies and activities should be conducted with respect for the artistic, archaeological and cultural heritage, which they should protect and pass on to future generations; particular care should be devoted to preserving and upgrading monuments, shrines and museums as well as archaeological and historic sites which must be widely open to tourist visits; encouragement should be given to public access to privately-owned cultural property and monuments, with respect for the rights of their owners, as well as to religious buildings, without prejudice to normal needs of worship;
3. Financial resources derived from visits to cultural sites and monuments should, at least in part, be used for the upkeep, safeguard, development and embellishment of this heritage;
4. Tourism activity should be planned in such a way as to allow traditional cultural products, crafts and folklore to survive and flourish, rather than causing them to degenerate and become standardized;

Tourism, a Beneficial Activity for Host Countries and Communities

1. Local populations should be associated with tourism activities and share equitably in the economic, social and cultural benefits they generate, and particularly in the creation of direct and indirect jobs resulting from them;
2. Tourism policies should be applied in such a way as to help to raise the standard of living of the populations of the regions visited and meet their needs; the planning and architectural approach to and operation of tourism resorts and accommodation should aim to integrate them, to the extent possible, in the local economic and social fabric;

where skills are equal, priority should be given to local manpower;

3. Special attention should be paid to the specific problems of coastal areas and island territories and to vulnerable rural or mountain regions, for which tourism often represents a rare opportunity for development in the face of the decline of traditional economic activities;
4. Tourism professionals, particularly investors, governed by the regulations laid down by the public authorities, should carry out studies of the impact of their development projects on the environment and natural surroundings; they should also deliver, with the greatest transparency and objectivity, information on their future programmes and their foreseeable repercussions and foster dialogue on their contents with the populations concerned;

Obligations of Stakeholders in Tourism Development

1. Tourism professionals have an obligation to provide tourists with objective and honest information on their places of destination and on the conditions of travel, hospitality and stays; they should ensure that the contractual clauses proposed to their customers are readily understandable as to the nature, price and quality of the services they commit themselves to providing and the financial compensation payable by them in the event of a unilateral breach of contract on their part;
2. Tourism professionals, insofar as it depends on them, should show concern, in cooperation with the public authorities, for the security and safety, accident prevention, health protection and food safety of those who seek their services; likewise, they should ensure the existence of suitable systems of insurance and assistance; they should accept the reporting obligations prescribed by national regulations and pay fair compensation in the event of failure to observe their contractual obligations
3. Tourism professionals, so far as this depends on them, should contribute to the cultural and spiritual fulfilment

of tourists and allow them, during their travels, to practise their religions;

4. The public authorities of the generating States and the host countries, in cooperation with the professionals concerned and their associations, should ensure that the necessary mechanisms are in place for the repatriation of tourists in the event of the bankruptcy of the enterprise that organized their travel;
5. Governments have the right – and the duty-especially in a crisis, to inform their nationals of the difficult circumstances, or even the dangers they may encounter during their travels abroad; it is their responsibility however to issue such information without prejudicing in an unjustified or exaggerated manner the tourism industry of the host countries and the interests of their own operators; the contents of travel advisories should therefore be discussed beforehand with the authorities of the host countries and the professionals concerned; recommendations formulated should be strictly proportionate to the gravity of the situations encountered and confined to the geographical areas where the insecurity has arisen; such advisories should be qualified or cancelled as soon as a return to normality permits;
6. The press, and particularly the specialized travel press and the other media, including modern means of electronic communication, should issue honest and balanced information on events and situations that could influence the flow of tourists; they should also provide accurate and reliable information to the consumers of tourism services; the new communication and electronic commerce technologies should also be developed and used for this purpose; as is the case for the media, they should not in any way promote sex tourism;

Right to Tourism

1. The prospect of direct and personal access to the discovery and enjoyment of the planet's resources constitutes a right

equally open to all the world's inhabitants; the increasingly extensive participation in national and international tourism should be regarded as one of the best possible expressions of the sustained growth of free time, and obstacles should not be placed in its way;

2. The universal right to tourism must be regarded as the corollary of the right to rest and leisure, including reasonable limitation of working hours and periodic holidays with pay, guaranteed by Article 24 of the Universal Declaration of Human Rights and Article 7.d of the International Covenant on Economic, Social and Cultural Rights;
3. Social tourism, and in particular associative tourism, which facilitates widespread access to leisure, travel and holidays, should be developed with the support of the public authorities;
4. Family, youth, student and senior tourism and tourism for people with disabilities, should be encouraged and facilitated;

Liberty of Tourist Movements

1. Tourists and visitors should benefit, in compliance with international law and national legislation, from the liberty to move within their countries and from one State to another, in accordance with Article 13 of the Universal Declaration of Human Rights; they should have access to places of transit and stay and to tourism and cultural sites without being subject to excessive formalities or discrimination;
2. Tourists and visitors should have access to all available forms of communication, internal or external; they should benefit from prompt and easy access to local administrative, legal and health services; they should be free to contact the consular representatives of their countries of origin in compliance with the diplomatic conventions in force;

3. Tourists and visitors should benefit from the same rights as the citizens of the country visited concerning the confidentiality of the personal data and information concerning them, especially when these are stored electronically;
4. Administrative procedures relating to border crossings whether they fall within the competence of States or result from international agreements, such as visas or health and customs formalities, should be adapted, so far as possible, so as to facilitate to the maximum freedom of travel and widespread access to international tourism; agreements between groups of countries to harmonize and simplify these procedures should be encouraged; specific taxes and levies penalizing the tourism industry and undermining its competitiveness should be gradually phased out or corrected;
5. So far as the economic situation of the countries from which they come permits, travellers should have access to allowances of convertible currencies needed for their travels;

Rights of the Workers and Entrepreneurs in the Tourism Industry

1. The fundamental rights of salaried and self-employed workers in the tourism industry and related activities, should be guaranteed under the supervision of the national and local administrations, both of their States of origin and of the host countries with particular care, given the specific constraints linked in particular to the seasonality of their activity, the global dimension of their industry and the flexibility often required of them by the nature of their work;
2. Salaried and self-employed workers in the tourism industry and related activities have the right and the duty to acquire appropriate initial and continuous training; they should be given adequate social protection; job insecurity should be limited so far as possible; and a

specific status, with particular regard to their social welfare, should be offered to seasonal workers in the sector;

3. Any natural or legal person, provided he, she or it has the necessary abilities and skills, should be entitled to develop a professional activity in the field of tourism under existing national laws; entrepreneurs and investors-especially in the area of small and medium-sized enterprises-should be entitled to free access to the tourism sector with a minimum of legal or administrative restrictions;
4. Exchanges of experience offered to executives and workers, whether salaried or not, from different countries, contributes to foster the development of the world tourism industry; these movements should be facilitated so far as possible in compliance with the applicable national laws and international conventions;
5. As an irreplaceable factor of solidarity in the development and dynamic growth of international exchanges, multinational enterprises of the tourism industry should not exploit the dominant positions they sometimes occupy; they should avoid becoming the vehicles of cultural and social models artificially imposed on the host communities; in exchange for their freedom to invest and trade which should be fully recognized, they should involve themselves in local development, avoiding, by the excessive repatriation of their profits or their induced imports, a reduction of their contribution to the economies in which they are established;
6. Partnership and the establishment of balanced relations between enterprises of generating and receiving countries contribute to the sustainable development of tourism and an equitable distribution of the benefits of its growth;

Implementation of the Principles of the Global Code of Ethics for Tourism

1. The public and private stakeholders in tourism development should cooperate in the implementation of these principles and monitor their effective application;

2. The stakeholders in tourism development should recognize the role of international institutions, among which the World Tourism Organization ranks first, and non-governmental organizations with competence in the field of tourism promotion and development, the protection of human rights, the environment or health, with due respect for the general principles of international law;
3. The same stakeholders should demonstrate their intention to refer any disputes concerning the application or interpretation of the Global Code of Ethics for Tourism for conciliation to an impartial third body known as the World Committee on Tourism Ethics.

TIES Global Ecotourism Fact Sheet

Size of Global Tourism

- As the largest business sector in the world economy, the Travel & Tourism industry is responsible for over 230 million jobs and over 10% of the gross domestic product worldwide.
- In 2006, Travel & Tourism (consumption, investment, government spending and exports) is expected to grow 4.6% and total US$6.5 trillion.
- If tourism were a country, it would have the 2nd largest economy, surpassed only by U.S.
- In over 150 countries (four out of five), tourism is one of five top export earners. In 60 countries, tourism is the number one export.

Global Growth of Tourism

- 1950: 25 million tourist arrivals.
- 1990's: Tourism grew globally at 7% per year.
- 2004: 760 million tourism arrivals corresponded to a 10% global growth.
- 2005: The number of international tourist arrivals recorded worldwide grew by 5.5% and exceeded 800 million for the first time ever.

- 2020: Global tourism is forecast to reach 1.56 billion international arrivals.
- Importance to Tourism in Developing Countries:
- Tourism is a principle "export" (foreign exchange earner) for 83% of developing countries, and the leading export for 1/3 of poorest countries.
- For the world's 40 poorest countries, tourism is the second most important source of foreign exchange, after oil.
- Over last decade, tourism has been "the only large sector of international trade in services where poor countries have consistently posted a surplus."
- International tourism in developing countries is increasing by 9.5% a year compared to 4.6% worldwide.
- Tourism "appears to be one of the few economic sectors able to guide a number of developing countries to higher levels of prosperity and for some to leave behind their least-developed country status."
- Negative Impacts of Tourism
- There are 109 countries with coral reefs. In 90 of them reefs are being damaged by cruise ship anchors and sewage, by tourists breaking off chunks of coral, and by commercial harvesting for sale to tourists.
- Cruise ships in the Caribbean are estimated to produce more than 70,000 tons of waste each year.
- An average 18-hole golf course soaks up at least 525,000 gallons of water a day-enough to supply the irrigation needs of 100 Malaysian farmers.

Fact Sheet: Global Ecotourism

Ecotourism: "Responsible travel to natural areas that conserves the environment and improves the welfare of local people" (TIES, 1990).

Since surveys rarely ask either travellers or businesses specifically about ecotourism, precise statistics are difficult to determine. Ecotourism is frequently lumped together with nature tourism and other forms of 'experiential' or 'alternative' tourism. These figures represent TIES best effort to put together an accurate assessment of the strength of ecotourism, particularly since 2000.

Size of Global Ecotourism

- Beginning in 1990s, ecotourism has been growing 20%-34% per year.
- In 2004, ecotourism/nature tourism was growing globally 3 times faster than the tourism industry as a whole.
- Nature tourism is growing at 10%-12% per annum in the international market.
- Sun-and-sand resort tourism has now "matured as a market" and its growth is projected to remain flat. In contrast, "experiential" tourism—which encompasses ecotourism, nature, heritage, cultural, and soft adventure tourism, as well as sub-sectors such as rural and community tourism—is among the sectors expected to grow most quickly over the next two decades.
- United Nations Environment Programme (UNEP) and Conservation International have indicated that most of tourism's expansion is occurring in and around the world's remaining natural areas.
- Sustainable tourism could grow to 25% of the world's travel market within six years, taking the value of the sector to £250 billion (US$473.6 billion) a year.
- Analysts predict a growth in eco-resorts and hotels, and a boom in nature tourism — a sector already growing at 20% a year — and suggest early converts to sustainable tourism will make market gains.

Economics of Ecotourism vs. Mass Tourism

- In Dominica, in the Caribbean, "stay over" tourists using small, nature-based lodges spent 18 times more than cruise passengers spend while visiting the island.
- In Komodo National Park in Indonesia, independent travellers spend nearly US$100 locally per visit; package

holidaymakers spend only half this. In contrast, cruise-ship arrivals spend an average three cents in the local economy.

- 80% of money for all-inclusive package tours goes to airlines, hotels, and other international companies. Eco-lodges hire and purchase locally, and sometimes put as much as 95% of money into the local economy.
- The daily expenditure of cultural tourists (over €70/US$90) is higher than visitors on a touring holiday (€52/US$67), beach holiday (€48/US$62), city break (€42/$US$54) or rural trip.

Consumer Demand

- o More than two-thirds of U.S. and Australian travellers, and 90% of British tourists, consider active protection of the environment and support of local communities to be part of a hotel's responsibility.

TIES Global Ecotourism Fact Sheet

- In Europe: 20%-30% of§ travellers are aware of needs & values of sustainable tourism. 10%-20% of§ travellers look for 'green' options. 5%-10% of§ travellers demand 'green' holidays.
- In Germany, 65% (39 million) of travellers expect environmental quality; 42% (25 million) "think that it is particularly important to find environmentally-friendly accommodation."
- Nearly half of those surveyed in Britain said they would be more likely to go with a "company that had a written code to guarantee good working conditions, protect the environment and support local charities in the tourist destination... [E]thical tourism will rightly be a big issue in the new millennium."
- A survey of U.S., British, and Australian travellers revealed that 70% would pay up to $150 more for a two-week stay in a hotel with a "responsible environmental attitude.

- In a U.K. survey, 87% of travellers said their holiday should not damage the environment; 39% said they were prepared to pay 5% extra for ethical guarantees.
- 53% of American travellers say their travel experience is enhanced when they learn as much as possible about local customs and culture.
- 95% of Swiss tourists consider respect for local culture to be highly important when choosing a holiday.
- Nearly a third (46 million) of U.S. travellers buy specifically from companies that donate part of their proceeds to charities. In Europe, where there is a strong and growing sustainable tourism movement, these figures are even higher.

Profile of Ecotourists in Europe

- Experienced travellers.
- Higher education.
- Higher income bracket.
- Age: middle-age to elderly.
- Opinion leaders.
- Ask & tell their friends & colleagues about trip.
- Are the most important source of trip information xxxiv.

Bibliography

Chandler, Harry and Carter, John: *Chandler's Travels: A Tour of the Life of Harry Chandler*, London, Quiller Press, 1985.

Conroy, B. : *Quality in Education and Training for Tourism*, London, Tourism Society, 1997.

Craig Zacker : *Networking: The Complete Reference*, Tata McGraw-Hill, Delhi, 2007.

Cukier, J. : *Tourism Employment in Bali: Trends and Implications*, London: Thompson, 1996.

Digumarti Bhaskara Rao: *International Meetings on Human Rights*, Discovery, 2001.

Donald M.: *Customer Service in the Hospitality and Tourism Industry*, Englewood Cliffs, Prentice Hall, 1994.

Eberts, Marjorie: *Careers in Travel, Tourism, and Hospitality*, Lincolnwood, VGM Career Horizons, 1997.

Elio, C.: *The Hospitality Law Desk Reference*, Miami, Southern Beverage Journal, 1994.

Fowler, Peter: *Heritage and Tourism: In the Global Village*, London, Retailed, 1993.

Ghimire, Krishna: *The Native Tourist*: Mass Tourism within Developing Regions, London, Earthscan, 2001.

Graham M S: *Language of Tourism*, The, Wallingford, CAB International, 1996.

Harish Kapadia: *Meeting the Mountains*, Indus, Delhi, 1998.

Her Majesty's : *Higher Education in the Polytechnics and Colleges, Hotel, Catering and Tourism Management*, London, DES, 1992.

Ireland, Lewis: *Quality Management for Projects and Programs*, Upper Darby, PMI, 1991.

Jennings, Gayle: *Tourism Research*, Chichester, Wiley, 2001.

Karski, A: *Urban Tourism* - A Key to Urban Regeneration?, 1990.

Kotler, Philip: *Marketing for Hospitality and Tourism*: New Jersey, Prentice-Hall, 1998.

Larkham, P J: *Building a New Heritage: Tourism, Culture & Identity in the New Europe*, London, Routledge,1994.

Laws, E. : *The ATTT Tourism Education Handbook*, London, Tourism Society, 1997.

Maitland, R: *Tourism Destinations, London*, Hodder and Stoughton, 1997.

Medlik, S. : *Tourism, Past, Present and Future*, London, Heinemann, 1981.

Negi, K.S. : *A Textbook of Hotel Management*, Wisdom Press, Delhi, 2011.

Pantelidis, I.S. : *Evaluating the Consumer in Hospitality*, Annual Research Conference: London, 2010.

Pearce, Douglas: *Tourism Today: A Geographical Analysis*, Harlow, Longman, 1995.

Prentice, R: *Conceptualising The Experiences of Heritage Tourists*, 1997.

Ritchie, J. R. B. : *Alternative Approaches to Teaching Tourism*, Guildford, University of Surrey, 1988.

Robert C.: *Cases in Hospitality Marketing and Management*, New York, John Wiley, 1997.

Rosemary, E.: *Managing Employee Relations in the Hotel and Catering Industry*, London, Cassell, 1995.

Rue, Nancy N.: *Choosing a Career in Hotels, Motels, and Resorts*, New York, Rosen Pub. Group, 1997.

Satyanarayana, N.R. : *A Manual of Library Automation and Networking*, New Royal Book Co, Delhi, 2003.

Slinn, Judy A: *Tourism: Management of Facilities*, London, Pitman: M & E, 1993.

Swarbrooke, J. : *Tourism and Leisure Education in the United Kingdom*, Tilberg, Netherlands, Tilberg University Press, 1995.

Timothy R.: *Cases in Hospitality Management: A Critical Incident Approach*, New York, Wiley, 1995.

Index

□□□